THE
EVERYTHING®
GUIDE TO
WRITING NONFICTION

Dear Reader,

I always loved to write and when I first began to write seriously, I wrote poetry, short stories, and even a novel. Write nonfiction? Too mundane. Yet shortly after my first poem and a short story were published, a strange turn of events took place. I began to write and publish nonfiction and ever since almost all my writing has been nonfiction.

So while I still occasionally mine the imagined world of fiction, I spend most of my time exploring the world in which we live, sometimes unearthing the past from which we stem, and pondering how to make for a better tomorrow. I have learned that far from being mundane, writing nonfiction is the most exciting and challenging quest a writer can undertake.

However, in order to succeed in transforming information, ideas, and observations into coherent and satisfying sentences good enough to be published requires attaining the knowledge and skills writing nonfiction demands. It is my hope that in this book I can share with you what I have learned over the years so you can achieve your goals as a nonfiction writer and enjoy the adventure along the way.

Sincerely,

Richard D. Bank

Welcome to the EVERYTHING® Series!

These handy, accessible books give you all you need to tackle a difficult project, gain a new hobby, comprehend a fascinating topic, prepare for an exam, or even brush up on something you learned back in school but have since forgotten.

You can choose to read an *Everything*® book from cover to cover or just pick out the information you want from our four useful boxes: e-questions, e-facts, e-alerts, and e-ssentials.

We give you everything you need to know on the subject, but throw in a lot of fun stuff along the way, too.

We now have more than 400 *Everything*® books in print, spanning such wide-ranging categories as weddings, pregnancy, cooking, music instruction, foreign language, crafts, pets, New Age, and so much more. When you're done reading them all, you can finally say you know *Everything*®!

QUESTION

Answers to
common questions

FACT

Important snippets
of information

ALERT

Urgent
warnings

ESSENTIAL

Quick
handy tips

PUBLISHER Karen Cooper

DIRECTOR OF ACQUISITIONS AND INNOVATION Paula Munier

MANAGING EDITOR, EVERYTHING® SERIES Lisa Laing

COPY CHIEF Casey Ebert

ACQUISITIONS EDITOR Lisa Laing

SENIOR DEVELOPMENT EDITOR Brett Palana-Shanahan

EDITORIAL ASSISTANT Hillary Thompson

EVERYTHING® SERIES COVER DESIGNER Erin Alexander

LAYOUT DESIGNERS Colleen Cunningham, Elisabeth Lariviere, Ashley Vierra, Denise Wallace

Visit the entire Everything® series at *www.everything.com*

THE
EVERYTHING®
GUIDE TO
Writing
Nonfiction

All you need to write and sell exceptional nonfiction
books, articles, essays, reviews, and memoirs

Richard D. Bank

Foreword by Jenna Glatzer, contributing editor, *Writer's Digest*

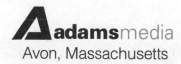

Avon, Massachusetts

*In memory of Louis Bank and in honor of his
great-grandson, Hayden Louis Bank.*

An Everything® Series Book.
Everything® and everything.com® are registered trademarks of F+W Media, Inc.

Published by Adams Media, a division of F+W Media, Inc.
57 Littlefield Street, Avon, MA 02322 U.S.A.
www.adamsmedia.com

ISBN 10: 1-60550-630-3
ISBN 13: 978-1-60550-630-2

Printed in the United States of America.

10   9   8   7   6   5   4   3   2   1

Library of Congress Cataloging-in-Publication Data
is available from the publisher.

This publication is designed to provide accurate and authoritative information with regard to the subject matter covered. It is sold with the understanding that the publisher is not engaged in rendering legal, accounting, or other professional advice. If legal advice or other expert assistance is required, the services of a competent professional person should be sought.

　　　　　—From a *Declaration of Principles* jointly adopted by a Committee of the American Bar Association and a Committee of Publishers and Associations

Many of the designations used by manufacturers and sellers to distinguish their products are claimed as trademarks. Where those designations appear in this book and Adams Media was aware of a trademark claim, the designations have been printed with initial capital letters.

*This book is available at quantity discounts for bulk purchases.
For information, please call 1-800-289-0963.*

Contents

Contents

Acknowledgments

What helps make this book special and a practical guide to nonfiction writers is the contribution made by the people who took time out from their busy lives to contribute samples or to be interviewed. My thanks to: Dan Rottenberg, D. L. Wilson, Ellie Slott Fisher, Cory Bank, Carlin Romano, Larry Atkins, and Nancy Gambescia. I would like to thank my agent, Carol Susan Roth, for her encouragement toward this project; to Lisa Laing, my editor, who was so receptive to this book and bringing it to fruition; and to Brett Palana-Shanahan who guided the manuscript through the developmental process.

Top Ten Things Every Nonfiction Writer Needs to Know

1. Writing nonfiction requires that your work be true and factual.

2. You can be creative writing nonfiction. Frequently, the techniques of creative writing are applicable to works of nonfiction.

3. Sometimes the work of a nonfiction writer has nothing to do with writing. You need to know how to research, gather facts, interview, and verify information.

4. In order to gain the trust and confidence of the reader that is crucial in writing nonfiction, you must write in a voice of authority.

5. Since there are so many nonfiction genres, you need to be able to identify the category in which you are writing and be familiar with its unique requirements.

6. It is important to know how to write a good hook because you must pique the reader's interest in the first few sentences so she will want to read on.

7. If you want to publish a nonfiction book, you do not have to write the book before seeking an agent or publisher but instead you must compose and submit a book proposal.

8. The odds of getting your work published may appear daunting but if you send your work to the right market and in a professional manner consistent with the protocol of the process, your chances for success will greatly improve.

9. Just because you write about a subject or experience once does not mean you cannot write about it again from a different perspective or in a different way.

10. Attending writers' conferences, workshops, and classes will improve your skills as a writer.

Foreword

I WAS IN MY twenties, and I'd written a bunch of screenplays that hadn't sold. Several times, I'd come this close to a sale, but things just hadn't come through. I wanted to find a way to earn a living as a writer, so I thought, "Well, I guess I'll do a little nonfiction writing until my big screenwriting career takes off."

The idea was to write for a few magazines, then give it up as soon as Mr. Spielberg came to his senses and hired me to write all his movies. But before long, I figured out something: being a nonfiction writer is . . . kinda awesome.

Wearing bunny slippers to work is not even the coolest part. The coolest part is that you get paid to learn about whatever you feel like learning. Just about anything you can think of that interests you will probably also interest other people . . . and if it does, there's a good chance you can find a market willing to pay you to share what you learn with their readers.

You can define yourself as a writer in so many ways depending on your personality and style. Some areas of writing are more suited to people who are outgoing and social, while others are perfect for people who would rather read research than do interviews. Some are right for people who love to travel, while others work fine from your living room.

As for me, I would never have had the rich life experiences I've had if I had shunned the nonfiction world. Among other things, I've hung out with Celine Dion until 3 in the morning while we worked on her biography, I've spoken with the man who Joe DiMaggio tried to kill because he was having an affair with Marilyn Monroe, I've been to a party where most of the guests were soap opera actors, I've done book signings and taught workshops, and I conquered my fear of flying because I was inspired by one of my interview subjects who had conquered his. I wrote books with people who awed me, like the first double-amputee to finish the Hawaiian Ironman, and I wrote articles about people doing great things in my community and across the world.

Then there are the perks like being among the first in line to review a new piece of software, book, or even (God bless you, Mr. Dyson) a vacuum cleaner. And the undeniable thrill that comes from seeing your byline on an article in a magazine or the spine of a book. That just never gets old.

I never went back to screenwriting. I found out that I was really suited to this kind of work and this lifestyle. Nineteen books and countless magazine articles later, I'm very proud to be a nonfiction writer, and very glad I picked a career that can grow and change with me.

What I like so much about this book is the way it shines light on possibilities you might not have considered before. You never know which experience is going to change your life for the better, or which assignment is going to lead to terrific new opportunities. I encourage you to grab a plate and think of this book as your buffet; try out several of the writing forms before deciding on your main dish. Do the exercises—even the ones that, at first, don't strike you as "you" at all.

I hope you will find the endeavor as enriching as I have.

Write on,

Jenna Glatzer

Contributing Editor, *Writer's Digest*

Introduction

SO, YOU WANT TO write nonfiction. Not a bad decision since four out of five of the several hundred thousand new books published annually are nonfiction. And on top of that, there are numerous markets for nonfiction besides books where you can send your work. Consequently, choosing to write nonfiction is a wise move if seeing your name and work in print is your goal.

If it is a nonfiction book you want to write, you may feel the challenge is a bit overwhelming. That's because people tend to fear the unknown. To overcome this, in the pages that follow, you'll explore all the different types of nonfiction books and learn everything you need to know so you have the confidence and ability to write a nonfiction book whether it's general, scholarly, or in a specific genre.

On the other hand, you may not be interested in a book-length project. Possibly, you want to try your hand at articles or journalism—perhaps a travel piece or covering a rock concert. You may feel strongly about an issue and want to persuade others to share your views, so you would like to write an opinion piece or op-ed. Along the same line, there may be a book or film or restaurant you want to tell people about by writing a review.

It could be that there is a subject of interest you desire to investigate and share with others and you want the writing to be eloquent, so it's a literary essay you have in mind. Or maybe, you'd rather write a personal essay concerning an experience you had that speaks to the reader or has a universal message. Sometimes, these personal essays are called "memoirs," which bring us to the subject of writing a book-length memoir possibly based on memories, notes, and jottings in that frayed journal you've kept over the years.

But whatever type of nonfiction you are thinking of writing, *The Everything® Guide to Writing Nonfiction* will inform you of all the categories of nonfiction and also enable you to bring your writing to the level where it's good enough to be published. We'll cover all the elements of nonfiction writing and the importance of getting the facts right and how to write in a voice of authority. You'll learn the importance of research, taking notes, conducting interviews, reconstructing memories, and knowing when you can take "literary license."

If you are concerned about hurting the feelings of people you want to write about, you will discover how to "disguise" your characters and events and not invade their right to privacy. You'll also be shown when an individual's right to privacy does not apply. And, of course, no one wants to be sued for libel, so you will be taught how to avoid a libel judgment. Sometimes, however, it's not a question of what is legal but rather a matter of doing the right thing, so a chapter is devoted to the ethics of writing nonfiction.

Special attention will be paid to every category of nonfiction and how to write in that particular genre with samples, excerpts, interviews, and writing exercises provided. If you also want to satisfy your craving to be creative and write in a style where the words flow like a well-written novel, creative nonfiction might be the genre for you, and that is covered in detail as well.

Finally, you'll learn of all the markets for nonfiction—whether articles, essays, reviews, opinion pieces, or books—so that you'll know exactly what to do when you are ready to share your work with the public. If it is a book-length project, you'll be shown how to write a book proposal, which is what editors, publishers, and agents want to review to determine whether your project is for them. And speaking of agents, we'll see how to go about finding the right one or if you should go it alone or even self-publish your book.

If you have given thought to one or more of these projects, then you have entered the exciting world of writing nonfiction. And though it requires work, dedication, and perseverance—it also can be very fulfilling and even a lot of fun. So, whether you have only entertained the notion, or have begun to write your first project, or even have some experience in writing nonfiction, *The Everything® Guide to Writing Nonfiction* will supply everything you need to get you started, train you in the craft of writing nonfiction, and give you a step up in getting published.

CHAPTER 1

Becoming a Nonfiction Writer

All you have to do to be a writer is write. But to be a good writer there is more involved. If you have the passion and desire to write and acquire the knowledge and techniques of proficient writing, you are on your way to transforming your observations and ideas into worthy prose. Choosing nonfiction as a genre opens a world of possibilities, but care must be taken to avoid crossing the line into fiction.

Writing Is a Passion

Perhaps writing is something you have always enjoyed since you were a child, or maybe you were drawn to writing in college. Possibly you took to writing in those spare moments during your hectic adult life when family and work demanded most of your time. On the other hand, writing may have entered your life in those "twilight years" when the free time you always yearned for finally became a reality.

In any event, the driving force that gets those fingers typing on the keyboard or scrawling with the point of pencil or pen is an overwhelming desire to transform into tangible form the spoken or unspoken word. That's what you feel. That's the craving you have. That's what makes you whole and satisfied at the end of the day. Writing is simply something you must do and that is why you want to write.

Telling It Like It Is

There are many genres for writers to work within but they all fall into two basic categories—fiction and nonfiction. While this may seem straightforward enough, you'll see the differences are not often clear. However, one thing all writing has in common is that it serves as an outlet for your passion to share your thoughts, observations, and feelings. One way this has been accomplished is through the telling of tales and narration of stories and when you get right down to it, that's what writing is all about—telling a "story" that may or may not be true. And sometimes, the "best" stories are the "true" ones!

FACT

"If you think about it, storytelling is, outside of breathing, eating, and sleeping, the most fundamental and time-consuming human activity there is. We listen to and tell stories all our lives."—Judith Nadell, John Langan, and Eliza A. Comodromos, *The Longman Reader, 10th edition*

If you have the desire to tell a story, whether it's to an audience or to just one person, then you are ready to write. The story can be about someone you know personally or an historical figure. It can be about building a boat and sailing it in the bay. It can be about the time you ran a marathon and another runner stopped to extend a hand when you tripped. Whatever the subject, even if it's true, it can still be a story.

You Can Be Creative Writing Nonfiction

Doesn't being creative mean making something up? Isn't writing novels, short stories, and poems an act of creativity while writing articles, biographies, and essays is just reporting the facts? How can you possibly satisfy your creative bent by writing nonfiction? Shouldn't you choose fiction instead?

Absolutely not! Try this exercise. Turn your computer on and take a look at that blank screen. Or, open the drawer where you keep your journal or writing pad and pick up a pen or pencil. Now, write something or strike those keys on the keyboard. Take a look at that screen or sheet of paper and you'll see that it's no longer blank. Now, while all it may be is a random assortment of scribbles or letters that make no sense whatsoever, the fact is, there is now something where once there was nothing and that is what "creating" is all about.

So, you can satisfy your desire to be creative by writing nonfiction and we'll explore this in much more detail in Chapter 19 when dealing with "creative nonfiction." The real question is, as with all creative outlets—is it any good? Which is what most of this book is about—helping you channel your creative juices into something you can be pleased with and proud of.

Getting Started and Filling the Blank Page

Transforming those nebulous concepts and pieces of information floating in your head into words and sentences that pervade your first page is one of the most personal processes there are. What works for one person will be counterproductive for someone else.

Nonetheless, there are some factors everyone should consider:

- Determine a time of day or night when you are usually prolific.
- Select a place that is conducive for you to write, keeping in mind where you are physically comfortable and not subject to interruptions.
- Make sure the tools of your trade are working and are at your fingertips, such as computer, pens and paper, reference materials, and so forth.
- Keep distractions at bay by turning off your phone and letting people know you do not want to be disturbed.
- Don't stare too long at that blank screen or sheet of paper; if need be, get up and do something else, letting you mind work in the background.

Take the Leap

Ultimately, you have to throw caution to the wind and just write. We all have built in censors that keep saying this won't work and that's too awful to put into print. This is not to say that editing and rewriting is not critical to the writing process, because it is. But at some point, you just have to get started and ignore the editor in the back of your head.

ESSENTIAL

"To write is to plumb the unfathomable depths of being. Writing lies within the domain of mystery. The space between two words is vaster than the distance between heaven and earth. To bridge it you must close your eyes and leap. Ultimately, to write is an act of faith."—Elie Wiesel from *Memoirs*

What will make it easier for you to take the leap and put the first words down on paper is to remember that they are just that—the first words of your first draft. They are not cast in stone and need not be perfect. They can—and likely will—be changed. In fact, very often the first beginning is excised from the final draft altogether. As long as it gets you started, it will have served you well. So, don't sweat your first beginning.

However, your "final" beginning is crucial and must grab the reader and make her want to read further. This is of utmost importance when it comes to shopping your work to editors and agents, as you will see in Chapter 22. To give you an idea, here are several beginnings for you to consider, although keep in mind what does and doesn't work is highly subjective.

"As Gregor Samsa awoke one morning from uneasy dreams he found himself transformed in his bed into a gigantic insect." (*The Metamorphosis* by Franz Kafka)

"Happy families are all alike; every unhappy family is unhappy in its own way." (*Anna Karenina* by Leo Tolstoy)

"He was called to the Torah, and before reciting the blessing he reached into his *tallis* bag, removed the silencer, aimed it at his temple, and pulled the trigger." (*The Golems of Gotham* by Thane Rosenbaum)

"Alexey Fyodorovitch Karamazov was the third son of Fyodor Pavlovitch Karamazov, a landowner well known in our district in his own day, and still remembered among us owing to his gloomy and tragic death, which happened thirteen years ago, and which I shall describe in its proper place. For the present I will only say that this "landowner"—for so we used to call him, although he hardly spent a day of his life on his own estate—was a strange type, yet one pretty frequently to be met with, a type abject and vicious and at the same time senseless." (*The Brothers Karamazov* by Fyodor Dostoevsky)

"Her name was Connie. She was fifteen and she had a quick, nervous giggling habit of craning her neck to glance into mirrors or checking other people's faces to make sure her own was all right." (*Where Are You Going, Where Have You Been?* by Joyce Carol Oates)

"Khrushchev was in power, or we thought he was, that month I spent as cultural ambassador and banjo-picking bridge between the superpowers, helping to stave off nuclear holocaust." (*Licks of Love in the Heart of the Cold War* by John Updike)

"There are two good things about living in a basement apartment. The first is that you can't kill yourself by jumping out the window." (*Kill Two Birds & Get Stoned* by Kinky Friedman).

Perhaps one or more of these beginnings have inspired you to achieve similar heights. Or, you are convinced more than ever that you might as well make the attempt because you can't do any worse than what has been written by others. In any event, give it a try. Without thinking for more than a minute, write a sentence or two as a beginning giving no thought to what may follow. Just do it. Now, put it away for another day. Maybe it will lead to something and maybe it will not, but even if it doesn't, remember this: You survived and are little the worse for wear for having written it. Just take that leap!

What Type of Writer Are You?

Just like most personality traits, there seems to be two types of writers—probably having to do with right-brain or left-brain dominance. There is the organized, meticulous, and disciplined writer and when you walk into his writer's garret, everything is in place, structured, and laid out for efficiency. We'll call this person Type A. Then there is Type B who is always full of ideas, whose mind wanders in all directions with different ways to turn a phrase, and when you walk into her writer's garret, it is strewn with books, papers, note cards, half-open bags of snack foods, and the computer is unplugged.

Naturally, you may fit somewhere in between and exhibit some traits of Type A and Type B but probably, one disposition dominates. The thing to remember is that neither temperament is better than the other. It's just a question of making adjustments so you can write and be productive.

If you are Type A, the toughest challenge you may face is coming up with ideas, so maybe what you need to do is leave your workplace and get out and about with nothing to do other than relax and be open to your surroundings. Let your mind flow. If you're Type B, ideas are not the problem. It's more likely that keeping track of them is the hard part, so having a small notebook handy to jot them down will be useful. When you get home, transfer the ideas to cards and a poster board or organize them on your computer.

The way you write will also reflect the type of writer you are. You may write page after page for hours without looking back or you may dwell on each word and sentence until it reaches perfection. But regardless of the style you employ, as you will see in the following, rewriting is at the heart of good writing.

FACT

"Tellers of stories with ink on paper, not that they matter anymore, have been either swoopers or bashers. Swoopers write a story quickly, higgledy-piggledy, crinkum-crankum, any which way. Then they go over it again painstakingly, fixing everything that is just plain awful or doesn't work. Bashers go one sentence at a time, getting it exactly right just before they go on to the next one. When they're done they're done. I am a basher."—Kurt Vonnegut, *Timequake*

Useful Techniques in Writing Nonfiction

Whether you are a Type A or Type B writer, the techniques you need to keep in mind as you write are essentially the same. There are many techniques applicable to writing nonfiction—some of them we have touched upon and others will be explored in more detail later. But here are some key points to bear in mind:

1. In writing nonfiction, professionalism is important and more attention must be paid to grammar, spelling, and punctuation than in writing fiction.
2. Be concise and respect word count limits.
3. While the canon of fiction writing, "show don't tell," sometimes applies, especially to creative nonfiction, typically you need not give it much consideration, but you must take care that when instructing or "telling," you do so in a compelling voice.
4. Spoon-feed the information and avoid inundating the reader with too much data and too many details at one time.
5. When you read your work for purposes of the rewrite, read from the point of view of the reader, not as the writer, so that nothing is assumed.

6. When rewriting and editing, don't be afraid to remove material—even an entire section—but keep it around because you may want to use it in another project.

Find Your Voice

Once you have begun to put words to paper you have reached the critical point of determining how it will sound to the reader. "Sound," you ask? "I'm not making a speech or having a conversation," you say. "I'm writing and the reader is reading."

If you are thinking these thoughts, try this exercise. Pick up anything but a newspaper article and read it and be aware of the voice in your head transmitting the words. It may sound like your voice but in fact it's the voice of the writer, which will only sound authentic if it reflects the writer.

ALERT

When rewriting and editing, don't be so critical that you will never be satisfied with what you have written. At some point, just be done with it and say, "It's as good as it's going to get." Otherwise, you'll never send out your work to be published.

In writing nonfiction, the voice is critical because the reader is asked to trust and believe that the material is true. The voice must be one of authority or at least be honest and believable. To make certain you are writing in your voice, write something and then try reading it aloud. If it sounds stilted or you are stumbling over the sentences or it just doesn't seem right, then you haven't found your voice. On the other hand, if the words flow out as natural as can be and seems to fit like a well-tailored suit, you're ready to write.

Is It Fiction or Nonfiction?

Okay, now you're set to go. Or are you? You better make sure it's nonfiction you're writing if that's your intent. This may appear to be a simple matter, but it is not. Despite the fact that nonfiction is based on facts and purported to be true and fiction arises from the writer's imagination, it is not a question of black and white but rather an issue cloaked in shades of gray.

How Can the Reader Tell the Difference?

Theoretically, only the writer knows for certain whether her work should be classified as fiction or nonfiction, and we'll get to this soon. But first, doesn't it seem probable that an attentive reader can discern the difference? See for yourself with these two excerpts from different books:

"The other white cook, Andy, lives on his dry-docked boat, which, as far as I can tell from his loving descriptions, can't be more than twenty feet long. He offers to take me out on it once it's repaired, but the offer comes with inquiries as to my marital status, so I do not follow up on it."

"This is the story of my older brother's strange criminal behavior and his disappearance. No one urged me to reveal these things; no one asked me not to. We who loved him simply no longer speak of Wade, not among ourselves and not with anyone else, either."

Can you say for certain which is fiction and which is nonfiction? The first excerpt is from Barbara Ehrenreich's *Nickel and Dimed*, a work of nonfiction about the time she entered the world of the "working poor" for a year. The second excerpt is the beginning of *Affliction*, a novel by Russell Banks that was subsequently made into a movie.

Now if you had picked the correct answers, ask yourself, "How did I know?" because it really is nothing more than a good guess on your part. As you shall see later in this chapter and again in Chapter 19, some works of nonfiction read like fiction and there are works of fiction that ring so true it is hard to believe they are not. The bottom line is that the reader can never be certain and must rely on the writer's representation in order to know whether it's fact or fiction.

Sometimes Only the Writer Knows

How many times have you watched a movie where the plot was so fantastic that were it not for the phrase "based on a true story," you would never have believed it to be true? On the other hand, how many times have you watched a movie that was entirely invented and you didn't enjoy it because it was simply "not realistic?"

The same standard applies to the written word—particularly essays and books. The problem is that while you know in movies many liberties are taken with the facts, you do not allow the same latitude with works of nonfiction because by definition, nonfiction means it is factual. But like movie scripts, in nonfiction only the writer of the words knows for certain from whence they came. Consequently, not only are there legal ramifications for the nonfiction writer who represents to the publisher that the work is true, but there are ethical obligations to the readers, which will be explored more thoroughly in Chapter 20.

Nonfiction Writing—Literary or Not?

There was a time when fiction was written one way and nonfiction another, making it easier for the reader to discern whether a work was nonfiction or fiction. However, with the growing popularity of what is called "creative nonfiction" (Chapter 19), where the techniques of fiction writing are applied to nonfiction, this is no longer the case. But as for standard nonfiction writing that applies to articles, reviews, and most nonfiction books, there is a distinctive style to writing nonfiction.

ESSENTIAL

Unless writing creative nonfiction, do not employ literary techniques such as foreshadowing and symbolism. Avoid the use of dialogue unless it is completely accurate and verifiable and only in a way that would represent reporting the conversation rather than creating a scene.

Bryan Burrough, who frequently writes for *Vanity Fair*, distinguished fiction from nonfiction this way: "Fiction is an art. Nonfiction is construction." While Burrough focused upon the notion that fiction writers build from their imaginations and minds and nonfiction writers were like builders of houses who gathered the lumber and nails and sheetrock and then labored to put them into place, there is another implication behind his definition which has to do with the writing style.

There has always been the idea that in writing nonfiction, so long as the rules of grammar are followed and the writing clear and comprehensible, what matters is the substance of the material. In writing fiction, however, the writing itself must be more artistic and literary to be considered fine fiction. While there remains a kernel of truth to this distinction, as you will see in surveying all the nonfiction genres, the writing of nonfiction has become anything but uniform and in some cases is just as "literary" as fiction writing.

Novels and Other Hybrids

Novels have been around for thousands of years and the novel is probably the most popular genre attracting writers. Almost every writer at one time or another wants to write the "Great American Novel." Maybe one of the reasons is that novelists have this mystique about them that impresses people. Next time you're at a social event, tell people you are writing a novel (doesn't even matter if it's been published), and watch those eyebrows rise in admiration. Then go to another group of people and say you've had a nonfiction book published about eighteenth-century Chinese art and notice how many yawns are stifled.

Historical and Autobiographical Novels

The nonfiction writer must know enough about novels to avoid the mistake of writing one inadvertently. This is very important especially when it comes to creative nonfiction. There are many categories or subgenres of novels such as the thriller, the romance novel, the literary novel, and chicklit, to name just a few. But the novels you should be aware of and not emulate if it's nonfiction you want to write—especially a biography or memoir—are the historical and autobiographical novels.

For fiction to succeed it must have a ring of truth, which is why some of the best novels are based on historical settings and characters or a real person's life. In the case of the historical novel, the novelist will likely do as much research as the nonfiction writer who is writing a book about a specific historical period or subject. But the major difference lies not in the research or even in the writing style but rather in the fact that the novelist is free to stray from accuracy for the sake of the narrative while the nonfiction writer may not.

FACT

The length of novels is usually between 60,000 and 80,000 words. However, some novels may be longer, especially if the author is established and doesn't have to concede editorial cuts to his manuscript. Novellas are short versions of novels generally between 20,000 and 40,000 words. Any work less than 20,000 words is a short story, though short stories average 2,500 words.

Nonetheless, you can learn a lot about writing memoirs, biographies, and history from reading autobiographical and historical novels, so here are several you might want to consider:

- *Coney* by Amram Ducovny
- *The Plot Against America* by Philip Roth
- *Exodus* by Leon Uris
- *This Boy's Life* by Tobias Wolff
- *Lincoln* by Gore Vidal
- *Call It Sleep* by Henry Roth
- *Dreamland* by Kevin Baker
- *Ragtime* by E. L. Doctorow

Hybrids Don't Fit in Either Genre

You would think by now that you've reached the point where at the very least you can detect the differences between writing fiction and nonfiction. Yet, some works of fiction seem so real that you just can't believe they're made up. Historical and autobiographical novels contain so much accurate and factual material that you cannot distinguish what is and isn't fictitious. And, as you shall see in Chapter 19, creative nonfiction is nonfiction, but you certainly can't tell that from the style of writing and techniques employed.

Even more of a conundrum, however, is that there are some books where you just never know one way or the other if it's fiction or nonfiction. Take, for example, Jack Kerouac's, *On the Road*, which up until the fiftieth anniversary of its original publication had always been considered a novel based on some of the author's experiences but is now sometimes portrayed as a memoir with acceptable embellishments and literary license taken. Or, consider Norman Mailer's *The Armies of the Night*, which won the Pulitzer Prize and the National Book Award and is considered to be one of the first and finest works of contemporary creative nonfiction. Yet, the subtitle is *History as a Novel, the Novel as History*, laying claim to both genres and yet exclusiveness to neither.

So, if you still feel somewhat uncertain about whether you may be writing nonfiction or fiction, what rules you must abide by, and which techniques you should adopt, think no further about it. At this point, you're as qualified as anyone to begin writing nonfiction and by the end of this book, no matter what sort of nonfiction you choose to write, your work will muster any scrutiny.

CHAPTER 2

The Categories of Nonfiction

Once you have decided to write nonfiction, a wide vista of opportunities is open. You may want to write a short opinion piece promoting the environment, a lengthy literary essay about Henry James, a seemingly endless family memoir, or a book based on your visits to all the major-league baseball parks. While you are free to move from one nonfiction genre to another, you should know what each genre involves in order to be successful.

Selecting a Genre

Now that you have made the decision to write nonfiction, there are two ways to go about choosing what type of nonfiction you want to write. On the one hand, perhaps you have always wanted to write a book, so a book project it shall be. Or, you opt for writing opinion pieces because you have been a regular reader of the op-ed page and now want to see your name in print while you present opinions which you passionately hold.

On the other hand, you have an idea and want to pursue it in some way but you're not sure what form it should take. For example, you love to travel, and you take several trips a year to unusual and even exotic destinations. You want to write about your experiences but you're not sure if you want this to be about just one trip or many trips or focus on the sights and sounds versus the practicalities of making the journey. You're thinking maybe an article or possibly a series of articles, a personal essay, or maybe even a travel book. You're just not sure.

In the first scenario, you have decided upon the genre but need the project to fill it. In the second scenario, you've got the idea but you're not sure in what shape it should be crafted. To succeed in either case, you must have a comprehensive understanding of the various categories of nonfiction—what they require, the type of subject matter, the style of writing, the protocols, and the forms of presentation—and then choose the genre best suited for you.

You could go about selecting the genre the way some people make decisions, like randomly throwing darts at a dartboard. But that rarely achieves the best results. So, a general survey of the options awaiting you is a good way to get started and the chapters that follow will explore the categories in more detail.

Be an Author of a Nonfiction Book

Naturally, the most ambitious project is to write a book. In Chapter 1, you learned a bit about novels—the appellation assigned to books of fiction. Nonfiction books do not have a special designation. They're simply called "nonfiction books" or sometimes just "books."

The primary distinction that separates nonfiction books from other works of nonfiction is the length, which is usually between 50,000 and 90,000 words. So, if you decide you're ready to undertake a project that requires composing 50,000 words or more and what you have in mind is based on fact and completely true, then you're ready to do a nonfiction book.

ALERT

If you decide you want to write a nonfiction book for publication, do not write the book! Agents, editors, and publishers make their decisions based upon a book proposal and not a complete manuscript. Write the book proposal first (see Chapter 23) and begin to circulate that.

A multitude of nonfiction book genres await you. Some of these categories are quite popular, with hundreds and even thousands of new titles published each year. Several of the following chapters will deal specifically with each of these genres. As for the remaining tens of thousands of nonfiction books published annually, they cover just about every subject under the sun, and you'll learn about these as well.

Popular Nonfiction Books

All "popular" nonfiction books, sometimes called "trade" or "mass market," share the trait that they are expected to sell well and reach a wide audience in the tens of thousands. This is the glaring distinction between this category and other nonfiction books. While there are some differences in style and content, for the most part, the techniques of writing nonfiction apply to all nonfiction books.

Obviously, what may be considered popular nonfiction today will not be trendy tomorrow. Consider "religion/spirituality" books that have some titles selling millions of copies—a genre that has taken off in the last twenty years. Books about physical fitness and exercise commenced their popularity after President Kennedy called upon Americans to become more physically fit.

On the other hand, some nonfiction has been widespread for many decades and even centuries. The publication of scholarly nonfiction has always been substantial. The interest in famous people has made biographies a popular genre over the years. And the catch-all category of general nonfiction has consistently produced thousands of books annually.

A Market for Almost Any Subject

Suppose your one passion and singular pursuit outside of work has been baseball cards from the 1950s. That's right, the cards that came in a wrapper with pink gum you first purchased for a nickel—not to chew the gum but to obtain the cards with each bearing the face of a baseball player accompanied by statistics. That's been the focus of your life and now you want to write a book about it. But who will buy such a book? Isn't this a pipe dream?

If you do a little research, you will find that there are thousands of people collecting vintage 1950s baseball cards who comprise a potential market for your book. What is more, there are several reputable independent publishers who cater to this specific market and would have interest in your project. Indeed, it is often easier to publish such "niche" books that target a small but specific and devoted following than works of general nonfiction that might appeal to a wide audience but where few actually purchase the book. Consequently, even if your subject appears to have a minuscule audience, do not shunt it aside because thousands of such books are published each year and there is no reason your book cannot be on that list.

Interview with Author D. L. Wilson

D. L. Wilson is the bestselling author of the thriller novel *Unholy Grail*, a university textbook *Apparel Merchandising*, and a cookbook *The Kitchen Casanova* that resulted in a national tour with interviews on *Regis* and CNN. Wilson, the former president and CEO of U.S. and European fashion companies and consultant to industries and governments in thirty-two countries has also written feature articles for *Writer's Digest* and the *Writer* magazine. His next book will be *Sirocco*, a novel.

RDB: As someone who has written both nonfiction and fiction, what similarities do you see and what major differences?

DLW: My fiction and nonfiction involve extensive research and both forms of book-length writing require tremendous dedication and countless hours of work, but that's where the similarities end. Both of my nonfiction books required great attention to detail. For the cookbook, each recipe had to be tested and retested and credit for all drawings and photos verified. The university text involved interviews with top fashion industry executives and each chapter included figures, photos, and cases in point to support the technical content. With my novels I had greater latitude regarding research, but since I try to produce works of fiction with content, I am very careful to find multiple sources of data to support critical concepts that help drive my plots.

The major difference I found in writing fiction, especially after writing technical nonfiction, is retraining your brain to be more right-brain oriented to release your creative muse. Nonfiction writing conditions us to focus on analytical and logical processes and fiction writing requires us to unleash our holistic, imagistic creative self.

RDB: Your two nonfiction books are in different genres (one for a general audience and one for students and scholars). In writing them, what differences stood out and in what ways was the process similar?

DLW: The textbook required a great attention to detail and a focus on concepts, planning, and execution principles that tied into other university courses. The cookbook had a more creative bent with photos of the various menus showing the final presentation for elegant dining experiences. Both books had to be structured to attract and retain the attention of the readers, but from different perspectives. The textbook had to provide a creative approach to understanding the development, execution, and delivery of fashion lines to prepare students to make successful decisions when they entered the competitive business world. The cookbook was a hands-on guide to preparing romantic dinners. In both cases the process involved creating carefully executed chapter-by-chapter outlines where the format and presentation focused on including all the details in a structure that met the overall goals for the book.

RDB: What different skills are required in writing articles as opposed to book-length projects?

DLW: Articles have to be tight, short, and to the point. They address a specific area of interest such as "What Fiction Editors Want" or "How Agents Work." If you are interviewing editors or agents for these types of articles you have to consolidate their responses into clear, concise answers to the focus of the article. In a book-length project you have more flexibility to include material to give the reader a broader perspective of the person being interviewed and how they came to their conclusions. Book-length projects require more complex writing skills than articles.

RDB: How do you come up with your ideas and topics for nonfiction projects?

DLW: I maintain an Idea File. If I read an article in a magazine or newspaper, see an interesting TV show, or hear an intriguing idea for a fiction or nonfiction project, I jot it down and place it in the file. Periodically I scan the file and highlight concepts that maintain my interest. I often go on the Internet and search for additional information to expand a topic. When I'm ready for a new article or a book-length project, I search through my Idea File and pick a concept and a backup concept and start the research process.

RDB: What are the more important tools in research and fact-finding?

DLW: In this day and age the Internet is a godsend for quickly locating research data and many supporting sources for that data. Google and other search engineers quickly guide you to a broad perspective of research sources. Another tool that is critical to accessing the hundreds of research files I create for a book-length project is a good searchable database. I create summary files for each research book, article, and Internet research material and save the files in a software program such as Info Select.

RDB: In what ways do your writing styles differ when writing nonfiction and fiction?

DLW: Nonfiction relies on the structural business style I used for over thirty years as an executive during my day job. It follows the sequential, analytical, logical, and verbal skills associated with the left-hemisphere functions of the brain. I found it much easier to lock into a comfortable style while writing nonfiction. The development of detailed outlines for my works of fiction also relies on my analytical skills. It's when I start the actual fiction-writing process that my style must make a dramatic shift. I use meditation techniques to help activate my creative, imagistic right brain. My detailed scene outlines help keep me focused in the right direction, but I've learned to listen to my muse if a creative swerve will boost the thrill and excitement of the read.

RDB: Which do you enjoy most—writing fiction or nonfiction?

DLW: I find that both forms of writing are enjoyable. They each have their strengths and weaknesses. I have recently been focusing on fiction since it opens exciting new creative areas that have lain dormant during my business career.

RDB: Any words of advice to the nonfiction writer?

DLW: Focus on topics for which you have a deep interest. To be a successful nonfiction writer requires passion. Passion that will support you through the tough times and bring you great satisfaction when you see your work in print.

Writing Articles Offers a World of Opportunity

Perhaps undertaking the commitment to write a book of several hundred pages that can be years in the making is not what you have in mind—at least not for now. You prefer addressing a number of subjects or even just one general topic approached from different perspectives, and the best way to do this would be something shorter than book-length and more to the point. If this rings true, you should seriously consider writing articles.

FACT

It is not unusual that following a series of articles on a particular subject, the writer authors a book. What can also occur is that after a book, the author writes "spin-off" pieces in the form of articles based upon different sections of the book or backed by the authority of having written a book on the subject.

Before writing an article, you must satisfy one or more of the following:

- You must be an "acknowledged expert" in the field.
- You have the requisite credentials such as a PhD or professional/ occupational background.
- An authority in the subject serves as a coauthor with you.
- Interviews with experts are included in your article.
- You have "life experiences" that qualify you to write the article, such as being a cancer survivor and writing about surviving cancer.

Everything you need to know about writing articles is developed more fully in Chapter 13, but the bottom line is that if it is your desire to inform and you wish to do so in something less than a book-length project, you should seriously consider writing articles.

Writing Reviews

In offering an assignment to write a book review, an editor said to me, "What could be better than reading a book that you would want to read anyway, receive it for free, write what you think of it, and get paid!" Can't argue with that, and the same applies to writing reviews of movies, the arts, theater, and restaurants.

The chief purpose of the review, like all nonfiction, is to inform. With novels, movies, and the theater, it is important to convey a summary without giving away the story ending. In reviews of nonfiction books, the essence of the book should be imparted, and in fact, reviews are often read as substitutes for reading the entire book.

While the reviewer's opinion is usually put forward, it should not be the focal point of the review. It is best to present objective information about the subject to allow the reader to make an informed decision whether to read the book, attend the play or movie, or dine at the restaurant.

Reviews are generally short pieces between 300 and 1,000 words. Sometimes they evolve into "review/essays" that use the subject of the review as a springboard for a more extensive article of several thousand words. For example, a review of Philip Roth's most recent book may continue to explore some common themes running through his other books, thus becoming a review/essay.

The Art of Persuasion—Writing Opinion Pieces

Do you feel the time has come for you to weigh in on the question of gun control? Abortion? Border security? Or maybe an issue more mundane like whether there should be a uniform dress code at the local high school. And perhaps you aren't satisfied voicing your opinions to a wall or shouting from the rooftops and you want to rally the minds of others to join your way of thinking. If so, then writing opinion pieces may be for you.

Opinion pieces are also referred to as "Commentaries" and "op-eds"—the latter reflecting their placement opposite the editorial page of newspapers. Writing opinion pieces and having them published is not simply a matter of putting your thoughts to paper. Length restrictions are rigid and vary—typically in the range of 300 to 700 words; timeliness is critical; arguments must be intelligent and persuasive without appearing dogmatic; and of course, the piece must be well written. There is much more you need to know if writing opinion pieces is to become an outlet for your nonfiction writing—all of which will be presented in Chapter 15.

The Craft of Writing Essays

Essays fall into three general categories but all are expressed in the first person. The first type of essay presents opinions and is written to "instruct" the reader. Though frequently less than a thousand words, opinion pieces are considered essays. The other two classifications are the literary essay and the personal essay.

The primary function of the literary essay is to convey information and knowledge, often accompanied by a message, in a piece that may be as long as 8,000 words. Though the subject may be narrow, the literary essay is designed for a wide audience and to deliver a universal message. If you want to write a literary essay, you need not be an expert in the subject but you must project a voice of authority that is best accomplished by a command of the facts. Though the writing should be literary and the material well supported, you can still write in a personal tone.

ALERT

You may make use of a personal experience and personal reflections in writing a literary essay. However, do not allow the personal experience to become the center of the piece and do not let your personal ruminations dominate the narrative, or you risk transforming it into a personal essay.

Personal essays (sometimes called "memoirs") take one or more related personal experiences or memories, dwells upon it, and brings forth a universal message or at the very least, something to which many readers can relate. As with all nonfiction, the personal essay must be of interest to the reader and not only to family and friends if you are seeking publication. Generally, personal essays run between 1,000 and 4,000 words. If longer, you are approaching the final nonfiction category—the memoir.

Writing Your Memoir?

Does writing your memoir sound intimidating? Covering all the ground that has made up your life from your earliest memories to what you had for breakfast today? And then inscribing it for posterity? Don't let such thoughts prevent you from the genre of memoir writing that has been around from time immemorial and never more popular than today. But memoir writing does not mean it must be your life story.

Like the personal essay, a memoir draws from personal experiences and thoughts. It can be about one experience or involve just a few hours of your life. Such memoirs are like personal essays if the length is around several thousand words. No absolute distinction appears to exist between personal essays and memoirs, and often it is nothing more than the call of an editor labeling a piece one or the other. But once you get into the tens of thousands of words and have entered the realm of book-length projects, the only thing your work can properly be called is a "memoir," which will be thoroughly examined in Chapter 18.

CHAPTER 3

The Genres of Nonfiction Books

Hundreds of thousands of nonfiction books are published each year—a tenfold increase from the new titles published annually near the end of the last millennium. With so many opportunities, there is no reason why your book can't join this list. But first, because there are so many kinds of nonfiction books, you must decide the genre in which you want to write and in order to do this, you need to become familiar with all the categories.

General Nonfiction

There are two ways to go about describing "general nonfiction." One approach is to say that general nonfiction is nonfiction that doesn't fit neatly into a specific nonfiction genre. The other method might be to say that general nonfiction is whatever is left over after all the books are listed in nonfiction categories. Either way, you would be right.

As a writer, you will find an advantage and a disadvantage in becoming the author of a general nonfiction book. On the plus side, since you are not limiting yourself to a specific nonfiction genre where certain protocols, writing styles, and techniques must be followed, you have more leeway and artistic discretion in crafting your book. On the negative side, go to a bookstore and browse the nonfiction aisles and try to find the shelves marked "general nonfiction." It's possible you'll never locate that section, because often it doesn't exist. This is why from a marketing perspective, as you will see in Chapter 23, a book generally is assigned to a genre and a target market.

An examination of a recent *New York Times* bestseller list shows that of the fifteen top nonfiction bestsellers, four were biographies/memoirs and eleven general nonfiction, of which five were political and three were humorous. The remaining bestsellers were books about the investigation of a serial killer, the influence of the mob over casinos in Cuba, and the "fleecing" of the consumer by the government, unions, and businesses. Clearly, there is a market for the general nonfiction book should this be your choice.

Books for Scholars, Students, and Professionals

If you are contemplating a book directed to students (textbooks), scholars, laypeople well versed and interested in a specific subject, or to members of a profession such as doctors, lawyers, and psychologists, then you must become well acquainted with this genre. Not only are the requirements for authoring this kind of book unique, but the substantive material and the style also differs from writing other nonfiction books.

You must make certain you have the requisite credentials in the subject such as a PhD in history if you're writing a book about the Enlightenment, or that you are a psychiatrist or psychologist if you're writing a book directed to mental health therapists. Another option is to collaborate with someone possessing the necessary credentials who will serve as your coauthor.

However, if you are qualified, writing scholarly and professional books is afforded many opportunities through the university presses and numerous general publishers. A great deal sets this genre apart from other nonfiction books, beginning with writing and researching the book, which you'll learn in Chapter 7, through the submission process (to be explored in Chapter 23).

ALERT

If you do not have the necessary credentials to write a scholarly book, interviewing experts in the field or having someone who is credentialed write a foreword will not suffice. Such alternatives work for other types of nonfiction but cannot satisfy students, scholars, and professionals.

Self-Help and How-To Books

The first advice book that was published in America appeared in 1817 and offered guidance to parents. Less than two centuries later, there are almost 80,000 self-help books one can purchase that bestow advice on widely diverse matters such as achieving "happiness," managing stress, tapping into your creativity, and obtaining "personal transformation."

While always a popular genre, self-help and how-to books underwent a significant change in the last several decades. There are now a smaller proportion of titles in the "how-to" category providing hands-on practical instruction in such matters as painting a room, drafting your own will, fixing your lawnmower, and writing a nonfiction book. Comprising the larger segment of this genre we now have more books that you might call ethereal and new-age, which cover issues like achieving personal fulfillment and enrichment, living the spiritual life, and relating to the world around you.

Nonetheless, if you are knowledgeable in the subject and can write within the parameters of this genre (which will be examined in Chapter 8), then writing a how-to or self-help book can be rewarding and a lot of fun.

Religion and Spirituality

Spirituality, religious feelings, and formal religion have been with humankind for thousands of years and so have books on the subjects. In the latter decades of the twentieth century with the dawn of the new millennium approaching, spirituality became a very popular genre. In recent years, traditional books about religion have constituted a large segment of this category with thousands of new titles published annually dealing with Christianity, Buddhism, Judaism, Hinduism, and Islam. Books about religious books such as the Bible and the Koran are popular as well.

The thing to keep in mind is that the range of subject matter in this genre is practically limitless. To give you an idea of the scope of subjects you can select, just consider titles of several bestsellers in this genre:

- *God Gave Us Heaven* by Lisa Tawn Bergren
- *Man's Search for Meaning* by Viktor E. Frankl
- *Where's Your Jesus Now? Examining How Fear Erodes Our Faith* by Karen Spears Zacharias
- *So You Don't Want to Go to Church Anymore* by Jake Colsen
- *The Power of Now: A Guide to Spiritual Enlightenment* by Eckhart Tolle
- *The Purpose Driven Life* by Rick Warren

As you can gather from some of the preceding titles, books about religion and spirituality do not have to be dry or scholarly. They can be conversational and directed to a mass audience. What is more, you don't have to be a religious scholar or cleric to write a book about spirituality. In fact, spiritual books often find themselves in the "self-help" and "health/mind/body" sections of the bookstore. Even writing a book dealing with religion does not require credentials unless it fits into the scholarly category. However, the book must be based on research and other acceptable methods of verifying your facts, which you will learn about in Chapter 5. So, if you want to explore the spiritual world, delve into the divine or mystical, or write a traditional book on religion, becoming the author of a book in this category may be for you.

Books about Health, Mind, and Body

Books about health, mind, and body comprise a major genre but they also cross over into the self-help and spiritual categories. So, for example, a book titled *A New Earth: Awakening to Your Life's Purpose* (by Eckhart Tolle) can be found in the health/mind/body section of the bookstore and also where books about spirituality and self-help are located.

The health/mind/body genre contains many subdivisions, including: mental health, death and grief, psychology and counseling, diet and weight loss, exercise and fitness, nutrition, and sex. If you want to write a book in this genre, you will find it helpful to have some degree of expertise. For example, if you want to write about nutrition or weight loss, you should be a nutritionist or in the medical field. If you want to write about grief recovery or breaking addiction, you should be a mental health professional. Of course, if your research, interviews, and possibly even your own real-life experiences are impressive, you may qualify to write such a book without a formal degree.

ESSENTIAL

Sometimes your personal experience will be sufficient to provide you with the voice of authority to write a health/mind/body book. For example, if you have completed several Ironman triathlons, you will likely be considered qualified to write about training for triathlons without having a degree in physical education or sports psychology or certification as a fitness trainer.

As you'll see in Chapter 10, books in this genre are written in a style similar to self-help books. In other words, you'll adopt a friendly, conversational tone while informing and instructing and, like self-help books, they are enjoyable to write. Consider some of the bestselling titles in this category:

- *Skinny Bitch: A No-Nonsense, Tough-Love Guide for Savvy Girls Who Want to Stop Eating Crap and Start Looking Fabulous!* by Rory Freedman and Kim Barnouin
- *Fit and Fabulous in Fifteen Minutes* by Teresa Tapp, with Barbara Smalley
- *Blink: The Power of Thinking Without Thinking* by Malcolm Gladwell
- *Fast Food Nation* by Eric Schlosser
- *Money and the Law of Attraction: Learning to Attract Wealth, Health, and Happiness* by Esther and Jerry Hicks

Parenting/Family/Relationships

If nothing else, parents, children, spouses, and the relationships among members of the family unit have always been, and likely always will be, a fertile subject providing an endless supply of fodder for books offering advice and guidance. Indeed, the "players" and participants have increased with the advent of "extended" families, "live-in" companions, "significant others," and "life partners." The demand for these books is practically insatiable, and if writing in this genre is your desire, you have chosen wisely.

Of course, as with most nonfiction, you should be an "authority" in the subject. But personal experience can be an acceptable substitute for an undergraduate or graduate degree. Consider a book on how to raise children with autism by a parent with an autistic child, or a book about entering the singles scene at the age of fifty-something written by a widow who found herself in that situation.

There are many subcategories in this genre, including: adoption, aging, parenting, family relationships, childbirth, fertility, and special needs. In the 1970s and 1980s many books were written about relationships between spouses and what to do when things went awry. In recent years, a large number of books in this genre have been devoted to fertility issues and raising children, as you can glean from some of the following bestselling titles:

- *100,000 + Baby Names* by Bruce Lansky
- *Happiest Toddler on the Block: How to Eliminate Tantrums and Raise a Patient, Respectful, and Cooperative One- to Four-Year-Old* by Harvey Karp, MD
- *So Sexy So Soon: The New Sexualized Childhood and What Parents Can Do to Protect Their Kids* by Diane E. Levin, PhD, and Jean Kilbourne, EdD
- *What to Expect When You're Expecting* by Heidi Murkoff and Sharon Mazel
- *10 Conversations You Need to Have with Your Children* by Shmuley Boteach
- *The Baby Book: Everything You Need to Know about Your Baby from Birth to Age Two* by William Sears, MD, and Martha Sears, RN

Biographies—Writing about the Lives of Others

The public's fascination with learning about the lives of others is voracious, as reflected in the countless stories concerning famous and sometimes not-so-famous people that regularly appear in periodicals, television programs, Internet sites, and even word-of-mouth gossip. Perhaps this is why one of the most popular genres is biographies. In recent years there has existed at any given time well over 15,000 titles to choose from. So, if there is someone whose life intrigues you and you want to immerse yourself in a book-length project to chronicle that person's story, writing a biography is a good idea.

In writing a biography, the research and reliability of the facts must be impeccable. However, you don't have to be a scholar or an expert in any given field. What matters most is that you know how to do the research (which you'll learn in Chapter 5 and then more specifically in Chapter 12) and that you apply all the relevant techniques of nonfiction writing, which you'll acquire in the next chapter.

FACT

While biographies do not have to be about famous people, most published biographies do have well-known individuals as their subject. In the United States, biographies abound regarding former presidents like John Adams, Washington, Truman, Theodore Roosevelt, and Franklin Roosevelt. In fact, it is possible that more biographies have been written about Abraham Lincoln than any other person in history.

Biographies about prominent persons cover the full spectrum. One best-seller list includes individuals as diverse as Albert Einstein, Karl Marx, Frederick Douglas, Warren Buffet, Robert Kennedy, and Madonna. However, you need not limit yourself to well-known individuals. As long as there is an audience for a particular person—frequently someone recognized in a specific community—a publisher can often be secured. You also should not be dissuaded from undertaking a biography simply because biographies have already been written about the subject of your proposed book. Indeed, there have been occasions when two or even three biographies about the same individual were published within weeks of each other.

Other Categories and Niche Books

If you have a book in mind that doesn't seem to fit into one of the genres discussed in this chapter or you don't have a specific idea and none of these categories appeals to you, do not despair. There are many other categories of nonfiction books that publishers seek which you can consider. Many of these genres have hundreds and even thousands of books published every year. To get you started, consider some of the following categories:

- Horticulture/gardening
- Art/architecture
- Business/economics
- Cookbooks/dining
- Government/politics/world affairs
- History
- Nature/environment
- Music/dance
- Hobbies
- Military/war

Still haven't found a genre that arouses your interest and yet you still thirst to write that book-length project? Then return to the techniques discussed in Chapter 1 and mine the world around you as well as your own inner thoughts and feelings. No matter what subject you come up with, if that's what you want to pursue, you should go for it. Even if it's something as narrow as existentialism and the mind of Woody Allen or the fifty best public libraries west of the Rockies, it will probably find a home in what is referred to as the "niche" market for books.

The important thing to bear in mind if you want to write a nonfiction book is that if this is your goal, you should go for it. You can determine the genre before or after the project is complete, although at some time, before you finish the final proposal or manuscript and begin to seek an agent or publisher, it would be best if you have reached a decision. When all is said and done, what matters most is that you write the book you want to write, keeping in mind the techniques and elements of good nonfiction writing.

CHAPTER 4

Elements of Nonfiction Writing

Now that you have decided the subject you want to write about and you know the nonfiction genre for your project; the moment has finally arrived to begin the actual act of writing. "It's about time!" you exclaim as you pull out pen and pad or flip on your computer, relishing the fact that this moment has finally arrived. But while this can be a fulfilling and enjoyable activity, you'll only succeed if you learn and apply the key elements common to writing all types of nonfiction.

Truth and Accuracy

You saw in Chapter 1 that the fundamental distinction between writing fiction and nonfiction is that the nonfiction writer must scrupulously adhere to truth and accuracy. You also saw how it is sometimes impossible for the reader to discern what is true and what is not, which means that the reader must rely on the writer's representations. Thus, it boils down to a matter of trust, and if you take upon yourself the role of a nonfiction writer, you are ethically bound to this responsibility. Perhaps because it is a question of trust, when a nonfiction writer is discovered to have fabricated the facts, the public outcry is loud and clear—especially toward journalists and memoirists.

ALERT

When relying upon interviews or experts in the subject, you cannot take what is said at face value. If something arouses a question in your mind, you must pursue it further to make certain it is accurate. Ultimately, the validity of your work falls squarely on your shoulders and you are the one who will be held accountable.

A Distinct Writing Style

When reading nonfiction, readers need to believe and trust the writer and that what is represented is true. One way this comes across is in the writing style. There are different techniques when writing fiction and nonfiction that will be explored in many ways throughout this book. As an example, consider the following two excerpts:

> "And then, while he was fortunately anchored to the edge of the bed, the vertigo took him by the ears, a shot of bile surged into his throat, and he felt as he had felt riding the waves as a kid after catching a big one too late and it broke over him like the chandelier at Asbury's palatial Mayfair, the great chandelier that, in dreams he'd been having for half a century, ever since Morty was killed in the war, was tearing loose from its moorings and falling on top of his brother and him as they sat there innocently, side by side, watching *The Wizard of Oz*."

"Just about a year passed before he began, all at once, to lose his equilibrium. In the meantime, he'd had the cataract removed—restoring to his left eye practically 20/20 vision—and he and Lil had gone to Florida for their usual stay of four months. In December, in Palm Beach, they even attended the wedding that Sandy Kuvin had invited him to the previous spring back when the brain surgeon had told me that unless we okayed the operation, in a relatively short time he'd be much worse off—back when I thought that he'd never see Florida again."

Although both of the preceding paragraphs describe older men, vacation resorts, infirmity, death, and even vertigo, the writing styles could not be more different. Try examining this for yourself and note the distinguishing characteristics. Did you notice that the first paragraph was one run-on sentence? How about word choice and the use of literary devices? The matter-of-fact tone present in the second paragraph as opposed to the tone of the previous excerpt? What else did you discern?

Would it surprise you to learn that both paragraphs were written by the same writer? The first excerpt is taken from *Sabbath's Theater*, a highly acclaimed novel by Philip Roth. The second excerpt is from *Patrimony*, Roth's nonfiction book about his eighty-six–year-old father suffering from a brain tumor. It was written only four years before *Sabbath's Theater*, so the difference in writing style has nothing to do with the passage of time but rather everything to do with the fact that in one book, Roth writes as a nonfiction writer and in the other as a novelist.

Facts Must Be Verifiable

Despite the importance of a bond between the reader and writer based upon trust conveyed through the writing style, the material presented must be demonstrable by independent sources. This can be accomplished by:

- Interviews
- Research
- Reliance on experts
- Observations
- Personal experiences

In the next chapter, you will discover how to utilize these resources effectively and ethically. You'll also learn the importance of having sources that are up to current standards.

Details, Details, and More Details

If you want to write fiction and you want it to have the ring of truth, you need to permeate the work with details. This is what brings the writing alive and makes it believable for the reader. With nonfiction, there can never be enough details to make the work complete, because that is the heart and soul of writing nonfiction.

Consider the following description of a group of firefighters in the best-selling and award-winning book *Young Men and Fire* by Norman Maclean (author of *A River Runs Through It*), which recounts the story of the Mann Gulch fire that claimed the lives of a brave band of firefighters:

> "They crawled out of their jump suits that made them look part spacemen and part football players. In 1949 they even wore regular leather football helmets; then there was wire mesh all over their faces, the padded canvas suit (with damn little padding), and logger boots. . . . Their work clothes, unlike their jump suits, were their own, and they were mostly just ordinary work clothes—Levis and blue shirts, but hard hats. None in this crew appeared in white shirts and oxfords."

Just think of what Maclean's attention to details accomplishes: the reader is drawn into the scene and narrative; the author conveys a mastery over the facts that results in a convincing portrayal of the events; the reader is made to feel that the author is believable and trustworthy because he took the time and trouble to gather this material. Details are the lifeblood of nonfiction and you must dispense them with skill and art.

You Must Write Well

Ever attend a writers' conference, a workshop, or a writing class? If not, it's something you should consider, and you'll learn more about this in Chapter 24. If you have participated in such a program, you may have been informed about some of the "rules" of proper writing such as: use semicolons sparingly and never when writing fiction; commas should be employed in moderation, only when appropriate, and in a series of three or more; a sentence should never end in a preposition even if it's the only thing you can think of.

To write well, one cannot be ignorant of the rules of language and grammar. You must know what is proper and what is incorrect before you can determine whether or not a particular rule should be followed or discarded for the sake of the writing.

The truth is that there are no absolute rules when it comes to writing well regardless what you may be told by a writing instructor or workshop leader. Some of the very best writing and most talented writers repeatedly violate the fundamental canons of grammar. What counts is whether the writing is effective, and this can be subjective and a matter of opinion. For example, it may be incorrect grammatically to end a sentence in a preposition, but sometimes to maintain a conversational tone or particular voice or get across a sense of realism in the dialogue, it is the best option.

Rules Vary in the Genres

When writing fiction, one has far greater latitude when it comes to grammar than writing nonfiction. Conformity to the rules of grammar varies among nonfiction genres. In some nonfiction genres, rules of grammar must be followed assiduously, such as in scholarly treatises, textbooks, and articles appearing in professional journals and newspapers. You'll have some flexibility regarding grammar if you're writing articles, reviews, and opinion pieces and even more latitude with memoirs, personal essays, and creative nonfiction.

The best way to know the degree of flexibility you have in adhering to basic principles of grammar in a specific genre is to become familiar with that genre. The most effective method to do this is to become well read in that genre.

Regardless of the nonfiction genre you select, there are some common grammatical mistakes many writers make which you should avoid. Here is a sampling:

- Do not confuse *that* and *which*. *That* is the restrictive or defining pronoun while *which* is the nonrestrictive or nondefining pronoun.

- Do not substitute *affect*, the verb, for *effect*, the noun.
- Avoid using an exclamation mark following a simple straightforward statement of fact. The exclamation mark should be employed for commands or true exclamations.
- Do not insert commas between cumulative adjectives.
- *Can* refers to an ability and should not be an alternate for *may*.
- *Irregardless* should not be substituted for *regardless*.
- At the end of a list introduced by *such as* or *for example*, do not end the list with *etc.*
- Avoid starting a sentence with the word *however* when the meaning is *nevertheless*.
- Omit needless words and use definite, specific, concrete language.

Point of View

If you want to write nonfiction, you must know about the different points of view at your disposal, especially since some nonfiction genres are written in one point of view while others must be written from a different point of view.

FACT

You must be able to control the point of view. Shifting from one point of view to another betrays the consistency of the narrative voice and can confuse the reader. Shifting points of view are rarely used in nonfiction and when this does occur, it is generally limited to books and employed by experienced writers.

The Four Points of View

There are four points of view from which you can choose to write: the first person, the second person, the third person omniscient and the third person objective. When writing in the first person, you are speaking directly to the reader and frequently use the word *I*. In the first person, you'll be conveying information that only you would possess. Typically, personal essays and memoirs are written in the first person.

Writing in the second person is an even more direct way to address the reader and commonly employs the words *you* and *yours*. How-to/self-help books and manuals are often written in the second person. This book is written in the second person.

The two remaining points of view are written in the third person. The third person omniscient is where the writer knows everything there is to know—like a mythical Greek god with an "all-seeing eye." Indeed, the writer can even enter the minds of the subjects in the work. For example, in a biography about Abraham Lincoln that is written in the third person omniscient, the reader may actually get a view inside Lincoln's head and experience what he is thinking. The third person objective does not have this capacity but describes things as they are seen from the outside. So in a biography about Lincoln written in the third person objective, the reader will not have access to Lincoln's thoughts.

ALERT

Whether intended or not, once you use the *I* word, you will have shifted from whatever point of view you had been utilizing to the first person point of view. This should only be done if this is your intention, so take care not to use the *I* word unless you have been writing in the first person.

Voice of Authority

In Chapter 1, you were advised to find your voice and write with that voice. But you also must make certain your voice manifests the authority that is so important in writing nonfiction. In Chapters 7 and 13, you will see sample excerpts from different writers written in their own distinctive styles, but all of them are written in a voice of authority. In order to write in a voice of authority, there are two things you must accomplish.

Write with Expertise

There are several ways you can become an authority on the subject of your project and demonstrate a mastery over the material. Obviously, you can validate yourself as an authority if you have already amassed this knowledge through earning an undergraduate or graduate degree or if you are a professional writing about a subject in your field. If this is not the case, there is another avenue open to you, which is to rely on experts through interviews and research, which shall be explored in the following chapter. Finally, your own personal experiences might give you all the authority you need about a particular topic.

ESSENTIAL

Do not avoid writing about a subject simply because you know very little about it. One of the wonderful things about being a writer is that it can be a learning process. W. H. Auden eloquently expresses this: "Writers write what they know. But they don't know what they know until they write it."

Remain Unassuming

The second prerequisite to enable you to write with a voice of authority is that your writing reflects the confidence you have in yourself and in your command of the subject. You must appear bold, decisive, and self-assured. Of course, this is not something you flaunt throughout the pages, because then you will not have the kind of voice a reader finds trustworthy and companionable.

For instance, picture yourself in a doctor's office with the physician explaining the diagnosis of your condition. The doctor can be aloof and speak in professional jargon, talking down to you, or she can be understanding and friendly, conversing in laymen's language to get the message across. Which do you prefer? Same goes for the voice of authority you employ.

CHAPTER 5

Getting the Facts Right

With truth and accuracy being the lifeblood of nonfiction, it is crucial that the writer get the facts right. There are a number of means to accomplish this, most or all of which you will use at some point in your work. Some of these methods have specific protocols such as research and interviews while others, like relying on your own personal experiences and observations, are less formal. You also need to know what pitfalls to avoid, such as copyright infringement and consulting experts who are not what they appear to be.

You Don't Have to Be an Expert

Think how little you would have to write if you had to be an authority on every subject you might want to write about. That is why the process that culminates in a finished and polished work of nonfiction, whether a short article or a 400-page book, begins as a learning experience and ends with the writer knowing more than when he began—even if he was an authority at the start. This is what makes writing nonfiction an exciting and rewarding adventure.

There are a number of methods you can utilize to obtain the knowledge you must possess in order to write and complete your project. While each of these procedures will be discussed separately in the following, you will generally find that you'll use more than one for any given undertaking. For example, in an article about the Olympics you might draw on your own experiences having observed previous Olympic events; interview current and former athletes, coaches, or officials; visit and observe the venue where it is held; and research the history of the Olympics. So in just one article, you may well avail yourself of all the tools at a writer's disposal to become knowledgeable in a given subject.

Personal Experiences and the World Around You

It can be said that writers do their best work when they are not at their desk. Once you understand that the writing process is so much more than the actual task of writing—putting pen to paper or making words appear on the computer screen—you can appreciate this statement. Writing entails not just looking at but actually seeing what is going on in the world and outside your front door. Once you do that, not only will you come up with ideas you might want to write about but you also will gain knowledge to enable you to write on a subject.

If you have kept a diary or journal, reviewing your entries from the past is a terrific source of information stemming from your own personal experiences. You also can use a journal or diary to record current impressions you reach about what you have recently observed that can prove helpful in future projects.

Writing is like drawing water from a well. If the well runs dry, there is no water to draw. This is the same for writing. Even if you have an idea, if there is nothing inside you—at least some information to bring substance to the idea—then it will linger and no words will pour forth. All you have to do is be open to what is happening around you, consider it with a keen eye and critical mind, and if worthwhile, store it away in your brain or write it down and file it where you can use it at some future time to prime the pump when you're ready to write.

Research

When you hear the word *research*, does it make you cringe? Do boring, tedious, time-consuming activities come to mind? It doesn't have to be that way. Research can and should be an exciting, intriguing journey—an exploration of the unknown where at the end of the trail you have amassed a treasure of knowledge. At least, that's how it can be and there are numerous venues for you to employ in this quest.

Despite the convenience, breadth, and scope of the Internet, you should not dismiss what the traditional brick-and-mortar library has to offer. You will generally find reference librarians eager to provide support, and you can save much time by having them assist you and steer you in the right direction.

FACT

Your local library, where you have access to journals, magazines, and books as well as online resources, is an excellent place to begin your research. However, you should also consider university and college libraries for more advanced research, although admittance for the general public is sometimes limited.

Naturally, there is no substitute for the Internet regarding convenience and the number of sources to be had. However, you must take care concerning the sources you utilize. Nonetheless, conducting a search of your subject or employing a keyword will instantly provide you with numerous sites to examine where you can gather the information you require. There are, however, a number of sites that are particularly useful for a writer conducting research, several of which are:

- *www.wordsmyth.net* has a dictionary and thesaurus for convenient reference.
- *www.meriam-webster.com* provides access to the *Encyclopaedia Britannica* as well as a thesaurus and dictionary for a monthly fee.
- *www.fedstats.gov* and *www.usa.gov* provide statistics and information on local and federal government entities as well as agencies and policies.
- *www.refdesk.com* supplies links to experts and reference facilities on almost any topic.

ALERT

Many editors restrict the number of Internet sources that may be cited in a work or how much web research can be relied upon. The reason for this restriction is that, for the most part, anyone can place anything on the Internet. You should always investigate the legitimacy and respectability of any source you use on the Internet.

Interviews

Another avenue open to you for obtaining the information you need is to interview experts or people with firsthand information about your subject. Many times such people prove an invaluable source for material that is simply not available otherwise because it never has been published. For example, suppose you want to write a biography about Elizabeth Taylor. You might want to contact people who worked with her professionally or knew her personally to learn more about her.

Aside from providing insight and clarification on key topics, interviews can also enliven your work. The presence of actual people on the pages make for a more dynamic experience for the reader. Quotations and anecdotes, especially when given extemporaneously, add luster to your piece. And not only are interviews entertaining for the readers but they can be fun to conduct, making your project that much more enjoyable an undertaking.

Setting up the Interview

The means of making first contact and requesting an interview have evolved over time and with technology. Today e-mail is perhaps the best way to contact your subject to request an interview. But whatever form of initial contact you employ, it goes without saying you should be polite, friendly, and get to the point. Don't be intimidated by the prominence of your subject and don't be afraid to ask for an interview. You will often find that the more well known the person, the more likely she will be to grant an interview. Once arrangements have been made, the time to begin your interview is before it even takes place.

Prepare, Prepare, and Prepare Some More

Despite the importance of interviews and the extent to which they are frequently employed, there sometimes exists a carefree attitude that all that needs to be done is to ask questions—sometimes without even having prepared them in advance. Yet, nothing is further from the truth.

ALERT

It is important to obtain the consent of the interviewee to have a phone conversation recorded. You can have this accomplished in advance with a written document but it is best to ask the subject at the outset of the interview with the tape running to confirm consent.

The first thing you must do to get ready for the interview is to have an idea of what shape your article or the relevant portion of your book will take and how the interviewee fits into it. In other words, do not simply make a list of questions. Give the matter a good deal of thought in advance. You should ask yourself what it is that you want to get from the interview. You also need to plan the arrangements: how it will be recorded; when and where it will take place; the length of time involved. Consider the following points as a partial checklist you can utilize to adequately prepare for the interview:

- Review biographical information and background material, such as articles and books about your subject or written by your subject.

- Confirm all arrangements that have been made including the time of the interview, the location (if face-to-face), and the means, such as tape-recording, e-mail, or phone.
- Formulate specific questions and/or an outline.
- Begin the interview with uncomplicated questions that will put your subject at ease and then move on in a logical order. Your questions need to go somewhere.
- Make sure your questions will elicit information that your readers need to know and that is pertinent to your subject.

The Interview

The actual interview should be an enjoyable and rewarding experience for both you and the interviewee. In the end, an interview is nothing more than two people getting to know each other. Although it's likely you'll learn more about your subject (which is the point of conducting the interview), you still will be revealing something of yourself even if only by the questions you ask. As for being nervous—don't be. There is no reason you should be. After all, you're the one asking the questions.

Of course, conducting an interview via e-mail won't yield the benefit of meeting the subject face-to-face. Nonetheless, it certainly is a convenient way to carry out the interview and overcomes geographical distances or arranging a mutually agreeable time and place. E-mail interviews also allow the subject more time to respond to your questions.

FACT

E-mail interviews have certain benefits: speed, convenience, and the elimination of the need to transcribe the answers. On the negative side, you must make certain the e-mail interview is promptly opened and answered and not left in your mailbox. Nor do you have the flexibility to follow up with new questions.

With the phone interview, you merely have to establish an appointed time to speak. You can take notes as well as record the conversation with the interviewee's consent. Other than meeting in person, the phone interview is similar to the face-to-face interview.

If you are well prepared, the interview should go smoothly. Make sure you review the questions and any notes beforehand. Ask questions that go somewhere even if it means adding a question to follow up on a response or varying your questions based on what you learn during the interview. Try to frame your questions so they need to be answered with more than a "yes" or "no." Finally, you should be polite, professional, and nonjudgmental, remaining in the background as an active listener.

After the Interview

Following the interview, you should rewrite your notes as soon as possible so they are complete and legible. It is important that you do this while the interview is still fresh in your mind. Even if you had recorded the interview, you should still transcribe it promptly.

You need not write the interview in the exact words of the interviewee. Feel free to edit, but do so prudently and only to bring clarity to the subject's answers. You may revise quotes as long as this is clearly indicated, and the end result should not stray from the meaning of what the subject said.

Avoid Copyright Infringement

Care must be taken when transforming your research into your own composition to avoid copyright infringement, which is the illegal misappropriation of work that is protected by copyright. You may only use copyrighted material with the permission of the copyright holder. This is secured by written agreement—usually a letter signed by the copyright holder—similar to the sample in Appendix B.

ESSENTIAL

Copyright infringement is not plagiarism. Plagiarism is the failure of providing acknowledgment to the author of the material and instead taking credit for oneself. The plagiarist falsely represents that someone else's work is his own, while the person who infringes upon another's copyright reproduces the work without permission. A copyright infringement may occur even with credit given to the author.

Without going into the complexities of copyright law, the most prudent course of conduct you should follow is to assume that everything you have come upon in written or tangible form has been copyrighted and you will need permission of the copyright holder to reproduce any of it or to expropriate its substance. You cannot assume that the author is the copyright holder. It can be the publisher or another party, but starting with the author—unless the name of the copyright holder is indicated—is a good idea.

The six defenses to copyright infringement are:

1. Fair use
2. Independent creation without knowledge of the other work
3. Use of public domain
4. Permission had been granted
5. Inexcusable delay to enforce the copyright
6. Statute of limitations to bring legal action had lapsed

If you can prove you created your work independently of the copyrighted material, you will not be liable for infringement. However, the burden will be on you to substantiate this, which can be difficult to do. Suppose you write an article for a local newspaper about feral cats and the best way to utilize "have-a-heart" traps to capture the cats without injury. A few months later you receive notice that you have infringed upon a copyrighted article in *Cat Fancy*, a magazine with national circulation, that appeared before your article and explained the same procedure. How do you prove you never saw the article? You can see how difficult proving your claim can be.

FACT

Copyright protection does not last forever and once expired the work falls into the public domain. Work created before January 1, 1978, is protected for a period up to seventy-five years. Work created after that date is protected for a period spanning the life of the author plus seventy years.

You would not be liable for copyright infringement if you secured permission; the copyright holder was tardy in bringing legal action; the time period for copyright protection had lapsed; or the material fell into the public domain. These are straightforward defenses that can be established. The more difficult and more frequently occurring issue arises when you maintain the right to make "fair use" of the material and therefore did not need to secure permission.

Fair Use

The concept of "fair use" is a defense to copyright infringement that permits researchers, scholars, educators, and the like to utilize small portions of copyrighted work for socially beneficial purposes without obtaining consent. "Fair use" has been relied upon throughout this book wherever you came upon an excerpt or quotation. You will note that acknowledgment has always been made to the author of the work to avoid the taint of plagiarism. On the other hand, samples that appear in Appendix A were accompanied by a signed permission to use the work.

The problem in relying upon the "fair use" doctrine is that the final judgment rests with the court in applying the standards to a specific case. Unfortunately, there are no clear demarcations and this can be a murky issue. For example, exactly what is a "small portion" of the work that has been utilized? Clearly, a few words will fall within the "fair use" protection and several pages will not. But what about one page? One paragraph? Two paragraphs? There is no guarantee what a court may hold when it comes to interpreting this gray area of the law. It is best for you to err on the side of caution. There are some guidelines, however, you can consider when making a determination about whether "fair use" is applicable:

- The less commercial your work, the more likely fair use will apply.
- The more didactic or scholarly your work, or if it is newsworthy, the greater the chances fair use can be relied upon.
- Using your own words or paraphrasing the material rather than quoting the work strengthens the case for fair use.
- The shorter the work relied upon—generally two paragraphs or less—the more likely fair use applies.
- Do not make use of the crux or major part of another's work.
- Provide appropriate credit to the author of the work.
- Your work should not compete in the commercial market with the work copied.

Reliance on Experts and Sources

While this has been said before, it merits repeating. Even though you have researched your subject thoroughly and you can cite a number of independent sources and experts in the topic at hand, ultimately, responsibility for the veracity of the material and facts falls upon you. You need to substantiate the credentials of your experts and the reputation of your sources. If need be, confirm the accuracy of the biographical information provided by your experts. This is easy to do by accessing the Internet.

As for the resources you rely upon, try to use both online and traditional sources. Encyclopedias and other general sources of information make for a good starting point, but if you are writing about a specific subject, you will need to delve further. Finally, make certain that your sources are up to date.

CHAPTER 6

Writing Nonfiction Books

Before becoming an author of a nonfiction book, you must decide what you want to write about and whether it is a book-length project. The next step is to map out your plan beginning with gathering all the material and information you will need and then outlining how this will appear in a book. Finally, you can settle in and commence the actual writing, bearing in mind the special skills and techniques you will rely upon to produce a professional book that will make you proud.

Selecting Your Subject and Genre

You saw in Chapter 1 some of the ways to arrive at a subject you want to write about. The important word in the previous sentence is *want*. Unless writing is your livelihood and you are presented with the topic to write a book for which you will be paid, it is important that you are enthused about the theme of your book.

Choosing the Subject

From the inception of an idea to putting down the first words to the day you receive the final galleys, you may be living with this book for several years. So, the project had better be important to you and something you "want" to do or else you might not have the stamina or desire to make it to the finish.

ESSENTIAL

"Writing a book is like falling in love or getting to sleep or finding a taxi in the rain. It'll come to you, but first you have to let it."—*Kill Two Birds & Get Stoned* by Kinky Friedman

You have already been told that you should be familiar with the subject of your book at the outset. Otherwise, you may not know where to begin the research or how to critically assess your sources. While you need not be an authority at first, by the time you reach the last page, you will have attained a degree of expertise in the field.

Choosing the Right Genre

Now that you have a subject with which you are familiar, it would be a good idea if you could determine the genre in which it fits. In Chapter 3, you saw some of the major genres and were informed that there are also numerous small and niche categories for all sorts of nonfiction books.

But if you can't seem to find the right genre, don't put your project on hold. You can make this decision later, although in some cases you do need to know at the beginning. For example, suppose you decide to write about the Watergate scandal that resulted in the resignation of President Nixon but you're not sure if you want to emphasize the characters and the drama or unearth new information, leaving you in a quandary as to whether it will be general nonfiction, creative nonfiction, or scholarly. In such a case, you won't be able to delay because if it's to be a scholarly book, the rigors of research must be observed and the writing style and tone is much different than general or creative nonfiction.

Ready to Write the Book—Almost

Now armed with the knowledge that you have your subject and genre, you're set to go. Or, so you think. However, there remains one more issue to be decided and even after that, it may be a long time before you begin to write the full manuscript.

Is There a Book Here?

Before you proceed further, you must honestly ask yourself whether the project you have in mind needs to be conveyed in 50,000 words or more. Keep in mind the writers' mantra that "less is more." While your idea and subject are superb and you are certain you have the ability to write about it convincingly, it just may be that the project can be as effectively expressed in an article or a series of articles.

It is not unusual for one article to lead to a second article on a subject and sometimes an entire series. With a proven track record of publication in the subject and having demonstrated an ability to write with authority on the topic, the result can be a book deal that expands on the articles.

There is also the question of marketability and securing a publisher for your book, which will be examined in great detail in Chapter 22. Beginning by writing articles on the subject (which will be explained in Chapter 13) is often a good strategic move to get you on the road to publishing your book.

It's Not the Book They Want to See

Many aspiring authors are surprised to learn that most publishers, editors, and agents do not want to see a book manuscript but instead require a book proposal. Consequently, unless you want to write the book whether it gets published or not, the point to remember is: "Don't write the book!"

You'll need a book proposal to shop your book project, and you'll learn how to do this in Chapter 23. Nonetheless, you must master every aspect of writing a nonfiction book in order to produce a first-rate book proposal, so we will continue with everything you need to know to write a nonfiction book.

ALERT

While the general rule is to write a book proposal to be marketed to editors and agents and write the book after a contract is signed, this is not always the case. Some genres and some publishers will require a complete manuscript before closing a deal. This is especially true of scholarly books.

Interview with Journalist and Author Dan Rottenberg

Dan Rottenberg has been the chief editor of seven publications and has written more than 300 articles for numerous magazines. A former *Wall Street Journal* reporter, he wrote an editorial-page column for the *Philadelphia Inquirer* for twenty years. Rottenberg is the author of ten books, including *The Inheritor's Handbook*, *The Man Who Made Wall Street*, and most recently, *Death of a Gunfighter: The Quest for Jack Slade, the West's Most Elusive Legend*.

RDB: You have written hundreds of articles and ten books. What have been the advantages and disadvantages of each?

DR: A book is a long-term project that may offer some semblance of immortality—one of the great compensations of writing. On the other hand, book publishing is a very capricious business. It's no easy thing to persuade people to spend $20 or $30 on your particular book, especially if your subject is obscure. That's especially true (as was the case with one of my books) when the publishing house is sold shortly before your book appears, and the editor, publicist, and marketing director all quit, leaving no one to champion your effort.

It's much easier to write an article for a magazine with subscribers who, while leafing through its pages, will stumble upon your article and may be enticed to read it. For that reason, in some respects magazine writers feel less subconscious pressure to hype their work than book authors feel. Such are the tradeoffs of the writer's life.

RDB: How do you go about determining the subjects of your books?

DR: I write for two reasons: for education and for immortality. So I look for subjects that interest me and where I can make a difference and learn something. Usually these are subjects that have been neglected by other authors. The great challenge is to find ways to interest people in important subjects that aren't necessarily sexy. (My Anthony Drexel biography, *The Man Who Made Wall Street*, was a prime example.) That said, I won't pursue a book project unless a publisher feels enthusiastic about it. I've kept projects on the back burner for years until I could light a fire under a publisher.

RDB: You have authored books over a span of thirty years. How have your research methods changed? Has your writing process altered over these years?

DR: Computers and the Internet have changed everything for me over the past thirty years. I used to type, cut, and paste (literally) and then retype a clean manuscript when I was finished. Aside from being labor-intensive, this process subconsciously inhibited me from polishing my prose. Thanks to computers, a change of a word here or there is no longer a big deal.

Similarly, I used to spend days researching a subject in the public library. Thanks to the Internet and e-mail, I'm able to access material and consult with experts all over the world within minutes. The "search" function on my computer is also an invaluable tool for sorting out information.

RDB: What changes have you seen in the book industry and among the publishing houses?

DR: When my first book, *Finding Our Fathers*, first appeared in 1977, 40,000 books were published annually in the United States. Now the figure is something like 280,000. Thanks to online publishing and the Internet, it's much easier to publish now, and much easier to find a niche for a specialized book. But it's much harder to attract the attention of respected book review outlets. Promotion is different as well. With *Finding Our Fathers*, I was sent on a twelve-city promotional tour, doing TV and radio appearances and public talks and signings. Today most books are sold over the Internet. It's a terrific sales tool, but I miss the public contact, which generated new ideas and new contacts.

RDB: Your most recent book, *Death of a Gunfighter, The Quest for Jack Slade, the West's Most Elusive Legend,* has been decades in the making. Can you share your passion and persistence with this project?

DR: One of my missions is to rescue deserving figures from obscurity. Anthony Drexel was one such figure; Jack Slade is another. I first encountered Slade in 1951 in the pages of *The Pony Express.* I was nine years old at the time and found myself instinctively drawn to this roughneck who, when handed a seemingly impossible assignment, fulfilled it beyond anyone's wildest expectations, only to be destroyed by the weight of the burden. I resolved to write a novel about him but eventually discovered that the historical Slade was far more extraordinary than anything my imagination could have conjured up. And so a childhood curiosity about Slade blossomed into a lifelong obsession to find and understand him. But it wasn't until about five years ago that I found a publisher who shared my enthusiasm, which was just as well, since the necessary research required the benefit of the Internet.

RDB: What are the most important qualities a writer should have to write a nonfiction book?

DR: Persistence, integrity, objectivity, organizational skills, and the ability to grasp the large picture. Writing a book is inevitably a huge project.

RDB: Any words of advice to budding authors?

DR: Ask yourself: What do you have to offer that no other author can offer? Maybe it's expertise in a particular subject. Maybe it's a perceptive eye. Maybe it's an analytical mind. Maybe it's a good ear for language. Maybe it's a love of words. Maybe it's a unique personal experience.

Also ask yourself: What book is worth a year or two (or five) of my life? If you're not really committed to your subject, maybe you'd be better off writing a magazine article and then moving onto some other subject.

Truth and Accuracy

Thus far, you have seen that truth and accuracy is the foundation upon which every nonfiction project rests. Nowhere is this more essential than in writing the nonfiction book. However, the other side of the coin is that in no other nonfiction genre is maintaining this standard more difficult. Clearly this is due to the extended length of a book and all the information and material included.

There is always room for some latitude from factual details and taking "literary license" in writing nonfiction, especially in creative nonfiction and memoirs where reliance upon memory is significant. However, scrupulous care must be made not to misrepresent or alter the essential accuracy and meaning of the material being presented. For example, if writing about a former teacher you had in elementary school whom you describe as being excessively overweight with glaring brown eyes peering through horn rimmed glasses balanced precariously on a hawkish nose but in fact you're not sure after all these years what the color of her eyes actually were or whether she was obese or merely on the chunky side, unless the description is vital to your work, chances are no harm done and it's within the realm of literary license.

You have seen in Chapter 5 the tools available to get at the truth and present the facts accurately. Suffice it to say, make the most of them—research, interviews, and experts. Remember to question and verify the accuracy and credentials of your sources. There is no place for misrepresentation even if only in several paragraphs of a 400-page book. You must be certain that what you present is bona fide.

Time to Get Organized

Now that you have completed the research, it's time to put it together in a way that is accessible as you move along with your writing. You may have already been organizing your material while collecting it but even then, chances are it's in need of a little tidying up.

Preparing your research material for writing is a lot like the editing you'll be performing on your first draft. You'll have to excise, delete, and store away for future projects that material you won't be using. You may also find the converse is true and that you need to explore some areas in more depth before you start writing.

The important thing is to have your material readily available at your fingertips. How you do this is up to you. You may have hard copies of everything or files stored on your computer or notes transcribed on index cards or even Post-its planted all over the walls. But the last thing you want to happen is to be in the middle of a sentence or an original idea or critical thought and have to start rummaging through your resource material in search of an item you know you must have.

The Outline

There are writers who prefer not to use an outline. While this can work for articles, essays, and shorter pieces, it is hard to write a nonfiction book without an outline. But here again, like the way you organize the material, there are no hard and fast rules regarding the form your outline should take, nor is it set in stone once you complete it. As you move along with your book, the outline can change. Remember, the outline is a guide to assist you in the journey of writing the book and since you were the one who created it, you can certainly alter the direction along the way.

A good starting point to compose your outline is the table of contents (TOC) that you will have written as part of your book proposal. In fact, your book proposal can serve as your outline with just some additional tinkering, or you may want to create a more traditional outline based on the proposal.

Time to Write

It may seem that this moment was never going to arrive but now that the research is complete, the material is organized, and you have a plan established, it's finally time to write. Everything you learned in Chapter 4 applies as you write your book. At the onset, you must determine your voice and writing style. As you have seen, if you are writing in a specific genre, you must adopt the voice and style required in that genre. If it's a scholarly book, you'll write in a professional tone with a first or third person point of view whereas if it's a how-to book, you'll write in a conversational tone from the first or second person point of view.

Regardless of the type of nonfiction book, your chief objective is to convey information and you must do this in a way that won't put the reader to sleep. The facts must be presented in a "readable" style. Remember, you're writing a book and presenting a large amount of information, so you have to take care not to overwhelm the reader at any given time. You don't want to be like the professor giving a lecture, going on and on, reading from prepared material, in a monotone, and never once deviating from a litany of facts. It's the same with your book—except all the reader has to do is put your book down if it gets too boring.

Finally, keep in mind that consistency is critical. It is not as difficult to avoid shifting points of view or changing tone when writing an article as it is with a book. Not only is it a matter of maintaining the same voice and point of view over hundreds of pages but you'll be doing so over a period of months or even years during the course of writing.

Editing and Rewriting

There is only one way when writing a book that you can ensure your voice has been consistent, the information is true and accurate, the material is readable, and the book is everything you want it to be—to rewrite and edit.

Rewriting to Fit Your Style

Remember in Chapter 1 where Kurt Vonnegut spoke about two kinds of writers: swoopers, who write on and on and then go back to rewrite; and the bashers, who struggle with a sentence at a time until they get it right? Whichever you are, you will be rewriting—it's just a question of where and when.

The first step in rewriting is to read your first draft. You must do so with a critical eye and from the point of view of a reader who knows nothing beforehand about what you—the writer—has to say. Feel free to make notes but try to read from beginning to end so you can grasp the big picture.

Obviously, if you are a swooper, you're going to rewrite a large amount of material at one time. With a nonfiction book, you may write the entire first draft without looking back or, you may rewrite each time you complete several pages or a chapter. It doesn't matter which approach you take so long as it works for you. Just keep in mind the skills and techniques discussed in Chapters 1 and 4 as you rewrite.

Editing Can Be Fun

Some say that in every editor there is a writer. The converse is probably true as well, that inside every writer is an editor waiting to red-pencil. The difference is that at the end of the writing process, every writer gets to be an editor, like it or not, and this is a crucial stage in writing the book. And yet, editing can be fun because you get to wear another hat—that of editor—and you get to pretend you are no longer the writer, because you must look at the work from a critical objective perspective.

FACT

When examining your work through the eyes of an editor, you have to do so on two levels. First, consider the big picture and what no longer belongs in the book or what else may be needed. Second, you have to get down to the details and look at word choice, grammar, spelling, and techniques.

There is much to take into account when editing your work and some of this—such as deleting and adding material—has been discussed previously. But here are some points to keep in mind when editing:

- Make certain the information is conveyed in a concise and comprehensible manner.
- The ideas and meaning should be clear and logical.
- Review the manuscript to be sure the point of view has not shifted and the voice remains authoritative and consistent.
- Review grammar, spelling, punctuation, and other writing mechanics, confirming that where there is improper usage, you have intended this for the sake of a good read.
- Make sure the language and word use advances the tone.
- Be satisfied that the book flows smoothly from one paragraph to another and one chapter to the next.

Writing Exercises

Writing a book is a formidable undertaking but it need not be an insurmountable one. If you want to write a book then you should do it and take pleasure in the process as well as relish the sense of accomplishment that awaits you when the final manuscript is in your hands. To help you get started, consider the following exercises.

EXERCISE 1

Just like every other writing project, writing a book begins with an idea. The difference, however, is that the subject must be book length. To see how this might work, go to that place where you receive your inspiration and on separate sheets of paper or index cards, write down five distinct concepts for a possible book. Put it away for a day or two.

EXERCISE 2

Now that you've had some time off, revisit the five ideas and see if you can come up with at least five subtopics for each and write them down. For example, you may have written "the O.J. Simpson Murder Trial," since it always fascinated you but the only subtopic you think of has to do with the size of the glove and you just can't come up with anything else. Now, maybe there is an article to pursue but not a book.

On the other hand, you also had an idea to write about hockey moms. In thinking further, you have no trouble coming up with subjects in that context including your own mother (you played youth ice hockey); how the mothers coped with the early hours of the games; how the mothers dealt with the profanities and abuse typically shouted in the stands; how the mothers handled seeing blood streaming down their child's face when hit by a puck; and how hockey moms felt the experience affected their own ability to handle tough situations. Clearly, you may have the makings of a book about hockey moms.

EXERCISE 3

The next step is to take the most promising of your five ideas and write a table of contents (TOC). If none of your ideas worked out and if you still want to write a book, just go back to Exercises 1 and 2 until you come up with something.

The TOC can form the basis for your book. Depending on the genre, you may have as few as a dozen chapters or as many as thirty or more. Don't agonize over the TOC. It is subject to change. Just see if you can compose an entire TOC and if you can, you're on your way to writing your book.

CHAPTER 7

Scholarly Nonfiction Books

While nonfiction writers ought to have some knowledge of their subject, authors of scholarly nonfiction must be authorities in their field. Although research standards are always meticulous, the tone and style of your book will depend upon which of three scholarly genres you select. At one extreme, your book will contain countless footnotes, but if written for a general readership, the writing will be less formal. Writing a scholarly book can be a stimulating experience as you learn more about the subject, share insights, and possibly propose innovative conclusions.

You Must Be an Acknowledged Authority

You have seen that writers of nonfiction should have some familiarity with their subject matter. For the most part, no more than this is required to write nonfiction. But when a writer proposes a scholarly nonfiction book, the publisher does not expect it to be a training experience for an apprentice.

FACT

Even though you possess substantial knowledge in the subject of your proposed book—perhaps as much or more than most authorities—your command of the material will not satisfy a publisher. It is necessary for you to be a recognized expert, generally with the most advanced degree obtainable in order to write a scholarly book.

Although a number of university presses carefully scrutinize the manuscript before it ever goes to production and frequently circulate the proofs for comments by other experts, many publishers do not undertake this review for a variety of reasons, not the least of which is the cost factor. Consequently, publishers rely on the author's representations that the book's content is accurate, which can be best ensured when the author possesses the appropriate credentials, such as a PhD in the field.

There can be instances, however, where your learning experience might result in a scholarly book. For example, it is not unusual for a doctoral dissertation to be expanded into a book that may even reach beyond academia. This occurred with *Hitler's Willing Executioners*, by Daniel Jonah Goldhagen, which grew out of his doctoral dissertation to become a bestseller.

Determine Your Audience

The audience whom you are addressing influences the type of scholarly book you will be writing. There are three categories of scholarly nonfiction books: the purely scholarly book; the hybrid scholarly book; and scholarly books for a general readership. You will have to decide which of the three you want to write before you begin because the style and tone depends upon the genre you choose.

Do not think the rigorous requirements for research and accuracy are less demanding if you decide to write a scholarly book for the general public. While the writing is not as formal and footnotes and sources not as exhaustive, the material must withstand the same scrutiny as any scholarly book.

The Purely Scholarly Book

The purely scholarly book is what most people think of when hearing the term "scholarly book." This is the type of book that is directed to an academic audience. The research must not only be precise but clearly noted in the manuscript.

What also distinguishes the purely scholarly book from other scholarly books is the writing tone and style. Given the clearly defined audience, the author is free to utilize the language and terminology unique to his field knowing that the readers will comprehend it.

If it's a purely scholarly book you have in mind, you should avoid certain pitfalls:

- Do not inundate the reader with footnotes.
- It is a given that you are an authority and this need not be proven by a deluge of references.
- Though purely scholarly, the writing should be clear and concise.
- Avoid dissertation-style writing that is frequently repetitious and forever summarizing what has gone before.

The Hybrid Scholarly Book

In between the purely scholarly book and scholarly books for a general readership lies the "hybrid," which shares certain characteristics with each of the other two genres. If you are going to write a hybrid scholarly book, you will have to conform to the same rigorous research standards as the purely scholarly book and your writing style will be very similar as well. However, you will be writing for an audience extending beyond the narrow scope of a particular discipline, so your book must be crafted accordingly. Your subject matter will be broader, reaching out to other disciplines, or you might present the material in a more general way because you believe the book's message is original enough to interest a specific segment of the public.

There are several things you should keep in mind when writing a hybrid scholarly book. The material should be placed in its widest context. This begins with an introduction that clearly explains what follows in the book. The initial chapters should be general with ensuing chapters delving into details. Finally, to capture the eye of a wide-ranging audience, chapter titles and the book's title should not be dry.

Scholarly Books for a General Readership

If you are an acknowledged authority in your subject and believe you have an original message that will attract portions of the public or you can present interesting information in a way that makes for a good read, then you should consider writing for a general market. It goes without saying that you must be prepared to substantiate your work to meet scholarly inquiry, but the delivery of the material is dramatically different from purely scholarly books.

ESSENTIAL

Scholarly books written to appeal to a general audience should not be oversimplified or written down to the reader. The target market for these books is comprised of intelligent people in search of serious books with unique concepts and new information. Though judiciously written, the writing style should not be inscrutable.

In some cases, scholarly books written for a universal readership will employ the techniques of creative nonfiction to make the book more readable and even entertaining. This is not to say the book enters the genre of creative nonfiction (which will be explored in Chapter 19) but only that some of the techniques of writing creative nonfiction will be applied. This sometimes occurs in the writing of biographies where characters are developed that readers care about. Another method that can make a scholarly book attract a broader audience is presenting an argument many people will find compelling, particularly if it addresses a contemporary issue.

Research Standards and Methodology

You saw in Chapters 5 and 6 how important maintaining truth and accuracy is to nonfiction and that research is one of the tools available to get at the facts. In scholarly nonfiction an even more stringent standard applies to research and acceptable sources. Moreover, each discipline may have its own set of rules for conducting research and the methodology to be followed. Suffice it to say that you should be knowledgeable in the research protocol regarding your project.

With scholarly nonfiction, your sources must meet the standards of your discipline. You need to verify the credentials of the experts upon whom you rely or interview as well as the suitability of written material. It is not likely you will find what you need at the local library or at the beginning of your search on the Internet. College and university libraries are still a good place to visit and care must be taken to verify the sources you rely upon, especially on the Internet.

Credit Your Sources

When to acknowledge sources is not always clear. Obviously you cannot credit every source you use since some may have only provided background material or minor facts. Nonetheless, the best guideline to follow is when in doubt, cite your source. Not to give credit when credit is due can trigger either copyright infringement or plagiarism or both. In Chapter 5 you were advised how important it is to avoid copyright infringement, which consists of the failure to obtain permission when required and can result in adverse legal consequences. Plagiarism can be another unwanted outcome and occurs when failing to acknowledge a source. Although not always having negative legal ramifications, a charge of plagiarism can be just as unpleasant.

FACT

An accusation of plagiarism damages one's standing and the reputation of the work. It is generally not, in and of itself, a violation of any law. However, normally in book contracts, the author agrees that there will be no plagiarism and therefore a violation of this standard would be a breach of contract, which does have legal consequences.

Plagiarism is presenting the material and concepts as your own without attribution to the source. If the material is in the public domain, while there is no need to obtain permission and no copyright infringement, there remain serious repercussions, especially when writing a scholarly book. Special care must be taken to avoid even the taint of plagiarism, which will be addressed in more detail in Chapter 20.

Excerpts from the Three Scholarly Genres

There is not always an absolute line dividing the three genres of scholarly books and it's not always easy to differentiate one from the other. The most reliable way to determine in which of the three categories a book fits is the manner of writing concerning language, tone, and technique, and it's this you should keep in mind when you set out to write a scholarly nonfiction book.

To give you an idea how different modes of writing are employed in the scholarly nonfiction genres, consider the following three excerpts. Each excerpt represents one of the three scholarly genres and it should not be difficult to discern the differences.

"In contrast to Freud's psychology, with its biological individualism and its innate competitiveness and aggression, Erich Fromm sees the key problem of psychology as 'that of the specific kind of relatedness of the individual towards the world and not that of the satisfaction or frustration of this or that instinctual need *per se.*' Following Karl Marx and Harry Stack Sullivan, Fromm sees people as *primarily* social beings, i.e. social in their very selves and not just in their needs." (*The Healing Dialogue in Psychotherapy* by Maurice S. Friedman)

"The main function of the dream is to preserve sleep. The experience one is aware of during sleep, which upon waking is referred to by the sleeper as a dream, is the end result of unconscious mental activity that, by its nature or intensity, threatens to interrupt sleep. Instead of waking up, the sleeper dreams, and sleep is protected. The conscious experience during sleep, which the sleeper may or may not recall after waking, is referred to as the *manifest dream.* The unconscious ideas, wishes, and feelings that threaten to wake the sleeper make up the *latent dream*." ("The Theory of the Unconscious" by Jack L. Solomon, MD, in *Psychoanalytic Psychiatry for Lawyers*, edited by Daniel B. Gesensway)

"The conclusion of this book is that anti-Semitism moved many thousands of 'ordinary' Germans—and would have moved millions more, had they been appropriately positioned—to slaughter Jews. Not economic hardship, not the coercive means of a totalitarian state, not social psychological pressure, not invariable psychological propensities, but ideas about Jews that were pervasive in Germany, and had been for decades, induced ordinary Germans to kill unarmed, defenseless Jewish men, women, and children by the thousands, systematically and without pity." (*Hitler's Willing Executioners* by Daniel Jonah Goldhagen)

Think about the differences not only in word choice but tone and style in the three excerpts. What about the clarity and simplicity or complexity in which the information is delivered? Does one excerpt presume a certain level of sophistication and knowledge in the subject? Is there an idea or argument put forth that might arouse public interest and debate?

It should be fairly easy to determine that the excerpt from Maurice Friedman's book is purely scholarly. The second "hybrid" excerpt is from a book directed to attorneys and those in the mental health field with the goal of explaining psychoanalysis and its practical applications. Note that the tone is instructional but not obscure and the language is comprehensible. As previously mentioned, the excerpt from Goldhagen's book grew out of his dissertation and is clearly scholarly but the boldness and uniqueness of his thesis (concisely stated in the excerpt), aroused so much debate that the book became a bestseller. You should be able to see how his style was directed to a general audience whose thinking he wanted to influence.

Writing Exercises

It should be clear by now that if you want to write a scholarly book, you have to decide whether it's purely scholarly, a hybrid, or for a general audience because the writing style is very different for each of the categories. It is also likely that if you write scholarly books, you may do so in more than one of these genres. So it's probably a good idea to master the respective techniques used in all three types of scholarly books. With this in mind, here are a few exercises you might want to try.

EXERCISE 1

Select a subject with which you are very familiar if not an actual expert. Write down a set of facts and information in the form of a list or outline. No more than a page is necessary. With this material in hand, write as if you are conveying the information and ideas to scholars and authorities in the subject. Don't worry about any reference notes; just concentrate on the writing style.

EXERCISE 2

Using the same set of facts as in Exercise 1, write for an audience that would include both the experts and laypeople with an interest in the subject.

EXERCISE 3

Again, with the same set of facts, write for the general public.

Interview with Nancy Gambescia, PhD

Nancy Gambescia maintains a private practice specializing in relationship and sex therapy. In addition, she teaches and supervises psychotherapists in the assessment and treatment of sexual dysfunctions and couples therapy. Dr. Gambescia is an approved supervisor and clinical member of the American Association of Marriage and Family Therapy and has coauthored four books: *Erectile Dysfunction*, *Hypoactive Sexual Desire*, *Treating Infidelity*, and *Systemic Sex Therapy*. Dr. Gambescia completed her clinical training at the Council for Relationships and received her doctorate at the University of Pennsylvania.

RDB: The subject matter of your books (sexual and relationship issues) lend themselves to a professional and scholarly readership as well as a general audience. What made you decide to write for the former group?

NG: To be honest, I was invited by a colleague to do some scholarly writing and I accepted without realizing the extent of my commitment. This invitation was based upon my clinical and teaching experience in the area of sexual intimacy. The books are intended for therapists; however, I often recommend them to clients. Everyone seems to relate to specific portions.

RDB: In writing your books, did you also try to make them accessible to a general readership or laypeople interested in the subject matter but who are not professionals in the field?

NG: Initially, I struggled to write in a comprehendible way. My editors helped me to write simply and clearly and now I am a true believer in making a concept palatable. Eventually, my goal was to write so that anyone could enjoy the books. Now after four books and ten articles, I am most proud of the works that my clients appreciate the most. One book in particular is *Treating Infidelity*.

RDB: You write as an authority in the field who is well credentialed. Do you still rely on research and other experts?

NG: Absolutely. The available research is the base of our treatment model that we call "Intersystemic." It integrates many theoretical and empirical systems. Moreover, clinical experience provides examples of the application of our model.

RDB: How do you go about your research?

NG: Much of the literature in the field is familiar to us. We conduct literature reviews. We read, review, and generate ideas from the existing literature. Moreover, we discuss the topics that we want to cover. In each of our books, there is a section on empirical research.

RDB: How do you employ case studies? Do you present them in a formal way or a more anecdotal tone that would appeal to a general readership?

NG: I like to interject short case studies to illustrate a point. Typically they are from my clinical practice, using data to disguise individuals. Sometimes I use excerpts from e-mail communications with permission. Some authors use long case studies. I think these can be tedious, so I use small bursts of information to give life to a treatment modality or clinical illustration.

RDB: Do you think you might write for a general audience and if so, how would you see your writing style differ from the professional books you have written?

NG: I do not anticipate writing for a general audience although I would like to do this with the infidelity book. The problem with this sort of idea is that there are over 200 books in print on this topic the last time I looked. Also, clinical writing does not utilize the kind of creativity contained in general writing. I know I could never write a novel because I do not believe I am truly a talented writer. I could, however, consider writing about clinical topics, omitting the more esoteric empirical research and using more examples.

RDB: Any words of advice to someone who wants to write a professional or scholarly book?

NG: Yes. Have a coauthor! One is never alone with another person to discuss, debate, edit, embellish, etc. I think that writing alone might be too isolating for me. I communicate with my coauthor every day, discussing everything from our personal lives to clinical cases.

CHAPTER 8

Self-Help and How-To Books

With almost 80,000 titles currently in print, the self-help and how-to book category is one of the largest nonfiction genres. Your book can join this list if you convey information or dispense advice with knowledge and authority in a well-written, comprehensible, and informal style. If you are not an expert in your subject, you can consider a coauthor or rely on research and professionals to give you credibility. Not only is there a vast market for self-help and how-to books, but writing one can be rewarding and fun as well.

One of the Most Popular Genres

Self-help and how-to books are as old as the history of literature. For millennia, authors have been dispensing advice and information, beginning with the Book of Proverbs to "Pilgrim's Progress" to Ben Franklin's maxims published in *Poor Richard's Almanack* to any one of the 80,000 titles available today.

ESSENTIAL

Self-help books are distinguishable from how-to books. Self-help books offer advice on improving oneself or some aspect of one's life while how-to books provide information on a specific subject or task. However, since some books share characteristics of both categories, the two types of books are considered one genre.

Since the style and techniques of writing self-help and how-to books is essentially the same, you don't have to decide in advance which of these books you intend to write. In fact, your book may end up in that gray area, sharing features of both kinds of books. However, you should be aware of the distinctions between the two categories.

Self-Help Books

Self-help books are supposed to do just what they say they will do—offer advice and information to the reader so the reader can help herself. This can involve almost any area of a person's life such as feeling better through exercise or improving relationships or developing a "can-do" attitude to achieve a given goal.

It is not unusual for self-help books to become bestsellers—especially when they suggest ways to achieve peace and tranquility or the ability to reach one's aspirations. Some examples of bestsellers are:

- *The Secret* by Rhonda Byrne, based on the premise that if you think it, it will come to be true.
- *One Month to Live* by Kerry and Chris Shook, a husband and wife team who suggest that because life is short, there is no time to waste when it comes to loving others.

- *The Purpose Driven Life* by Rick Warren, who advocates that one can find meaning in life through God.
- *Yes!* by Noah J. Goldstein, Steve J. Martin, and Robert B. Cialdini offers fifty ways to improve the powers of persuasion.
- *The Power of Now* by Eckhart Tolle is a guide to personal growth and spiritual enlightenment.

How-To Books

How-to books are like instruction manuals but are written in a style that is enjoyable and accessible as well as informative. These books will educate the reader on almost any topic from building a small boat to competing in triathlons to writing one's will. For example, consider some of the following bestsellers:

- *Women and Money* by Suze Orman not only encourages and instructs women how to intelligently manage their assets but suggests this is an empowerment tool as well.
- *How Not to Look Old* by Charla Krupp provides techniques to appearing youthful.
- *The 4-Hour Workweek* by Timothy Ferriss demonstrates how to create intellectual property and make a great deal of money in relatively little time.
- *Deceptively Delicious* by Jessica Seinfeld lists tips and recipes to fool children into eating right.
- *The South Beach Diet Supercharged* by Arthur Agatston is a guide to weight loss.

Be an Authority

As you know by now, to write nonfiction you must have a voice of authority. In the previous chapter, you learned that in order to write scholarly books, you need to be an expert in the subject. As for other nonfiction books, it can be enough to rely on experts and research. Writing self-help and how-to books lies somewhere in between these two standards. Without a doubt, you will have to possess some credentials to write a book in this genre.

Otherwise, you will not be able to earn the reader's trust, which is indispensable for any self-help or how-to book to be successful. But so long as you are conversant in the subject and can present the material based on experts and research, you should not hesitate to write a book in this genre if that is your goal. The process is also an excellent learning experience and you'll likely come away from the book as an expert in the subject yourself.

ALERT

If you possess the necessary credentials and are an authority on your book's subject, you can write from your own knowledge and experience. However, even if you are an expert, publishers and readers will almost always expect independent sources to support your positions and this should be included in your book.

There is another option for you to consider if you want to write a self-help or how-to book and are not an expert in the field. You can entertain the option to write the book with a coauthor who is a recognized authority. The situation may also arise where a publisher or agent or the authority himself approaches you to coauthor a book in the role of the writer. There are pros and cons to writing with a coauthor that you should consider before reaching a decision.

Is a Coauthor for You?

When one author is an expert in search of a writer and the other author is a writer in search of an expert, there is a greater likelihood for a successful outcome than in other areas of collaboration because each is in need of the other. By contrast, two writers writing a play or a novel will not be able to define their roles with the same clarity that an authority and writer can on a book project. Establishing who is responsible for what is crucial for the relationship to be successful.

There will always be the possibility for stumbling blocks such as personality clashes, different habits for meeting deadlines, the division of responsibility, and when decisions must be made jointly. However, you can alleviate these potential pitfalls by adhering to the written agreement between you and your coauthor. Despite this downside, in addition to matching an authority with a writer to produce a book, there are benefits to having a coauthor.

QUESTION

Do I need a written agreement with a coauthor?
Absolutely! A legally binding agreement (sometimes furnished by the publisher) benefits both authors. The agreement will spell out the responsibilities and obligations of each of the authors to prevent confusion and disputes. The agreement will also establish sharing of expenses and compensation as well as provide deadline dates.

Writing by its nature is a solitary process. Having another person who can serve as a sounding board and from whom new skills and knowledge can be learned is a wonderful opportunity. The division of labor can result in a better outcome with more time left for each author to perform their assigned task. The best way to ensure a positive experience is to be comfortable on a personal level with your coauthor and establish the ground rules in the beginning.

Writing the Book Should Be Fun

Writing a self-help or how-to book is like having a conversation with the reader. If you have information to share or a message to convey you're going to want to deliver it in an easygoing manner and not appear distant or aloof. After all, if you bore the reader or make the book cumbersome to read, all the reader has to do is put the book down and walk away. This is not what publishers want nor will it result in achieving your objective to deliver the information or get your point across.

FACT

All self-help and how-to books are written either in the first or second person point of view. This makes it easier to adopt a conversational tone in the book. Keep in mind, as always, not to shift from one point of view to the other.

Now that you have reached the stage when the actual writing commences, kick off your shoes, relax, and settle in at your computer or with pencil in hand and begin a conversation. Like any real-life conversation, from time to time, you will want to address the reader directly. But when writing a book, since you obviously don't know the reader's name, call the reader "you," which is common to this genre and helps define the second person point of view.

Writing Techniques You Need to Know

For the most part, the writing methods you learned in Chapter 4 apply but you need to make particular use of some of those techniques when it comes to writing self-help and how-to books. When writing in this genre, your goal is to inform and enlighten in a user-friendly and entertaining manner. The best way to accomplish this is to make ample use of lists and anecdotes.

Lists

Lists are a great way to break up text, organize information, and effectively detail something that may otherwise be rather complicated. There are various types of lists but the most popular in self-help and how-to books is probably the "bulleted list," which has a dot or an asterisk before each item. Like all lists, each point is indented. Another common list is the "numbered list," which is any list including a progression of numbers, letters, or other elements that are aligned. You may also find yourself utilizing a "checklist," in which each point is set off with a small checkbox.

The type of list you select depends upon its function. For example, if you want to inform the reader of items that should be packed for a vacation, you would use a checklist so the reader can check off each article as it is placed in the suitcase. On the other hand, if it's a matter of providing important points of information, you will probably do so with a bulleted list.

Anecdotes

Anecdotes are an important ingredient in self-help and how-to books. What is more, they can be fun to write because their function is to present the material in an engaging way. Anecdotes can serve as a vehicle to convey information or help you prove your point. Anecdotes need not be factual. They can be based on a true occurrence in part or completely fabricated. If the anecdote is true, it must be accurate in all respects. The fun part takes place when you write the narrative using your imagination and techniques in writing fiction.

ALERT

When writing an anecdote that is based upon an actual incident and real people—as many anecdotes are—it is necessary that you either obtain permission from the individuals depicted or disguise their identity so they are not recognizable. You also must keep in mind not to commit libel if the characters in your anecdote can be identified.

Excerpts to Ponder

As you have seen, there is a particular writing style and specific techniques that advance the goal of conveying information or delivering a message in an accessible and lucid manner. Consider these excerpts that exemplify some of the tools you will employ in writing a self-help or how-to book.

"The following guidelines summarize most editors' advice for drafting a one- or two-page query letter about a nonfiction manuscript . . . .

- State your specific idea. . . .
- Explain your approach. . . .
- Show how what you have to say is fresh and different from other things already in print. . . .
- Cite your sources. . . .
- Estimate length. . . .
- Mention your connections and qualifications. . . .
- Convey some sense of your enthusiasm for the project. . . ."

This excerpt from Judith Appelbaum's *How to Get Happily Published* provides an illustration of a bulleted list that is common in self-help and how-to books. You may find this excerpt particularly useful in drafting a query letter.

Break Up the Text

Since a high priority in this genre is to publish books that are user friendly, easy to navigate, and make for an enjoyable read, the text in self-help and how-to books is occasionally broken up with a particular piece of information that either doesn't quite fit, is so important the author wants it to stand out, or simply presents a concept with a new twist. In the *Everything* series, you see this in the sidebars consisting of E-Facts, E-Alerts, E-ssentials and E-Questions. In other books, this is accomplished in different ways, but the end result is the same with the short phrase highlighted in some fashion.

For example, in *How to Write a Book Proposal*, the author, Michael Larsen, utilizes what he calls "hot tips." Here is a sample:

> "HOT TIP: Avoid footnotes in your proposal. They are distracting and will make your proposal (and your book) look academic. If your book will have footnotes, make them blind footnotes, divided by chapter, that readers can find at the end of your book. If you use them in your sample chapter, include them at the end of the proposal. Avoid asterisks, which also interrupt the flow of the text."

Tell a Tale

Here's where you can be creative and craft a story or spin a yarn to make a point. As you were informed, anecdotes can be true or fabricated either in whole or in part, but either way they can serve up a message in an entertaining and effective fashion. Consider the following anecdote from *How to Deal with Your Lawyer* by Richard D. Bank.

> "Manny and Max were not only partners in a thriving business but brothers as well. Between Manny and Max, things deteriorated to the point where, although in the same office, neither spoke to the other and they communicated through employees.
>
> "Fortunately, closing the company and liquidating the assets at much less than value was avoided because of an all night negotiating session in my office. One brother sat in the library with the company's accountant. The other brother paced the halls, his wife goading him on. Both insisted that I, counsel to the corporation, be the only attorney present.

And so I shuttled back and forth between the two until an agreement was hammered out. One brother bought the interest of the other at a fair price and both were spared litigation.

"This tale is usually convincing proof to all my clients that such agreements [Buy-Sell Agreements] are necessary."

The clients' real names were changed but everything else in the incident is accurate. By using characters and concrete circumstances, the anecdote serves to emphasize the need for having partnership or stock restrictive agreements.

Writing Exercises

You have seen that some of the techniques employed to write nonfiction are particularly useful when writing self-help and how-to books. But the thing is that writing in this genre can really be quite enjoyable. Try one or more of the following exercises and see how you like it.

EXERCISE 1

In the third person, write one or two paragraphs about something you know as if you are explaining it to the reader. In other words, show the reader how to go about accomplishing a task or becoming better at doing something or achieving a certain lifestyle. Now, rewrite it in the form of a bulleted list—maybe half a dozen items or so. Just convey the essence and make sure the writing is crisp and concise using words sparingly.

EXERCISE 2

Once again, pick a subject in which you are knowledgeable—perhaps the same subject you used in Exercise 1—and write an anecdote to convey one of its main points. The anecdote should be no more than two or three paragraphs and can be real or imagined or a combination of both. All that matters is that the story exemplifies an important point and delivers it in an entertaining and concrete way. Have fun writing it!

EXERCISE 3

Go back to the paragraph or two you wrote in Exercise 1. Now, in the first person, have a chat with the reader and feel free to use both the *I* and *you* words. Convey the material in a clear style and get your point or information across.

FACT

Writing in a conversational tone is not limited to self-help and how-to books. It can be employed writing all kinds of nonfiction and fiction with the possible exception of purely scholarly. You may even "discover" your voice writing in this style and use it in all your writing.

To help you with setting the right tone, after you complete your first draft, read aloud what you wrote as though you were talking to someone. See how it sounds and if it flows as a conversation should. Note where you stumbled or substituted some words or omitted other words and rewrite if need be. Then read it aloud again. Once you're satisfied, you will have begun to master the writing style of self-help and how-to books.

EXERCISE 4

Take the final draft from Exercise 3 and rewrite it in the second person. This means you cannot employ the *I* word, but feel free to use the *you* word. You may find it's a bit more difficult to maintain the conversational tone writing from this point of view but it can be accomplished with some practice.

CHAPTER 9

Books about Religion and Spirituality

One of the major genres, books concerning religion and spirituality are as old as the Bible and will likely be written so long as humans seek something beyond the material and ordinary. Although many of these books are written by experts, you don't have to be an authority to write a religious or spiritual book if you have a unique personal experience or a vision that appeals to a segment of the public. If you choose this genre, you'll have to master its writing techniques and recurrent inspirational style.

A Time-Honored Tradition

One of the oldest of all books, the Bible remains one of the bestsellers of all time. *The Varieties of Religious Experience*, considered a masterpiece written by the philosopher and psychologist William James, was first published in 1902 and has never been out of print. But the number of varieties of religious experience James wrote about pales in comparison with the diversity and range of books in the genre today.

FACT

Books considered to belong in the religion and spirituality category are frequently included in other genres such as inspirational and self-help. Likewise, books in other genres may find themselves listed as religious or spiritual as well. Because of cross-listings, the total number of books arrived at by adding the various genres will exceed the actual number of books in print.

There are more than 79,000 religion and spirituality titles available for purchase. Most of these books inform readers about a specific religion, an aspect of religion in general, or a spiritual path. There are even books that are critical of religion but ironically, because of the subject, are found in this category. One recent example is the bestseller *American Theocracy: The Peril and Politics of Radical Religion, Oil, and Borrowed Money in the 21st Century* by Kevin Phillips.

Popular Religion and Spirituality Books

In more contemporary times, the religion and spirituality books that have lined the shelves to be snapped up by an eager public have been those books focusing on religious and mystical feelings that inspire and guide the reader to a sense of tranquility. Sometimes these books promote action and encourage the reader to improve some aspect of her life or the lives of others. To give you an idea of the kinds of books that comprise much of this genre, here is a list of some contemporary bestsellers:

- *The Love Dare* by Stephen Kendrick and Alex Kendrick is a guide to love in which the author takes the reader on a forty-day journey of devotional experience that results in returning one's heart to loving one's spouse.

- *Caged Virgin: An Emancipation Proclamation for Women and Islam* by Ayaan Hirsi Ali recounts the author's experience as a Muslim woman so that oppressed Muslim women can take heart and seek their own liberation.
- *Called Out of Darkness: A Spiritual Confession* by Anne Rice is an intimate memoir of the author's Catholic girlhood, her unmaking as a devout believer, and her return to the Church.
- *Everyday Grace: Having Hope, Finding Forgiveness, and Making Miracles* by Marianne Williamson demonstrates that with an attitude of hope, a call to forgive, a celebration of miracles, and the promise of strength and grace, sacred feelings can be found on ordinary ground.
- *Experiencing God: Knowing and Doing the Will of God* by Henry and Richard Blackaby and Claude King suggests how one can develop a more intimate relationship with God.
- *The Five People You Meet in Heaven* by Mitch Albom is a novel that explores the unexpected connections of our lives and the idea that heaven is more than a place but is actually the answer.

ALERT

Should the book you are planning to write not deal directly with religion nor appear to be spiritual, do not assume it will be excluded from the genre. If the focus of your book has to do with the incorporeal and particularly if it is inspiring, you should write it as if it belongs in the religion and spirituality genre.

Target Your Audience

It is always important to identify the audience your book is intended to reach and this is especially so from the publisher's perspective for marketing purposes. However, you as the author need to know your audience from the start when writing a religious or spiritual book.

Religious books about a specific religion generally have one of two purposes. If the book is designed to not only educate and inform the reader about the religion but also to provide guidance and instruction hoping to encourage the reader to take the religion more seriously and actively prac-tice it, the audience will usually encompass members of that religious group. However, if the gist of the book informs and educates the reader about the religion with no other goal than to educate, the book will have a wider audi-ence. There is also the possibility such a book may find itself classified as a scholarly book dealing with the subject of religion, in which case you would have to write the book consistent with what you learned in Chapter 7.

FACT

If your book is about one religion, it may be suitable for a publisher who specializes in books about that religion. For example, there are hundreds of publishers that publish Christian books exclusively while other publishers concentrate on Judaic or Eastern religions. These publishers know their market well.

Writing for the General Public

If the purpose of your religious book is to inform—even if only about a specific denomination—your book might have a more extensive market than the members of a particular religion. Should this be what you have in mind, you should assume that the reader knows little if anything about the subject.

Unlike books about religion that may or may not appeal beyond mem-bers of one specific denomination, spiritual books almost always target a broad audience. If you review the preceding list of bestsellers, with the pos-sible exception of Anne Rice's memoir, you'll see that the primary purpose of these books is to inspire without promoting one religion over another. Of course, this is not to say that religious books do not inspire, but only that they do so in a sectarian way while spirituality books approach the subject in a nonsectarian fashion. So, if it's a spirituality book you want to publish, keep a general readership in mind when you write.

You Can Never Have Too Many Endorsements

God in the Wilderness, Rediscovering the Spirituality of the Great Outdoors with the Adventure Rabbi by Rabbi Jamie S. Korngold contains no less than seventeen endorsements—two large blurbs on the back cover written by a professor and a rabbi and fifteen "advance praises" offered by authors, scholars, theologians, business executives, and editors. It goes without saying that you can never have enough words of support for your book from the right people—particularly if your book is in the religious and inspirational category and you do not have wide name recognition.

ALERT

Do not confuse a "blurb" with a "foreword." Blurbs are endorsements that typically consist of one or two sentences praising the book and are located on the back cover, the inside jacket, or in the front matter of the first few pages. A "foreword" is an introductory note written by a well-known authority and is typically several pages in length.

Just who are the "right people?" In a nutshell, the more famous the better. However, if you cannot convince someone prominent to write a blurb, pursue individuals with impressive credentials. For example, if you're writing a book addressed to Catholics, you should request endorsements from members of the clergy, theologians, and scholars of Catholicism. If you're writing an inspirational book, anyone renowned or with impressive credentials in almost any field should be considered.

Because you do not have to be an authority in the subject to write a religious or inspirational book, having experts praise your work and provide the book a degree of legitimacy is critical. Even more important when you do not have the appropriate credentials is to have a foreword written by a well-known authority. Of course, you can consider a coauthor who is an expert in the subject but if you do, bear in mind what you learned in Chapter 8.

How to Write Religion and Spirituality Books

Aside from books about religion that are meant to educate and inform and may even cross the line with scholarly books, writers in the religion and spiritual genre frequently write very personal books derived more from their hearts than their heads. As a result, while being an acknowledged expert in your subject never hurts, you can establish your voice of authority by drawing from your own personal experiences as well as that of others.

ESSENTIAL

Since you do not have to be an acknowledged authority to write a contemporary spirituality or religion book, what matters most is your writing. While the general techniques in writing nonfiction apply, you must be able to convey the information and your message in a style that inspires and enriches the reader.

Consider the previous list of bestsellers. Ayaan Hirsi Ali relies on her own struggle to free herself from the oppressive grip of fundamental Islam to guide other women to do the same. In a different vein, Anne Rice writes of her internal conflicts with Catholicism. Neither Ali nor Rice are theologians or religious experts but because they are good writers and can utilize the techniques of the genre, they are able to convey their messages effectively.

Uplift the Reader

If you are going to write a religious or spiritual book other than one purely to educate, you should plan on making the reader feel better about things by the time the last page is turned. For the most part, people seek out spirituality and religion so they can be elevated above the mundane. In order for your book to attain this effect, your writing style and tone has to reach the reader and evoke these emotions. In other words, you must write in an uplifting and encouraging style.

ALERT

While many religion and spiritual books inspire, do not confuse such books with the inspirational genre. Inspirational books come from a wide range of experiences often unrelated to religion and the spiritual: the paraplegic who completes a triathlon; the blind golfer; the African-American woman born into poverty to become governor of her state.

Mastering the writing skills of spiritual and religion books can be accomplished in the same way you would become adept writing in any genre; read in the genre and practice some of the techniques. With this in mind, study the following excerpts as examples and try your hand at the exercises that follow.

Excerpts That Inform and Inspire

Joe Eszterhas grew up a streetwise kid to become a journalist on the police beat who later wrote dark, violent, and sexually graphic films like *Basic Instinct* and *Jagged Edge.* So, you wouldn't think such a person would have the expertise or authority to write a book on religion or spirituality. Yet, Eszterhaus did write such a book based upon his own experience and employing his skill as a writer.

After battling throat cancer and addictions to alcohol and cigarettes, Eszterhas found God. In *Crossbearer,* he writes about his newfound faith in a very down-to-earth and sometimes humorous way. His introspection and honesty depicting his dilemma is something many people can relate to. Think about other techniques he utilizes to present the issues in an easy-to-read style.

"I didn't even really know how to pray. . . . Part of it was that I felt myself to be *presuming* God's favor in our new relationship. I thought to myself: Yeah, right, I reject Him so long ago, and then, after forty years of not just ignoring Him but of trashing Him in my writings, I'm suddenly back and talking to Him as though nothing had interrupted our relationship, saying 'How ya doin', God? Haven't seen you in a while—what's up? Everything cool?'"

An Authority Writes Spiritual Advice

By contrast, perhaps because he is a foremost authority on the subject of spirituality and the embodiment of Buddhism, the Dalai Lama writes in a formal tone but nonetheless delivers the information clearly and concisely. In the following excerpt from *The Art of Happiness: A Handbook for Living,* which he coauthored with Howard C. Cutler, MD, how to attain the first step of seeking happiness is explained.

> "*So, the first step in seeking happiness is learning.* We first have to learn how negative emotions and behaviors are harmful to us and how positive emotions are helpful. And we must realize how these negative emotions are not only very bad and harmful to one personally but harmful to society and the future of the whole world as well. . . . And then, there is the realization of the beneficial aspects of the positive emotions and behaviors. Once we realize that, we become determined to cherish, develop, and increase those positive emotions no matter how difficult that is."

Could these writing styles be more different? And yet, they belong to the same genre of books. The explanation for this disparity is that in writing a book where your voice of authority is derived from your personal experiences, you must draw the reader into your world in an intimate and informal style, while if you are an authority, you're already established and need to instruct and explain in a comprehensible and orderly manner.

Addressing Two Beliefs

Sylvia Boorstein is an example of the middle ground between the previous two excerpts. This is because as a psychotherapist and teacher of meditation she is somewhat of an authority in her own right. Yet, she also draws on her personal experiences using her skills as a writer to write in a genial fashion. The following excerpt is from *That's Funny, You Don't Look Buddhist: On Being a Faithful Jew and a Passionate Buddhist.*

> "I am a Jew because my parents were mild-mannered, cheerful best friends who loved me enormously, and they were Jews. It's my karma. It's good karma. My parents' love included respect, admiration, high expectations, and a tremendous amount of permission. . . .
>
> I am a prayerful, devout Jew because I am a Buddhist. As the meditation practice that I learned from my Buddhist teachers made me less fearful and allowed me to fall in love with life, I discovered that the prayer language of 'thank you' that I knew from my childhood returned, spontaneously and to my great delight."

Compare Boorstein's writing style and tone with the previous excerpts. To the extent it informs, it does so in a clear and direct way similar to the Dalai Lama but the tone is far more personal. Yet, it doesn't reach the informal, humorous, and gritty voice of Eszterhas because unlike Eszterhas, she is trained and educated in the subject.

Writing Exercises

If it's a religious or spiritual book you want to write, you have seen there are several styles and tones to consider. The techniques you apply depend on the type of book, your audience, and whether you are writing more as an authority or from personal experiences and beliefs. The following exercises are designed to help you explore these alternative writing styles.

EXERCISE 1

Decide upon a specific subject involving religion or spirituality with which you are knowledgeable or can obtain information through a bit of research. Pick a topic that will address a contemporary and fairly general readership. Generate a page or two of notes on the subject. Some examples: should priests be allowed to marry; techniques for successful proselytizing; connecting with nature.

Write a page or so on the topic with the aim of informing the reader and as a writer with a great deal of knowledge in the subject—perhaps even an authority. Avoid any anecdotes or anything personal about you.

EXERCISE 2

You can pick a new subject or use the same subject from Exercise 1, but this time, play the role of a writer who is not a recognized expert and again focus on informing the reader. Feel free to disclose anything about yourself or the experience of others but keep in mind, the purpose is to inform.

EXERCISE 3

Follow Exercise 2, except while being informative, your goal is to persuade and/or inspire the reader.

CHAPTER 10

Health, Mind, and Body Books

Books about health, mind, and body cover a wide range of subjects such as psychology, yoga, beauty, diet, running, and medications. In fact, if you want to write in this genre, there is hardly a topic that won't fit. As with most genres, you'll need to master its distinct style, tone, and writing techniques. Because the subject deals with the reader's health and well-being, more than any other class of books, you must be an authority or have your work supported by experts.

A Varied Genre

It's not likely you'll find a genre that can boast of so many diverse books as the health, mind, and body genre. In part, this is because the public's interest in such books and a willingness to buy books that help improve physical and mental well-being is almost insatiable. The other reason has to do with the myriad of subjects. For example, here is a small sample of the categories within this genre:

- Beauty
- Death and grief
- Diet and weight loss
- Disorders and diseases
- Exercise and fitness
- Medicine
- Men's and women's health
- Psychology and counseling
- Sex

FACT

There are so many subjects in the health, mind, and body genre that within the numerous subgenres there are even more categories to be found. For example, books concerning nutrition are subdivided into books about maintaining a healthy diet, weight loss, foods providing energy for exercise, and foods promoting mental alertness.

If you want to write a health, mind, and body book, you should clearly identify and define your subject. However, don't be disappointed to find that there are other titles already in print on the same material. This is not a problem at all and will be addressed more specifically in Chapter 23, where you will learn about the book proposal. The important thing to remember is that once you have your subject and have pigeonholed it into the right category you need to know how to go about writing a health, mind, and body book.

Writing the Health, Mind, and Body Book

Once again, since this is a nonfiction genre, the basic skills of writing a nonfiction book apply. But like all types of nonfiction books, this group has its own distinctive features that you need to consider.

Because health, mind, and body books frequently cross over into the self-help and how-to category, the writing techniques are very similar, and what you learned in Chapter 8 is generally applicable here. Consequently, you'll make ample use of lists and anecdotes when conveying information, instruction, and advice. The tone of your book should also be personal and straightforward while maintaining your voice of authority. Of course, to speak as an authority you'll generally need the credentials or other experts to back you up.

Experts Are Essential

What sort of book can be more important than one providing information and advice about how to attend to one's own well-being? Many generations ago, when people wanted to know about their health, whether physical or mental, they would visit their doctor or perhaps read an article or even consider the effectiveness of magical elixirs sold by a shaman to cure their ills or make them feel omnipotent. In recent years, books have proliferated in this popular and expanding genre, yet one constant remains. The reader has to have confidence in the person providing the information and guidance, so expertise is essential in writing a book about the health, mind, and body.

ESSENTIAL

If you are relying on others to provide the expertise for your book, whether a coauthor or someone interviewed, you need to establish that the person has the proper credentials. It is not enough to be satisfied with an "MD" following the name. You need to verify that the medical school is accredited and the doctor is currently licensed.

You're the Expert

As you saw in Chapter 3 when you were introduced to this genre, you can be the expert so long as you have the required credentials or experience. If the book involves health, you don't have to be a doctor so long as you are qualified in the field, such as a licensed social worker specializing in addiction writing a book for people with addictive disorders.

If your book does not rely on medical or scientific issues, there can be situations where you can establish yourself as an authority without any formal degree or training. Generally however, such authors will have achieved a measure of renown such as the beautiful screen star writing a book on beauty tips or the Olympian gold medal winner writing a book on her sport.

ALERT

Whenever offering advice or guidance, particularly involving exercise, some attention must be paid to potential legal liability. It is a good idea to qualify your suggestions and to have a disclaimer—perhaps in the front matter—that consultation with a physician is advisable before beginning any program.

With the exception of people whose name recognition is so extensive that their name on the cover will guarantee substantial sales regardless of their knowledge of the subject, an author must have attained some degree of proficiency in the subject to write a book in this genre—even if the book is written with a coauthor who is credentialed. Should you decide on a coauthor to bolster your voice of authority, revisit Chapter 8 dealing with this issue.

Forewords and Blurbs

You learned in Chapter 9 how valuable a foreword and blurbs can be to the success of a book. In no other genre are forewords and blurbs more relied upon than in books about health, mind, and body. Even if you are an authority on the subject, having other experts or prominent people praise your book not only legitimizes the book but positively impacts the sales—a factor publishers tend to appreciate.

Forewords

Naturally, you'll want to consider an accredited authority to write a foreword, especially if your credentials are weak. For example, if you are a licensed social worker with a practice in grief counseling, you would do well to consider a psychologist or psychiatrist to write a foreword. Sometimes however, even the expert can use a foreword from someone less credentialed.

Consider the book *Framework: Your 7-Step Program for Healthy Muscles, Bones, and Joints.* The author is Nicholas A. DiNubile, an orthopedic surgeon specializing in sports medicine with an impressive professional resume. Nonetheless, a foreword written by Governor Arnold Schwarzenegger, a former bodybuilder and movie star, while not necessary to establish the expertise of the author, certainly helped sales.

Blurbs from a Variety of Sources

It goes without saying that the more famous the source of the endorsement, the better. You might also think that blurbs should be written by people who possess a great deal of knowledge about your book's subject. While this is mainly true, it is not an absolute, especially when it comes to notable people. In Dr. DiNubile's *Framework*, there is an endorsement by the well-known basketball player Allen Iverson.

FACT

Authors provide an excellent pool of potential sources for your blurbs. Indeed, they need not have a direct correlation to the subject matter. Consider the bestseller, *Tuesdays with Morrie*, a book listed in this genre, where the author, Mitch Albom, obtained blurbs from M. Scott Peck, MD, Rabbi Harold Kushner, Bernie Siegel, MD, and Amy Tan—all bestselling authors.

As a general rule, the more your book involves medical science, the more you need blurbs from experts. In the 1970s bestseller *P.E.T., Parent Effectiveness Training*, by Dr. Thomas Gordon, a prominent blurb was obtained from the renowned psychologist Carl Rogers. Another source for blurbs is to reprint a portion of a favorable book review generally obtained from a reviewer after receiving an advance copy of your book before the release date.

The people you would want to consider for endorsements will depend upon the type of book you are writing. Consequently, it is important you know into which subcategory your book fits. To help you do this, a review of some of the major groups in this genre follows.

Books about Medicine and Health

While blurbs from experts are important if your book is about medicine and health, you still need to be an authority to write this type of book. This is particularly true if the focus of the book is to provide information on medical issues. On the other hand, you have more flexibility regarding your expertise if the topic is not critical to major health questions such as beauty or diet, which are subgenres unto themselves.

Medical Books

Books about medicine are almost always written by doctors. Very often, they are written for people in the health profession. Indeed, there are several publishers that publish medical books exclusively. Nonetheless, many of these books are purchased by laypeople who have interest in a specific area of medicine.

QUESTION

Do medical professionals need to learn to write for the public?
Most medical professionals, especially doctors, do not write in a style geared to a general readership. While they can learn to do this, it is common for a coauthor or a ghostwriter to be assigned to the project so the book will be easily understood by a lay audience.

A few recent titles that have sold well should give you an idea of medical books that target both a specific and general audience. The *PDR Nurse's Drug Handbook* details 1,500 commonly prescribed drugs and provides a good source of information to someone wanting to know about a particular prescription. *The American Medical Association Family Medical Guide* is designed to provide basic information on diseases, their diagnosis, and treatments, while *Healthgrades Guide to America's Hospitals and Doctors* informs the public about physicians and hospitals.

Diet and Nutrition Books

With almost 31,000 titles, diet and nutrition books are one of the biggest categories in the genre. This should come as no surprise given the concern people have about what they eat and how it affects their health along with the fact the majority of people would like to shed some pounds.

Because so much of this information can be obtained through research, you don't have to be an expert, although it certainly does help. Diet books in particular, which are frequently written more like self-help books with strands of humor woven through the pages, are often authored by lay writers.

ESSENTIAL

Sometimes you can attain a degree of expertise in the subject just by researching and writing extensively in the field. Such is the case of David Zinczenko, editor in chief of *Men's Health* magazine, who coauthored *Eat This Not That! Thousands of Simple Food Swaps that Can Save You 10, 20, 30 Pounds—or More!* and *The Abs Diet.*

One of the bestselling diet books, *Skinny Bitch*, is written by Kim Barnouin, a former model with a degree in holistic nutrition, and Rory Freedman, a former modeling agent who is self-taught in the field. But their book took off because of the brazen tone and attitude in which it was written in order to get women to become thin.

Beauty Books

You might imagine that beauty books only provide instructions about what type of makeup to wear, the sexiest clothes to buy, how to cover up male pattern baldness, and similar subjects, but you would be wrong. While there are books like these, typically such topics are the focus of articles in glossy magazines. Books about beauty go deeper and it might be a subject you want to write about.

For example, a recent edition in the "You" series of books is *You: Being Beautiful: The Owner's Manual to Inner and Outer Beauty* by Michael F. Roizen, MD, and Mehmet C. Oz, MD. Another bestseller is *The Mind-Beauty Connection: 9 Days to Reverse Stress Aging and Reveal More Youthful, Beautiful Skin* by Amy Wechsler, MD, a book that shows how to "de-stress" your skin.

Exercise and Fitness Books

The exercise and fitness book genre contains about 31,000 titles. There is a large crossover of books with the beauty genre, because a person who exercises is likely to look good and a person who is proud of their appearance has no qualms about going to a gym. There are numerous subcategories of exercise and fitness books, the largest of which are:

- Injury prevention
- Running and jogging
- Pilates
- Weight training
- Yoga

ALERT

Do not confuse books about exercise and fitness with the sports genre. Sports books inform about a specific sport and often one aspect of that sport, such as a baseball book about a particular team. Sometimes sports books provide instruction, such as how to play a better round of golf, in which case they may cross into the fitness/exercise category.

While many books in this genre, especially exercise, are written by authors with a medical background or physical fitness training, a large number of authors base their authority on their personal experience and success in a specific area. One of the top-selling books about running and jogging is *50/50: Secrets I Learned Running 50 Marathons in 50 Days—and How You Too Can Achieve Super Endurance!* written by Dean Karnazes, who is known as the "Lance Armstrong" of the running world. Like a number of athletes whose writing skills may be lacking, Karnazes authored the book with Matt Fitzgerald, his collaborator.

Psychology and Counseling

By far, the largest category in the health, mind, and body genre is psychology and counseling. There are 178,000 titles that are listed in this group. The more popular subcategories are:

- Child psychology
- Developmental psychology
- Mental illness
- Psychoanalysis
- Social psychology and interactions
- Sexuality

Many of these books not only provide information but also encourage self-help. Authors in this genre are almost always experts. For example, a one-time number one bestseller in this category is *Change Your Brain, Change Your Life: The Breakthrough Program for Conquering Anxiety, Depression, Obsessiveness, Anger, and Impulsiveness* is written by Daniel G. Amen, MD, a clinical neuroscientist and psychiatrist. Yet because the book provides do-it-yourself care filled with "brain prescriptions" from cognitive exercises to diet, it is written in the style of a how-to book despite the author's impressive credentials.

Categories of Mental Health Books

There are numerous subcategories within the topic of mental health books. Many books are traditional in their approach and are almost always written by psychiatrists, psychologists, and licensed therapists. These books provide information but may also offer guidance in mental health treatment and even self-help techniques.

Other mental health books are sometimes called "pop psych," meaning that they reach out to a wide audience in contemporary and popular parlance. For the most part, these books are also written by authorities in the field.

Books promoting the notion that mental health can be attained through exercise are growing in number. Based on the premise that the mind and body are connected and one affects the other, these books show how to improve one's emotional well-being through such exercises as yoga, running, and Pilates and are often written by experts in fitness rather than the medical field.

Excerpts from a Wide Range of Books

Because of the vast number of health, mind, and body books and the substantial number of topics, writing styles vary considerably within the genre. Reviewing several techniques and voices will help give you ideas of how you should write your book, but before getting started it is always wise to read several books similar to the one you intend to write.

Upbeat and Genial

Imagine yourself in a gym with a fitness trainer. Does a monotone voice counting backward from fifteen as you crunch out your reps motivate you? Is the voice one you can stand for more than a minute? Or, would you prefer an energetic, enthusiastic, and personal voice encouraging you? Same goes for writing an exercise book, as exemplified in this excerpt from the beginning of *Fit and Fabulous in 15 Minutes* by Teresa Tapp, with Barbara Smalley.

> "Hi, I'm Teresa Tapp.
> "Fit and fabulous in fifteen minutes? I know what you're thinking. It sounds too good to be true and even a bit sensationalized, doesn't it? Well, get ready, because in this book, you're going to discover that 'yes you can!'
> "Welcome to T-Tapp, the wellness workout that works wonders for your body, mind, and spirit. I take a rehabilitative approach to fitness and spent nine years creating this workout—plus over two decades perfecting it."

Can't have a more personal tone than T-Tapp, can you? But note that she immediately establishes herself as a person with experience and as someone the reader can trust.

Personal and Professional

You've seen how most books in this genre are written by recognized experts and professionals. But this is not to say that the tone is cerebral or written in the way one would write a scholarly book. The writing must be clear and personal yet also establish a voice of authority. Consider how Richard M. Restak, a neurologist and bestselling author, accomplishes this in the following excerpt from his book *Older and Wiser: How to Maintain Peak Mental Ability for As Long As You Live.*

"*Older and Wiser* will give you the information you need in order to keep your brain functioning at its peak throughout the mature years. Everyone can benefit from reading this book, primarily individuals forty and older. After age forty, the brain undergoes a series of changes that modern brain science, neuroscience, now understands sufficiently well that we can establish guidelines for preserving, even enhancing, our brain's performance during the later years of our lives."

Purely Personal

Sometimes, based on your own life experience and with no degrees or credentials, you can write a book in this genre. When you do, the voice is as personal as it can get. Consider the following excerpt from *The Athlete's Way* by Christopher Bergland, a world-class endurance athlete who has won the longest nonstop triathlon in the world three times and holds the Guiness World Record for treadmill running—153.76 miles in twenty-four hours.

"I have spent the past two decades exploring my own motivation and what motivates other people, and I am excited to share everything I have learned here. This book offers hundreds of reasons that will inspire you to exercise. Sport turned my life around and continues to inform my life—I know the power exercise has to improve daily life and to change your life. That is why I am a zealot about this program."

Notice how Bergland not only piques the reader's interest and curiosity to want to know how exercise turned his life around but even more important, how the reader can do the same, thus making the book a page turner.

Writing Exercises

If you want to write a book in the health, mind and body genre, remember that you want to write with a voice of authority yet in a personal and friendly way. Writing a book in this genre should be fun, so if you try one or both of the following exercises, do it with gusto!

EXERCISE 1

Select a physical activity you have engaged in such as jogging, biking, playing tennis, or baseball or even working out at the gym. Now whether or not you consider yourself to be an expert, imagine that you are an authority and write a few pages encouraging the reader to participate in the activity and how to do it well. Don't hesitate to draw on your own experiences.

EXERCISE 2

No doubt, there have been times when you struggled with adversity or endured difficult situations and conditions. Perhaps it was the loss of a loved one and dealing with grief, or your own depression about facing a new day, or losing a job and having to find new employment, or just raising teenagers! But it was something you overcame and you got on with your life. If what helped you over the hump came from within your own psyche and not religious faith (that's another genre), write several pages about how you accomplished this, keeping the reader in mind as someone to whom you pass on this advice.

CHAPTER 11

Parenting, Family, and Relationship Books

The family unit and the relationships among its members has always been a topic of interest for readers, especially with the advent of "extended families," and "significant others." While many of these books are written by acknowledged authorities, if you choose to write a book in this genre and don't possess the expertise, in many instances you can do so by relying on research, interviews, and your own experience. Writing a parenting, family, and relationship book can be an enjoyable experience since stories and anecdotes are frequently employed.

The Categories Within the Genre

It's important to know what subjects lay within the genre and which topics belong elsewhere. You should give the term "family" a broad definition and be inclusive. In addition to writing about parents, children, grandparents, and siblings you can also include stepparents/children/siblings and significant others or life partners.

ALERT

Do not confuse relationships among members of the family unit as used in this genre with "relationship" books, which are another group. Relationship books, sometimes found under sex or self-help books, generally have to do with dating or maintaining a good relationship with a significant other, although they do cross over into this genre, especially when affecting family members.

There are many subcategories within this group of books and because the degree of expertise you will need to write a book in this genre varies, you must know exactly where your book belongs. To help you focus on a possible subject, a brief survey of some of the major areas should give you a useful overview.

The Divisions of the Genre

There are many types of books within the parenting, family, and relationship genre. With more than 13,000 titles, books about the family in general are the largest category and include:

- Adoption
- Child rearing and development
- Fatherhood
- Motherhood
- School-age children
- Sex education
- Marriage

The topic of "family issues" is the next largest category with almost 3,000 titles addressing problems encountered by family members such as divorce, infertility, and addictions. Pregnancy and childbirth is a subgenre unto itself as are books about children with special needs such as ADD/ADHD, Down's syndrome, learning disabilities, children's diseases and disorders, and mental illness. Finally, with people living longer and new issues and concerns arising, so many books are written about the elderly that they are now categorized as books about aging and eldercare.

A complete review of all the subjects within this genre is not only unnecessary; it is impractical. However, by examining several select categories you will be able to see the different writing styles, methods, and expertise you will need to write a book in any subject of this genre.

Getting the Family Started

Two people living together who have formed a relationship, perhaps joined by marriage, a civil union, or a commitment, is the embryo for the family unit but it is only when children arrive that a "family" is formed. Sometimes, difficulties arise in reaching this stage and people tend to turn to books for guidance. Once conception is achieved, books provide another source for information and advice. Consequently, books about infertility, pregnancy, and childbirth are popular subjects within the category of family issues.

ESSENTIAL

Even when the approach to overcoming infertility is unconventional, such as applying Taoism and unifying mind and body to enhance fertility, the author needs to have some expertise. Such is the case with Daoshing Ni, the author of *Tao of Fertility*, who is a doctor of oriental medicine, a licensed acupuncturist, and has earned a PhD.

Trouble Conceiving

Infertility appears to be a growing problem, or perhaps it's just discussed more openly. In any event, there are 142 books in print on this subject. If you want to write a book about infertility, you need to be an expert in order to gain the confidence of the reader about this very important concern.

Sometimes infertility books are textbooks but because they are written so clearly they are widely read by the general public. A prime example of such a book is *Clinical Gynecologic Endocrinology and Infertility* by Leon Speroff, MD, and Marc A. Fritz, MD. Even *The Fertility Diet* is authored by two medical doctors, Jorge E. Chavarro and Walter C. Willett, along with a coauthor, Patrick Skerrett, who is the editor of the *Harvard Heart Letter.*

Growing a Family

A person could spend every minute of every hour of the nine months of gestation reading one pregnancy book after the other and still not finish. Unlike dealing with the issues of infertility, pregnancy is generally an upbeat time, so the books are written accordingly while presenting useful information.

FACT

You can write a pregnancy book without having medical credentials so long as the material is basic and incontrovertible. You'll likely write with a casual voice and even be entertaining at times. A prime example of such a book is *What to Expect When Your Wife is Expecting* by Thomas Hill, the creative executive for Nick at Nite and TV Land.

You do not have to be an authority in the subject but may rely on research and interviews to support your work, although you will need an expert involved with your book in some capacity. For example, *Great Expectations* is written by Sandy Jones, an author of parenting books, and Marcie Jones, a freelance writer, but written under the editorial guidance of a medical doctor and the director of nurse midwifery at Emory University.

Child Rearing and Development

In the general family category, child rearing and development covers all common concerns parents might have when it comes to raising their children. The largest number of books in this subject has to do with raising infants, babies, and toddlers. Generally these books are written by acknowledged authorities who sometimes combine their own parenting experience with their professional training. An example of this can be found in the bestseller, *The Baby Book: Everything You Need to Know about Your Baby from Birth to Age Two*, written by William Sears, a pediatrician, his wife Martha Sears, who is a nurse, and their two sons, both medical doctors. William and Martha Sears also drew on their personal experience raising several of their children on the theory they advocate in the book—"attachment parenting."

However, if your writing is strong enough, you can author a book in this genre by researching and having an expert or two associated with your book. The author of the What to Expect series, Heidi Murkoff, and her coauthors, who are all writers, secured a foreword from a medical doctor for *What to Expect the First Year*, which became a bestseller.

Children with Special Needs

Moving up the age ladder in families, there is more opportunity to write from personal experience. Consider the bestseller, *Louder Than Words*, in which the author, Jenny McCarthy, tells of her successful efforts to save her son from autism. Indeed, receiving many favorable responses from readers, McCarthy wrote a follow-up, *Mother Warriors*, in which she shares stories from parents with autistic children.

However, if you are not an authority, be prudent dispensing advice. Relating your experiences and observations and allowing the readers to draw their own conclusions is the wiser course. For instance, if you have a child with attention deficit disorder, you can write about how your family managed and perhaps even share successful coping strategies, but leave it to books written by experts such as *Healing ADD* by Daniel Amen, MD, to suggest that in some instances the standard treatment of Ritalin makes matters worse.

The Couple—the Lynchpin of the Family

The family unit begins with a couple but the emotional attachment between these two people will not always remain as it existed at the start. There are many factors that can put stress on this relationship, not the least of which are other family members—children, in-laws, stepchildren, ex-spouses, and so on. Once strained, a source for help people frequently seek is books and there are more than enough to choose from.

Many of these books have a positive spin and attempt to lead a couple to a warmer and more intimate relationship, such as the long-time bestseller *The Five Love Languages: How to Express Heartfelt Commitment to Your Mate*. Like the authors of most books in this category, Dr. Gary Chapman bases his advice on his clinical experience as a marriage counselor.

ALERT

Although sometimes cross-listed in the parenting, family, and relationship genre, books about divorce belong more in the self-help and how-to category or sometimes in law/business books. Divorce books focus on the failed relationship and not how to save the marriage. Most divorce books, to at least some degree, confront legal issues and need to be written by an attorney.

Naturally, there are instances where nonexperts write of relationships—those successful and those that failed. However, for the most part, the author is someone famous and the book is purchased more to secure a peephole into the celebrity's life than for purposes of gaining credible advice. A recent example is *A Promise to Ourselves: A Journey through Fatherhood and Divorce* by Alec Baldwin. Like most celebrity books, a ghostwriter, Mark Tabb, worked with Baldwin.

Aging and Eldercare

As the population ages, books about aging and eldercare will proliferate even more than they have to date. There are essentially three types of books in this subgenre, and you only need to be an expert in one of the groups. If you are going to write about specific physical and/or mental conditions, you must be an authority. For example, you could not write *The 36-Hour Day: A Family Guide to Caring for Persons with Alzheimer Disease, Related Dementing Illnesses, and Memory Loss in Later Life* unless you possessed credentials similar to the book's authors, Peter V. Rabins, MD, a professor of psychiatry, and Nancy L. Mace, MA, a mental health professional.

However, if you want to write a resource book such as one that details sources available to the elderly in securing home care or health benefits, all you need to do is research and use the tools you learned in Chapter 5. Of course, some professional experience would help, as would blurbs and a foreword by experts.

The third area in this subgenre is books written by adults with elderly parents who are dealing with their own personal experiences. Essentially, such books are memoirs, and you'll learn more about this in Chapter 18.

Writing a Parenting, Family, and Relationship Book

Because this genre is so diverse with numerous categories and subtopics, the writing style and techniques can vary. Nonetheless, the tone should be personal. While exhibiting a voice of authority, you should sound accessible. With few exceptions, even if you are a professional, do not write for your peers but for the general public unless it's a scholarly book you want to write.

ESSENTIAL

Since many books about parenting, family, and relationships find themselves sharing shelf space in the self-help and how-to section of the bookstore, you generally need to follow the writing skills you learned in that genre. Make ample use of lists and anecdotes, and feel free to draw on your own experience.

Although you will be writing as though you're having a conversation with the reader, you need to establish yourself as an authority. If you possess the expertise, you can do less research and rely on fewer experts, studies, and statistics than if you lack the required degrees and credentials. When writing about your conclusions based on research, do not be too technical and make sure your interviews make for a good read.

Excerpts That Show Diversity

Writing styles and techniques will vary from category to category within this genre and you need to examine books similar to the one you intend to write. But to give you an idea of what you should be thinking about, consider the following excerpts.

"When Billy was 5 years old, his mother took him to the pediatrician because of his high activity level and difficult nature. The doctor told Billy's mother that there was nothing the matter with the boy and that she should take parenting classes. The mother left the pediatrician's office in tears. . . . When he was in third grade, Billy came to my office for an evaluation. Billy had classic ADD: He was inattentive, distractible, disorganized, hyperactive, and impulsive. I placed him on medication, talked with the school on effective classroom management techniques, and had his parents attend a parenting group. . . . Six months after ADD treatment, Billy was a different child." (*Healing ADD* by Daniel G. Amen, MD)

"Because baby is getting a little older [8 weeks], you may be planning to take him out of town to meet his grandparents or other relatives. As you pack, think about what you'll need. For the diaper bag, consider the following:" (*Your Baby's First Year Week by Week* by Glade B. Curtis, MD, MPH and Judith Schuler, MS)

"No gimmick or quick road to effective parenthood, the 'no-lose' method requires a rather basic change in the attitude of most parents toward their children. It takes time to use it in the home, and it requires that parents first learn the skills of nonevaluative listening and honest communication of their own feelings." (*P.E.T. Parent Effectiveness Training* by Dr. Thomas Gordon)

"My conclusion after twenty years of marriage counseling is that there are basically five emotional love languages—five ways that people speak and understand emotional love. . . . Once you identify and learn to speak your spouse's primary love language, I believe that you will have discovered the key to a long-lasting, loving marriage." (*The Five Love Languages: How to Express Heartfelt Commitment to Your Mate* by Dr. Gary Chapman)

All of the excerpts are written by experts in their respective fields and yet they are written with a personal voice, conveying information and advice in a down-to-earth and comprehensible way. If the professionals can do it, certainly the lay author can.

You should be able to see how the standard techniques of writing nonfiction have been used even in the preceding brief excerpts. Dr. Amen told a story about a patient of his; a checklist was used in *Your Baby's First Year*; Dr. Gordon clearly explained what is required to become a better parent; and Dr. Chapman established his authority as an expert, setting the stage to explain his philosophy on maintaining loving relationships.

Writing Exercises

The exercises that follow require that you approach the genre from one of two perspectives. In the first exercise, you'll write from your own experience to validate your proficiency in the subject and the advice you provide keeping in mind this should be an easy and entertaining read. In the second exercise, if you lack professional experience, consider a bit of research to give you the knowledge you need to write the piece and imagine yourself as an authority. Feel free to make a list or relate anecdotes and use other techniques common to nonfiction writing.

EXERCISE 1

Unless you live on an uninhabited island, chances are you have some current familial or romantic relationship going on, but even if you do lead a solitary existence, there must have been some relationship in the past. Write several pages about that relationship whether it involved parent/child, child/parent, siblings, spouse/significant other, or extended family members and draw from your experience to offer some concrete suggestions and advice to the reader.

EXERCISE 2

Even if you are not an authority on the subject, for purposes of this exercise, you are one now! It's not an exam, so total accuracy doesn't matter; what counts is that you express yourself well, with a confident voice of professional authority. Select any one of the topics in this genre that interests you and with which you have some fluency or expertise, do a little research if need be, and offer information and guidance to the reader. Don't get carried away with your "new" degree. Keep your voice friendly and try writing a list or an anecdote.

Interview with Journalist and Author Ellie Slott Fisher

Ellie Slott Fisher is the author of *Mom, There's a Man in the Kitchen and He's Wearing Your Robe: The Single Mother's Guide to Dating Well without Parenting Poorly* and *Dating for Dads: The Single Father's Guide to Dating Well Without Parenting Poorly*, and she is currently working on a new book, *It's Either Her or Me: A Guide to Help a Mom and her Daughter-in-Law Get Along*. She is a contributor to the anthology *Single Woman of a Certain Age* and is a former editor and reporter for United Press International. Ellie has been featured in numerous national magazines. She has drawn from her own dating experiences to communicate and empathize with people in similar situations.

RDB: You have a background as a journalist and magazine writer. How did you come to write books on family dynamics, dating, and similar subjects?

ESF: As a journalist, I've always written about the lives of others. I am a private person and I never expected to write about my own experiences, reveal personal details of my sex life or bra size! But when I was in my thirties, my husband died suddenly, leaving me with two small children and no clue as to how to re-enter the dating world I had so long ago, and blissfully, given up. Consequently, when I began dating, I made mistake after mistake, even remarrying briefly, and then divorcing. I began writing books on relationships and single parenting because I wanted to help others avoid some pitfalls of being a dating single mom or dad.

RDB: Since your degree is in journalism and not the subject matter of your books, did you need to rely on experts and, if so, to what extent? Had you considered a coauthor who is an authority?

ESF: I have never been interested in a career in psychology because I felt I could be most helpful writing of my own experiences, as one single parent to another. Editors and publishers, however, want a professional expert to lend credibility to self-help books. In all of my books, I interview psychologists, medical doctors, attorneys, and other experts for their professional advice. At the same time, I maintain a raw, honest edge by being no different from my readers.

I never considered coauthoring because my books are personal narratives. It's also very important to me to be in control of the advice I give my readers. I understand what it's like to be a responsible parent who acts irresponsibly while in the midst of a passionate romance.

RDB: What type of research did you do for your books?

ESF: In addition to interviewing experts for all my books, for the Mom book, I spoke with single moms, their children, and the men who date single mothers. For the Dad book, I interviewed or surveyed 100 single dads and their children. My third book, which deals with how all the females get along in a guy's life, specifically his mother and his girlfriend, includes interviews with the mothers, sons, girlfriends and wives, and psychologists.

RDB: How did you utilize interviews, anecdotes, and people's stories?

ESF: My three books are primarily fueled by people's stories. I love a good story. If I can give readers examples of other people's trials and tribulations, then they will be able to relate to me and to my writing.

RDB: Is your writing style different when writing your books as opposed to writing articles?

ESF: As a journalist, I am adamant about not injecting myself into a magazine article, choosing instead to present the facts and interviews of those intimately involved in the subject matter. But as the writer of my books, it's impossible not to divulge personal information. And, in fact, how can I expect the people I interview to be honest with me if I don't come clean about myself?

RDB: What did you do to promote your books?

ESF: As most writers will tell you, promoting a book is our least favorite part of the process. I've been fortunate that both my publishers assigned me a publicist. Although they will assist you in scoring television and radio interviews and in receiving some magazine and newspaper coverage, you must persevere. For example, I gave the publicists the lists of local media—broadcast and print—and local bookstores so they could arrange appearances for me. Between my publicist's connections and my contacting everyone I knew even remotely connected to the media, I managed to get some good publicity, including appearances on the *Today Show* and NPR.

RDB: Any words of advice to someone contemplating writing a nonfiction book for the first time?

ESF: As I tell the college students I teach, nonfiction must be well organized and well conceived. Start with an outline and develop that into an extensive chapter-by-chapter outline. If you run out of ideas by Chapter 3, then maybe you need to rethink your topic. You also need to research the market and determine whether any published books are like yours, and if so, why yours is different, and if not, what makes yours sell? Research your audience thoroughly, because if you lack one, no publisher will buy your book.

CHAPTER 12

Writing Biographies

Because people have always been fascinated about the lives of others, biographies have consistently been a widely read genre. What is more, should you want to write a biography you do not have to be an expert in a specific field. What you do need to master is how to gather the necessary information; how to make your subject come to life for the reader; and how to write in one of the recognized styles for biographies. Telling someone's true story can be an enriching and enjoyable experience.

A Consistently Popular Genre

In a way, each person's life is a story. People love stories and perhaps that explains why the biography has always been one of the bestselling genres. People are also intrigued by the lives of others—the famous, the infamous, and even the not-so-famous if the story is compelling. If you decide to write a biography, it will likely be an endeavor that is fulfilling and fun.

ESSENTIAL

"Stories . . . told you how people felt, what they saw and heard, and how they lived. That was the important thing: They were part of a world, one that maybe didn't exist anymore, but that was the only way you could know it."—Henry Roth, *Mercy of a Rude Stream*

Biographies not only inform the reader about a person's life, but they also open a window to the world in which that person dwelled. Sometimes, it's the time period or an historical event or the people the subject came into contact with that's intriguing, which is why a biography can be written about an individual who, in and of herself, is not very well known. So, if there's someone's life story that fascinates you or the era in which your subject lived intrigues you and your subject is the perfect vehicle to explore that world, it just might be that writing a biography is for you. If this is the case then you are looking at an enormous market for your project.

Many Categories to Choose From

By some counts, there are more than 56,000 biographies in print. However, the figure is high because booksellers provide wide latitude for crossover among the genres of biographies, autobiographies, and memoirs. Since you'll learn about writing memoirs in Chapter 18, the term *biography* here usually means the account of a life written by someone other than the subject.

There are numerous divisions in the biography genre. Some of the most popular categories are:

- Celebrities
- Historical biographies

- Scientists and inventors
- Politicos
- Sports and adventure
- Scholars and specialists
- Family memoirs
- Business biography

Biography's Most Popular Categories

The categories in the biography genre can be all-encompassing or quite narrow, targeting a small but receptive market. For example, in the limited category of local politicos, a biography about a popular mayor of a small city in Oklahoma would sell well among the city's citizens, so it's not unlikely a publisher could be secured. But for the most part, biographies are written about well-known people who are the subjects of the larger categories.

ALERT

The subject of a biography need not be human. For example, the bestseller *Dewey: The Small-Town Library Cat Who Touched the World* is written by librarian Vicki Myron, who found Dewey stuffed into the library's book slot on the coldest night of the year. The book recounts the cat's nineteen-year life that inspired people all over the world.

Life Stories about Celebrities

People are interested in the lives of celebrities, as can be seen from all the magazines and tabloids covering these icons and the 4,000-plus biographies written about them that are readily available. Indeed, a number of biographies are marketed, if not actually written, with the salacious in mind. For example, in writing the summary for *Doris Day: The Untold Story of the Girl Next Door* by David Kaufman, the publisher describes the book as "scintillating tales of fame, beauty, money, tragedy, sexual ambiguity, and sexual conquests."

Frequently, these books are authored by the celebrity/subject himself with the help of a ghostwriter. Sometimes the celebrity writes of his own life experience with another person who is technically the subject of the book, thus making it more of a biography than a memoir. A recent example is the bestseller *Big Russ and Me*, in which Tim Russert writes of his life with his father. More common however, it's another person who writes the biography.

Historical Biographies

With more than 10,000 titles in print, historical biography is one of the largest categories in the genre. Some historical periods provide more fertile grounds than others for finding subjects, such as the years leading up to the founding of the United States and the early decades of the nation during which figures like Franklin, Washington, Jefferson, Adams, and Hamilton lived, of whom hundreds of biographies have been written.

FACT

The timeliness of your subject can be a factor in choosing whom you want to write about. For example, *The Snowball: Warren Buffet and the Business of Life* by Alice Schroeder became a bestseller when the financial markets were in turmoil and people sought guidance and inspiration from the life of this successful financier.

If you decide to write about a person of whom a number of biographies have been written, you should try to concentrate on a unique aspect of the person's life or write about the subject from a different perspective, perhaps focusing on a different time period in that person's life. Alison Weir has done this repeatedly with her subjects, including Henry VIII, Eleanor of Aquitaine, and Britain's royal families.

Scholars and Specialists

Along with books about scientists and inventors, biographies about scholars and specialists are often written by experts in the subject, unlike other books in the genre, where being an acknowledged authority is not required. For example, *Pascal's Wager: The Man Who Played Dice with God* was written by James A. Connor, who holds a PhD in literature and science.

However, do not be dissuaded from writing a biography about a scientist or scholar if that is your desire. Many of the biographies that have been written about Albert Einstein are by authors who were neither scholars nor scientists. It is also possible that a nonexpert is better suited for a particular biography, depending on the approach and perspective of the project. For instance, a book on the life of Alan Turing, the English mathematician who cracked the Enigma codes of World War II and whose career ended after his arrest for violating antihomosexual laws, needed an author who could convey the suspense of breaking the code and the drama of the criminal charges. Hence, David Leavitt, neither scholar nor mathematician but rather an author of novels and short stories, proved perfectly suited for the project.

Politicos and Sports Figures

Books about politicians abound and with 10,000 titles, it is one of the largest groups of biographies. In addition to the regular stand-bys that are timeless—Lincoln, Theodore and Franklin Roosevelt, Benjamin Franklin, and John and Robert Kennedy—contemporary politicos are always ripe for a biography.

It is not unusual for active politicians to pen their own memoir/biography usually with a ghostwriter, and this is also the case for celebrated sports figures such as the renowned basketball coach John Wooden who, with Steve Jamison, wrote *Wooden: A Lifetime of Observations and Reflections On and Off the Court.* Typically however, biographies about sports figures are written by someone other than the subject and generally the book needs to go beyond playing the game. In *The Express: The Ernie Davis Story* by Robert Gallagher, the biography of the scholar/athlete is set against the backdrop of the civil rights era in which he lived.

Selecting Your Subject

The first thing to consider when deciding upon the person to write about is whether you are truly interested in him. Sometimes, you'll settle on someone with whom you share common interests, which can provide the added benefit of establishing your qualifications to write the biography. Let us suppose you have always been a biking enthusiast and have even competed in races and now would like to write a biography of Lance Armstrong. Your interest and experience in biking helps make you suitable to write the biography.

There is another more important reason you must be attracted to the subject of your book: since it's likely you will be immersing yourself in the life of your subject for two years or more, you had better find her interesting!

ALERT

If the subject of a biography designates you to write the biography, the book can be promoted as "an authorized biography," which provides access to much information and encourages people to agree to be interviewed. Without an endorsement, it is improper to employ this term, although sometimes, for marketing and sensationalist purposes, the phrase "unauthorized biography" is touted.

Another consideration in choosing whom you write about concerns the issue of cooperation. If the subject is alive, having his cooperation would be beneficial not only in interviewing the subject but in gaining access to information and the ability to interview others. Should the subject be deceased, securing the assistance and support of the estate or heirs can prove invaluable for similar reasons.

You're a Detective

Your job as a biographer involves several critical responsibilities but the first and foremost is to gather information that is accurate and interesting to readers. In order to do this, you need not be an expert in any specified field, but you will have to draw on the skills you acquired in Chapter 5 in addition to using certain methods especially useful to researching biographies.

Reliable Research Tools

Much depends on whether your subject is alive or dead and if deceased for how long. Should the person you are writing about be living, you will want to try and interview him. You'll also want to interview family and people that know him or knew him if recently deceased. Bear in mind how important it is to prepare for the interview and be familiar with the methods for interviewing in Chapter 5.

If your subject has been deceased for many years it may be necessary to forgo interviews and rely upon other standard sources for information such as books and articles by or about your subject as well as official records and documents. In addition to the usual sources of information, there are research tools that work particularly well in writing biographies.

Supplementary Resources

The longer your subject has been dead and the better known your subject, the more likely it is there have been biographies previously written. Examining these books can make for a good starting place to commence your research, although you must keep in mind what you learned in Chapter 5 about plagiarism. You'll also have to make sure that your biography brings new information to light or offers a different perspective on the subject.

FACT

Since the advent of the telephone, people have relied less on writing letters to communicate. Formal correspondence has become even more infrequent with the Internet and communication making use of e-mails, most of which are not transferred to hard copies and are eventually purged. Hence correspondence, an important source of material for biographers, is less and less available.

A second source relied upon by many biographers is correspondence. Naturally, if there are diaries or journals maintained by the subject and you can access this material, you will have the pleasure of learning about your subject from her own words. But correspondence can also give you this insight, and you can gain access either from your subject directly, from the estate or family if the subject is deceased, from the correspondents who may possess these letters, or from an institution where the letters are held.

Be Creative

Think of writing a biography as an adventure while preparing to explore the life of your subject. It should be challenging, informative, and a great amount of fun. Do not feel constrained to limit yourself to a specific research tool; use anything that can bring results. For example, in writing *The Six Wives of Henry VIII*, Alison Weir relied on earlier biographies, letters, memoirs, account books, and diplomatic reports to produce great scholarship and an accessible book bringing these women to life.

Breathe Life into Your Subject

You should approach writing a biography with the idea that you are writing the "story" of a life. In fact, it's very much like writing about a character in a novel except that everything must be true. Employing the techniques discussed in this chapter, you need to get under the skin of your subject and inside his head and make him come alive in your book. While this is not always the case, you will find it is the way most biographers work.

QUESTION

Should I write a biography as though it was fiction?
While you may employ some techniques of fiction writing in your biography, especially if it's creative nonfiction, you need not do so. The important thing is not to present your subject as a one-dimensional person but rather as a complex and sometimes conflicted human being.

Three Styles of Writing Biographies

The writing style you employ will depend upon the type of biography. If you are writing a scholarly biography that is largely directed to an academic audience, then you can write in the style discussed in Chapter 7 for scholarly nonfiction even though some laypeople might read your book. For the most part, however, biographies are written for a general audience and you need to apply all of the writing skills you learned in Chapters 4 and 6, paying special attention to maintaining a personal voice and presenting your subject in a compelling way that will retain the reader's attention.

There is a third style of writing biographies that is becoming more common with the growing popularity of creative nonfiction and that is writing a biography employing some of the skills utilized in writing fiction. In Chapter 19, you will be provided an overview of how creative nonfiction is written.

Excerpts of Three Writing Styles

Styles differ in writing biographies that are scholarly, general, or creative nonfiction. Three excerpts follow. Can you discern the differences?

"Buber's readiness to do justice even to those who opposed and insulted him does not mean that he was 'objective' in the usual sense of the term, i.e., that he detached his reason from the rest of his person. It means rather that even in involving himself in the situation, he did not lose sight of the side of the other and was ready to pay sincere respect to any quality of greatness that he encountered." (*Martin Buber's Life and Work: The Early Years, 1878–1923* by Maurice Friedman)

"At 17, Franklin was physically striking: muscular, barrel-chested, open-faced, and almost six feet tall. He had a happy talent of being at ease in almost any company. . . .

"Franklin arrived at Philadelphia's Market Street wharf on a Sunday morning. . . . In his pocket he had nothing more than a Dutch dollar and about a shilling in copper, the latter of which he gave to the boatman to pay for passage. They tried to decline it, because Franklin had helped with the rowing, but he insisted. He also gave away two of the three puffy rolls he bought to a mother and child he had met on the journey." (*Benjamin Franklin: An American Life* by Walter Isaacson)

"'I am heir apparent, you know,' Adams reminded Abigail after arriving in Philadelphia for the opening of the Fourth Congress.

"The prospect of Adams succeeding Washington had been ever-present for seven years, but now, separated again by hundreds of miles, they addressed themselves to the growing likelihood of his actually becoming President, exchanged thoughts and feelings on the challenge in a way that apparently they never had before, and that perhaps they would have found impossible except at a distance." (*John Adams* by David McCullough)

Although not intended exclusively for a scholarly audience but for anyone interested in the life of the philosopher Martin Buber, Maurice Friedman wrote the three-volume definitive biography of the man and his philosophy in a style one might call challenging and far from an easy read. On the other hand, consider how Isaacson depicts the young Franklin by furnishing information and providing description to acquaint the reader with the physical appearance and personality of his subject in just a few sentences.

Midway between these examples, McCullough presents the life of John Adams in a style representative of general biographies. While McCullough conveys the material in a straightforward fashion without embellishment from literary devices, the reader is invited to see below the surface of the soon-to-be second president and even witness tension over the impending responsibility.

Writing Exercises

These exercises will familiarize you with the process of writing a biography more than honing a particular writing style. By this time you should be adept at writing in a personal tone with a voice of authority and employing the techniques for any specific category of biography. Which of the three styles is most applicable to your exercise depends on your subject matter.

EXERCISE 1

Select a subject either living or dead but who was alive during your lifetime and of whom you have some memory. It is not necessary the person knows or knew you but only that you know of the person. Try to conduct one or two interviews with people who know or knew your subject either directly or from afar and if you can, secure an interview with your subject. Rely on your own knowledge of the person and employ only a minimum of research other than interviews.

Write several pages about your subject keeping in mind you are not a journalist but a biographer and you need to make the person three-dimensional. Do not try to squeeze an entire lifetime into the piece but keep the time frame short, concerning yourself more with what the reader can learn about your subject and at the same time providing a good read.

EXERCISE 2

Repeat Exercise 1, but this time your subject must have died before you were born. You'll need to rely on more research, although depending on the circumstances, interviews might still be an option. Although you have no living recollection of your subject, you must get to know her and bring her to life for the reader.

CHAPTER 13

Writing Articles

Writing articles presents an unlimited world of opportunity. There is not a subject under the sun that does not lend itself to becoming the focus of an article, so you can write an article about almost anything and find a potential marketplace. However, coming up with the right ideas, knowing how to obtain the facts you need, and then crafting the piece professionally is not something that comes without the know-how you will learn in this chapter.

So Many Topics

The image of the writer staring at the blank screen or empty page and help-lessly waiting for inspiration for something to write about is a concept you are surely familiar with (and quite possibly has happened to you on one or more occasions). In actuality, writers are like explorers who gaze out at an entire hemisphere of undiscovered and unchartered territory. The task then is to know where to look and how to find subjects for your writing.

Getting Ideas from the World Around You

Charles Reich, the author of the 1970s bestseller *The Greening of America*, wrote that being a writer "meant being a thinker and even a philosopher, exploring and loving—a quiet calm person who was open to life, open to all the influences and experiences that came his way." There is no better way to mine the world for subjects to write about then simply being "open" to the world around you—the sights and sounds, the people you come into contact with, the conversations you overhear, the news on the Internet or broad-cast over the television or radio.

FACT

The newspaper is a great source for potential topics to form the basis of an article. Papers with wide circulation provide material that may appeal to a national audience, but don't forget your local paper as a source for articles—especially human-interest pieces.

Keep your eyes open for political, sporting, cultural and other events you might want to attend and cover. Visit places of interest but don't dismiss the most mundane—a neighborhood park or schoolyard or shopping mall. Even standing in line at the deli counter of the supermarket may provide fod-der for your next article. The thing is to keep your eyes and ears receptive to what is around you and as Reich implores, "be open."

Getting Ideas from Inside You

Sometimes, however, it's not what is "out there" but what is stirring in your own mind that may be the basis for an article. To explore what lies "within," make a space in your life for some "down time" when you can just think and let your mind wander and see where it takes you. Don't be dismissive of any thought that comes. Jot them all down and evaluate them later. One or more may be the next article you write.

If letting your mind just meander doesn't seem to work, consider those subjects you know something about—things that interest you like a hobby such as stamp collecting or having a passion for fine wines. Perhaps the subject may be work related, such as a high-school guidance counselor who wants to share tips for students seeking entry into colleges.

ALERT

When using your own experience as a springboard for an article, remember that it is not a personal essay or memoir you are writing. The focus must be on providing information and material of interest to the reader and your own experience should only be anecdotal.

Do not feel limited to writing only about what you know. There may be something that you want to learn about that will take you on an adventure of discovery and that you can share with the reader. This is where getting the facts and research becomes very important, as you will see in this chapter.

Some Subjects to Consider

If being "open" to the world around you or your own mental meanderings does not give rise to material then you may need something more specific to get you going. The best way to determine a topic might be to consider some of the genres of article writing and see what flows from there.

QUESTION

How do I find topics that are suitable for articles?
Go to the magazine section of the bookstore and peruse the categories of magazines as well as the table of contents in the issues. Read articles that draw your attention. Examine the magazines and the categories listed in trade books such as *Writer's Market*.

Make a list of the different types of magazines. It's not as daunting as you think. You'll soon see that some genres are very popular with many magazines published in that category, such as health and fitness, parenting, religious, travel, sports, and business. Once you select one of these general categories, you may then want to narrow the subject further. For example, if you are drawn to sports publications, you might want to focus on magazines devoted to running or biking or golf.

Now that you have a subject, you may think you have reached the end of your search. And in some cases, this is correct. However, if you have a desire to have the piece published, you must ask two more questions: Is this something other people will want to read? Is this something an editor will want to publish? Usually, if the answer to the first question is "yes," then the second answer also will be in the affirmative—it's just a matter of finding the right editor and publisher, which you will learn more about in Chapter 22.

Getting the Facts

Even though you have the subject that will form the basis of your article, you're still not ready to write. Articles contain information and facts and you must master the art of gathering the facts you will need for your article.

Basically, the tools you were informed about in Chapter 5, such as interviews and research, and the skills to use them, is what you will employ in writing articles. Depending upon the article you write, you may rely more on one method of fact finding than another. For example, if you a certified financial planner with an MBA and you are writing an article on allocating assets with retirement in mind, you will be your own best expert and draw from your own knowledge. But even in this scenario, you will find some editors asking you to interview other experts or cite sources.

ALERT

Sometimes, depending on the subject, relying exclusively on research and interviews no matter how thorough will not be enough. For example, in writing a nature article or travel piece, nothing takes the place of actually going to the natural setting or to the destination of your travel article and experiencing the environment firsthand.

Of course, in addition to interviews, research, and your expertise, you can draw upon your own experiences in getting the facts right. But remember, unless it is a memoir or personal essay you are writing, this cannot be the main source of your article.

Writing a Professional Article

With your subject clearly in focus and all the substantive data you will need within reach, the time has finally come when you begin the task of writing. This is not to say that all you have done before this point was not important. Mining the world and your interior life for ideas, selecting the subject for your piece, and gathering all the facts and information required is part of the writing process and being a writer. It's just that now the time has arrived when the craft of writing comes into play and to do this effectively, while there are no absolute rules, there are guidelines you should keep in mind as you go about putting words to print.

Structure of the Article

There are five ways to structure your article. They are:

- The inverted pyramid
- The double-helix
- The chronological double-helix
- The chronological report
- The storytelling model

Think about how you read a newspaper: you scan the captions and then read the first paragraph or two to get the gist of the article and then read further if you want to know more of the details. That's the inverted pyramid style of writing used by journalists, in which what's important comes first. The double-helix also presents facts in order of importance but it alternates between two separate sets of information. For example, suppose you are writing an article about the two national political conventions. You'll first present Fact 1 about the Democrat convention, then Fact 1 about the Republican convention, then Fact 2 about the Democrats, Fact 2 about the

Republicans, and so on. The chronological double-helix begins like the double-helix but once the important facts from each set of information have been presented, it then goes off to relay the events in chronological order.

FACT

You may choose any structure in which to write your article but keep in mind that you should not use the inverted pyramid unless you are writing for a newspaper. Once you select a structure, you must remain with that structure throughout the article.

The chronological report is the most straightforward structure to follow since it is written in the order in which the events occurred. The final structure is the storytelling model, which utilizes some of the techniques of fiction writing, so you would want to bring the reader into the story right away even if it means beginning in the middle or even near the end and then filling in the facts as the story unfolds.

Hooking and Reeling In the Reader

Remember in Chapter 1 where some noteworthy "beginnings" were presented and how the one and only thing they had in common was to grab the reader from the start and make her want to read more. The term for this device is the "hook." And that's what you must keep in mind in writing the first sentence or two of your article. You must make it interesting enough to pique the reader's curiosity and interest and want to read on.

In writing articles, the "hook" is a component of what is called the "lead." If you select a structure where you must begin with facts that are the most important or the first to have occurred in time, you still should write in a way to make them compelling.

You were also told in Chapter 1 that sometimes you just have to let it out and write a beginning just to get you started and that possibly later, the first beginning may be dropped altogether with another written in its place. The same method applies with writing articles, so don't become fixated on the beginning. There is time enough, as you will see in the following, to substitute just the right hook and lead when you rewrite and edit.

The Three Components of an Article

Like every form of writing, articles have a beginning, middle, and end but with articles, they are generally referred to as the introduction, the body, and the conclusion. The introduction serves the function of presenting and familiarizing the reader with what is to follow and generally should be no longer than one or two paragraphs. If it is longer than this, you need to edit it. You may have dwelled too long on introducing yourself to the reader or discussing background material.

The body of the article presents the reader with facts and information that is the purpose of the piece in the first place. Naturally, in terms of word count, it represents the bulk of the article. Keep in mind that unless you are writing an essay for a journal or a scholarly treatise, articles are meant to be practical, so do not overlook the importance of instructing the reader even though you may not be specifically writing a "how-to" article.

Finally, don't forget the conclusion, which is not to be confused with the ending. By definition, every written work has an "end," but that means it is merely the place where the writing ceases to continue. It is important that you wrap things up for the reader—perhaps a summary of the salient points even if no more than a paragraph.

Techniques in Writing Articles

Most of the techniques you saw in Chapter 1 apply to writing articles—particularly grammar, punctuation, and word count. There are also some techniques that are particularly important when it comes to writing articles.

ALERT

You must respect the parameters of the word count when you receive an assignment to write an article. Space is a critical factor facing editors when it comes to magazines and other periodicals. Don't have an extra fifty words and leave it to the editor to decide what to excise or be short a hundred words assuming some extra spacing can pad what is missing.

Tone and Voice

While your writing should reflect your "voice" that was developed in Chapter 1, it is important that the tone of your article be consistent with the publication in which it is to appear. For example, a humorous, carefree style combined with compatible language would be an appropriate tone if you're writing a piece on how to avoid bad blind dates for a readership of twenty-somethings but not suitable if you're doing an informative article on Alzheimer's for *AARP Magazine*.

And speaking of "voice," when writing nonfiction—especially articles, it is often important that you write with a voice of authority. Even if you are not an expert in the subject of your article, the reader needs to trust that you know what you are talking about. To do this you need to sound confident and also dispense facts and information. Avoid couching your claims with "possibly" or "perhaps" and similar limitations. On the other hand, just because you are an expert does not mean you have to sound superior and talk down to the reader. The voice can and should be friendly and accessible.

Bullets and Anecdotes

When you hear the word *bullets*, you probably think of the slugs of lead that blast from a gun. It's no coincidence that this is the term used to describe lists that appear with dots or asterisks placed before them in some books and many articles. Bullets are meant to quickly dispense important information in a way that stands out. You will find many bullets in this book and you'll probably need to create some in the articles you write.

Anecdotes are common in nonfiction. They belong exclusively to nonfiction because they are true (you'll see how to protect yourself from potential legal liability about the people depicted in your anecdotes in Chapters 20 and 21) but more important, they can be fun to write and in an entertaining way convey useful information. While in a book anecdotes may cover several pages, in an article they should be no more than a paragraph or two.

Be Your Own Editor

You may think that just because you are dealing with an editor you don't have to pay much attention to editing and you can leave that to the editor.

However, in most cases the editors of magazines and periodicals are overwhelmed with many tasks—sorting through queries and proposals, acquiring articles, establishing the terms of assignments, editing specific articles and sometimes entire sections of the publication, and even writing articles themselves. What editors want to see when an article is submitted is a polished piece that has been rewritten, reworked, and edited by the writer so it's just about ready to go to production.

Less Is More

You know the saying "less is more." Nowhere is this more appropriate than in writing articles. What was said in Chapter 1 about being concise and eliminating material that doesn't belong—no matter how important or wonderfully written—applies tenfold to writing articles. You have to be like a butcher cleaving the fat from the beef even if it means you might take a bit of meat with it.

ESSENTIAL

In rewriting and editing, it's not always a matter of removing material. There may be gaps that demand more information, which you can spot if you read the piece from the point of view of the reader. So bear in mind that the editing process can also mean adding to the article.

On your first rewrite, it will probably be easy to see where you have gone off on a tangent or gotten a bit too personal. That means that any material that makes for a good conversation but is not needed for the article should be cut. The more difficult problem is determining what facts and information should go. In this case, anything that is not necessary to the story, even if it is extremely interesting, should be deleted.

Be Consistent

It should be fairly easy to detect your writing style and tone of voice after the first or second paragraph. Whatever the tone of voice, you must be consistent and maintain it throughout the article. In writing fiction, it is almost an absolute rule not to move from one point of view to another—especially with short stories. This is even more unequivocal when writing articles.

If you see the tone has changed from the beginning to something else later in the article, go back and see what style works best. Don't automatically think you must abide by the way you began the piece. It may just be that while you were writing you unconsciously deviated from the original style because it just wasn't working. The thing to remember is that you must have only one style, tone, and point of view.

Excerpts to Ponder

Now that you know what to look for, critically reading and examining articles in magazines, newspapers, and other periodicals is an excellent way to develop and improve your own skills in writing articles. It goes without saying that reading makes you a better writer and there is much to be learned by examining both the strengths and weaknesses of other writers' material. While this is not meant to be a substitute for your own exploration of this genre, consider what can be learned from just the following excerpts.

> "Michael Phelps and his astounding performances have so thoroughly dominated these 2008 Beijing Olympics that it seems the Games' motto ought to be altered to 'One World. One Dream. Eight Golds.' Phelps continued his historic medal-mining this morning, capturing the 200-meter butterfly, his pet event, and then helping the U.S. romp to an 800 meter freestyle relay victory. The times in both were world records." (*Philadelphia Inquirer*, August 13, 2008)

This cover article that appeared in the sports section written by Frank Fitzpatrick about the gold medal record holder Michael Phelps is a perfect example of the inverted pyramid structure so typical of journalists but something you would not employ when writing other nonfiction. You can see how it begins with a general statement and then delves into the particulars involving first the medals won and then more specifically, the times of the events.

> "The Georgian army, suffering massive casualties in the face of overwhelming Russian firepower, retreated from the break-away region of South Ossetia yesterday. Russia ignored those calls [for a cease fire] and continued to bomb targets deep in Georgia." (*Philadelphia Inquirer*, August 11, 2008)

In the first sentence, the reader is informed of important information about the Georgian army. In the next sentence, there is information about Russia. This is typical of the double helix structure as the article goes on with these two strands—one from Georgia and the other from Russia.

"I first encountered 'Tricolor' in an English garden, where it glowed like a multicolored beacon. I was torn between loving it for its beauty and utterly rejecting it for its gaudiness. Being a polite young man, I asked the garden owner what that particular lovely plant was, and she replied, 'St. John's wort.' Gaudy or not, this small shrub really caught my eye with its graceful, arching form and pink, green and yellow foliage. I vowed to bring it home and try it in my garden." (*Fine Gardening*, October 2008)

In what person is this excerpt from Allan Armitage's column written? You should recognize from the *I* word that it is written in the first person, but even without this clue, you should be able to discern that much of the writer is present in this article. Although it could be the beginning of a personal essay or memoir, the piece goes on to inform the reader about the particular plant. The colorful description and the bit of dialogue reflect typical techniques of writing creative nonfiction that you will see in Chapter 19, but because of the subject matter and information, it is indeed an article.

Writing Exercises

Now that you know everything you need to enable you to write nonfiction articles, the fun part has finally arrived. You can begin to write your article! Although you will see in Chapter 22 that in many instances you try to secure an assignment in advance of writing the article, in other situations you must write the article first. But in any event, you might as well become accustomed to writing articles, so here are a few simple exercises to get you started.

EXERCISE 1

Actually, this is not a "writing" exercise at all because there is no writing involved. Go wherever it is you go and do whatever it is you do to come up with your ideas—a subject to write about that would make for a good article. Take as long as you like and don't make it too narrow. So, for example, if it has something to do with pets, focus on dogs but not one specific breed.

EXERCISE 2

Now that you have your subject, it's time to write the hook. Don't give the hook too much thought—no more than a couple of minutes. You're supposed to be creative here, so let it flow—no self-censoring, at least not yet. Write down three different hooks of one or two sentences each.

EXERCISE 3

Okay. Now take a break of at least an hour but no more than a day or two. Return to your writer's garret and select what looks to you like the best hook. Beginning with the hook you just picked, continue to write 120 to 150 words in a couple of paragraphs. Congratulations, you have just written your lead and introduction to your article. Don't edit or rewrite. Go away and don't come back for at least an hour but not more than a day or two (just like before).

EXERCISE 4

Return to your introduction and edit and rewrite it as many times and in as many ways as you want. You can take everything out if need be and feel free to add. But the end result should be between 80 and 100 words, a perfect length for an article of 1,500 words.

EXERCISE 5

This is also not a "writing" exercise. Take a break of at least a couple of days and return once again to your introduction. Is it something you want to write about and turn into an article? If so, review this chapter once more and go for it. Write the article. Not sure? Then put it where you file all those ideas and potential pieces you may write about and revisit later. Definitely not interested no matter what? Then delete it or toss it or tear it into little bitty pieces. No harm done. There never is if you enjoyed the process of writing. Just move on to your next project.

CHAPTER 14

Writing Reviews

Writing reviews affords a writer an excellent opportunity to break into print and there are many categories to choose from: books, movies, theater, restaurants, art, and music. Regardless of the subject of your review, the chief purpose is to inform and though you can render an opinion, it should be supported by facts. You also need to be cognizant of the ethical conduct expected of reviewers. While there is a writing style applicable to all types of reviews, you must adhere to the specific requirements of each category.

The Genre

When you contemplate where to go to dinner or browse the aisles in search of a book or ponder which movie to rent or which play to attend, you generally do not make the decision in a vacuum. You'll probably consider what you have heard from others—people you respect, friends, and family. Sometimes however, word of mouth hasn't made the rounds—especially if the movie has just been released or a new restaurant has opened. Because you don't want to leave it solely to chance, you might seek out a review in your local paper or a regional magazine or go on the Internet. This is why there has always been and likely always will be a strong market for reviewers.

While some knowledge or expertise in the subject of your review is always helpful, it is not a prerequisite to write a review. What you do need to know is how to write a review, which is what you will learn in this chapter.

FACT

Having written and published a number of book reviews does not give you much of an advantage if you decide to write reviews of restaurants. There is little room for moving from one category of reviews to the other and it is best to concentrate and develop a reputation in one area.

There Is Much to Review

With so many books published each year and publishers clamoring to have their books reviewed, there is a robust market for book reviews and as a reader and writer, you will find many opportunities to freelance in this area. Unfortunately, when it comes to other subjects—restaurants, music, theater, art, and movies—editors frequently have a specific individual in mind, often someone on staff, to write a review, although you can still establish yourself as a freelance reviewer specializing in any one of these categories.

Some General Tips

Regardless of the subject of your review, there are some basic guidelines that apply that you should follow. First and foremost is the need to project an aura of professionalism, because without it, your opinion will not be taken seriously. To accomplish this, make sure your review contains a good deal of information, facts, and well-thought-out insights.

ALERT

Be aware that some of your readers will have a different viewpoint than you. They may hate what you are reviewing when you love it or love it when you hate it. Keep this in mind as you write your review. You may even want to mention the types of people who might like or dislike the subject.

Here are other general tips you should remember when writing reviews:

- When reviewing anything with a story such as a novel, movie, or play, lay out the plot but do not give away the ending.
- Know the audience who will be reading your review and write with those readers in mind, considering their interests and demographics.
- Be sure to express your opinion but make sure you have supported your position with facts and logic.
- Make sure you have the background information so you are familiar with the subject and terminology.
- Be certain the tone and style of your review fits in with the publication for which you are writing.

Inform and Opine

The main purpose of any review is to provide the reader with sufficient information so she can decide for herself whether to buy the book or attend the play or dine at the restaurant. Your opinion is also important or the reader would be seeking out a newspaper or magazine article instead of a review, but your opinion will only be valued if it is supported by facts and information.

It is imperative that you write objectively when presenting the subject and do not allow your opinion to impact the portion of the review that must be a dispassionate discourse. For example, if you are writing a review of an art exhibit but are deeply offended by two of the works, which you consider pornography, you cannot allow this to influence your discussion of the other objects of art on display.

ESSENTIAL

Your opinion should be discernible in two ways in the review. First, feel free to state your opinion outright, but this should be done only once or twice. Second, your point of view can be more subtly suggested as you write the piece by using side remarks while presenting objective information about the subject.

Balancing Objectivity and Subjectivity

The best way to maintain a balance of objectivity and subjectivity is to be aware that there is no such thing as a "right" or "true" or "correct" opinion. An opinion is just that—an opinion and not a statement of fact. The thing about opinions is that there will be other opinions in opposition to the one you hold and none of them are true. Consequently, as a reviewer, be respectful when presenting your viewpoint.

An example of several reviews of the same play should help you maintain your humility as a reviewer. In a recent review of *Monster* appearing in the *Philadelphia Inquirer*, the critic Toby Zinman mercilessly panned the play while at the same time Lesley Valdes wholeheartedly praised it in *Broad Street Review*. Suggesting that both critics missed the point of the play, in a third review also appearing in *Broad Street Review*, Jim Rutter wrote: "But Valdes's thorough endorsement should have paid more attention to what Zinman rightfully criticized about the production values; and Zinman, for her part, failed to see that in an age when most people admit that they would rather die than live in broken bodies, Bell's play not only updated the *Frankenstein* themes, but provides the perfect metaphor for our vitality obsessed times."

Three reviews of the same production by three different critics with three different opinions. What is important is that all of the reviewers supported their argument with facts and logic, which makes it worthy of consideration for the reader, with whom lies the final decision whether or not to see the play.

Ethics of Reviewers

Because the principals of the First Amendment governing freedom of speech and the press is held in such high regard, writers are largely at liberty to write what they want and express themselves as they wish free of constraint. Of course, this is not without some limitations such as liability for committing libel or violating the right to privacy, as you will see in Chapters 21 and 22, or going beyond the protection of the First Amendment. But by and large, writers are not bound by ethical codes unless voluntarily agreeing to a code of ethics that may be required when joining a particular association of writers.

FACT

You must disclose any personal connection with the subject of your review, such as the author being a personal acquaintance or an actor in a play being a relative. Depending upon the editorial policy of the publisher, you will be compelled to mention the relationship in your review or be prohibited from writing the review altogether.

An exception to this general state of affairs is that journalists are bound to a code of conduct. Those reviewers who are journalists are consequently obliged to adhere to these principles. Because many reviewers are not journalists, the ethics of reviewers are general and informal. Nonetheless, there are some standards you would be wise to follow:

- Do not allow any preconceived bias to affect your appraisal of the subject.
- Be objective when presenting the facts and information such as describing the plot of a movie, the substance of a book, or the experience of the actors in a play.
- Divulge any personal association you have with anyone involved in the subject of your review.
- You should make a full disclosure if you do not complete the book or make an early exit from an exhibit, movie, or play, or not finish the meal in a restaurant.
- Other than a complimentary copy of the book or passes to the show, etc., you cannot accept any remuneration for writing the review.

Book Reviews

One of the few remaining opportunities for freelancers to be published in newspapers and tabloids is to write a book review. Magazines and journals continue to provide a ready market for book reviewers. While you need to have some experience or familiarity with the subject, the most important factor in having a book review published is your ability to write well and know what is required in this genre.

ALERT

While there is generally no "subject" to speak of in a novel or other work of fiction, you need to have credentials as a fiction writer to review a fiction book. Novels are regularly reviewed by published novelists; short-story collections may be reviewed by short-story writers; and published plays might be reviewed by playwrights.

Reviews of Nonfiction Books

Unlike most reviews where the reader reads the review to help make an informed decision to buy the novel or attend the performance or dine at the restaurant, readers of reviews of nonfiction books often read the review in lieu of the book. Consequently, your review should convey the gist of the book without holding anything back. The task for the reviewer of a nonfiction book is to inform the reader.

Feel free to refer to other material, facts, and books that complement or contrast the book under review. You can go beyond the book to provide additional information to make the review even more informative. It is not unusual for a review to evolve into what is known as a review/essay that takes the book as the starting point and then continues as an essay discussing the subject in more depth, which will be explored in Chapter 16.

One Review—Two Books

Sometimes if the subject matter is similar, you can write one review for two or more books. This frequently occurs when two or more biographies are released about the same person or a timely topic might spawn several books, such as a recent presidential election.

At other times, the connection between two books is less explicit, like the review written by Christopher Buckley in the *New York Times Book Review* of *Crossbearer* by Joe Eszterhas and *Called Out of Darkness* by Anne Rice, both of which were discussed in Chapter 9. When the link between the books is not obvious, you should make the connection known early in the review, as Buckley does in the beginning of his review:

> "Joe Eszterhas's 16 movies have grossed something like $1 billion. Anne Rice's novels have sold something like 75 million copies. So when writers with this economic mojo write memoirs about their return to the Roman Catholic faith of their childhood, attention must, and perhaps should, be paid."

Interview with Literary Critic Carlin Romano

Carlin Romano is the longtime literary critic of the *Philadelphia Inquirer*, critic-at-large of the *Chronicle of Higher Education*, and a former president of the National Book Critics Circle. Over the years his criticism has appeared in the *Nation*, the *New Yorker*, *Harper's*, *Slate*, the *Weekly Standard*, and other national publications. Romano has taught philosophy at Yale, Yeshiva University, Williams College, Bennington College, Temple University, and the University of Pennsylvania.

RDB: How did you become involved in writing book reviews?

CR: I regularly read book reviews growing up, in publications ranging from the *Times Literary Supplement* to the *New York Times*. I wrote my first one for the *Princeton Forerunner*, a Princeton undergraduate newspaper, and tried to do some at every paper I worked for in my twenties, including the *Washington Post* and the *Village Voice*. When I joined the *Philadelphia Inquirer* as a cultural writer, I began doing them for the *Inquirer*'s book editor. That put me in a position to succeed her, and I've been doing them ever since.

RDB: How do you determine what books to review?

CR: A mix of considerations that include personal interest in the subject, importance of the book or author in the marketplace and culture, size of the book versus time available to read it, and the feeling that I have something to say about the subject or writer.

RDB: What do you set out to accomplish in writing the review?

CR: In regard to content, a tight report of the book, some sensible evaluation, a contextualization of the book within ideas that matter to it. Stylistically, some snazzy phrases or sentences, a fetching lead, a coherent little essay from top to bottom.

RDB: How do you balance objectivity and subjectivity? How much of a review involves your opinion?

CR: Reporting of the book should reflect objectivity and fairness in description, but subjectivity infuses the process from start (choosing the book) to finish (assessing it). Most accurate answer to the second question is: All of it.

RDB: What comments do you have about the ethics of reviewing books?

CR: It's a complicated matter that I've explored twice in lengthy survey/reports for the National Book Critics Circle. A sample question from my surveys: "Is it ever okay to review a book without reading the whole thing?" You can see that such a question leads to further questions. Those surveys are available from the NBCC.

RDB: Is there a distinctive writing style you employ in writing reviews?

CR: I try to keep it lively, accessible, open to wordplay and wit, well-reported, not dumbed down.

RDB: Any words of advice to writers who want to write book reviews?

CR: Join the National Book Critics Circle, read its blog (Critical Mass), download a copy guide to book-reviewing opportunities.

Movie/Theater Reviews

Unlike book reviews—especially those of nonfiction books—where the primary purpose is to inform and an opinion is consigned a secondary role, reviews of movies and theater focus more on the critique. Readers of these reviews want to know what the critic thinks of the production and they take this into account when considering whether to attend. That is why a play can close on Broadway after opening night if the critics slammed it or a movie goes almost directly to video if the reviews were dreadful.

This means two things if you want to write movie or theater reviews. First, you must be someone whose opinion matters to the readers and therefore you ought to have some authority or expertise. Second, unlike book reviews, while you must provide a plot synopsis without disclosing the ending, be free to appraise the storyline, the actors, the set, cinematography and so on.

ESSENTIAL

Since movie and theater reviews are frequently brief—sometimes less than a few hundred words—you have to work hard to summarize the storyline. While you cannot discuss every subplot and character description in your review, make certain you convey the main plot and discuss the major characters.

Examine how in just a few short paragraphs movie critic Steven Rea of the *Philadelphia Inquirer* summarizes the movie *Pride and Glory*:

"*Pride and Glory* stars Colin Farrell and Edward Norton as two of New York's finest. Norton's Ray Tierney is a smart, straight-arrow detective, heading a task force to catch the killers of four ambushed police in a Washington Heights walkup. His dad, Francis Tierney, Sr. (Jon Voight), is chief of detectives. Ray's brother, Francis Jr. (Noah Emmerich), is the captain of the squad that just lost its men.

"And Farrell, nostrils flaring and arms flailing in serious over-acting mode, is Jimmy Egan, fellow cop and member of the Tierney clan by marriage. . . . He's all tears and rage at the hospital, looking on as one of his brethren hangs by a thread.

"But as Ray sets out to find the perpetrators, O'Connor's camera cuts to Jimmy and his cohorts torching the suspected shooter's getaway car. Uh-oh, the killings were an inside job, and the unthinkable has been thunk: rogue cops, drug ripoffs, extortion and worse."

Restaurant Reviews

Like reviews of movies and the theater, people read dining reviews to help them decide whether or not to patronize a particular establishment. While the opinion of the reviewer is important, the reader wants to know not only the quality of the food but the type of food; the cost; whether reservations are necessary; the efficiency of the servers; and the ambience. Consequently, there is a good amount of information you must convey in writing a restaurant review.

FACT

Unlike most nonfiction genres, to write movie, theater, and food reviews, you are not required to have a degree or vocational experience to validate your authority—rather your reputation comes with experience. In many cases, an editor assigns a reporter the task of reviewing movies and not infrequently, this becomes the start of a career and a movie critic is born.

But despite the need to provide information, reviews are by nature a balance between subjectivity and objectivity, and one negative experience may impact the review. Is this appropriate? Is it ethical? That would depend upon whether or not the nature of the affront reflects upon the quality of the establishment.

Consider the case of the dining critic Craig LaBan who after a "pleasant first meal" returned to the restaurant for a second culinary encounter. Laying the groundwork for his scathing review, he diced the appetizers and the ambience as well as the primi (the pasta course) and the forty-five-minute wait preceding the main meal.

When the entrée was finally served, the veal chop his guest had ordered without sugar because of an allergy was "glistening with a sweet brown shine of fig gravy." Although the waitress and owner were apologetic, they re-served the chop a second time by rinsing it under water and could not understand that it might still cause an allergic reaction.

In any event, on a scale of one to four bells, no bells were awarded. Not a good omen for a new restaurant.

Writing Exercises

Writing reviews can and should be a lot of fun. The exception would be if you are the sort of person who hates to say anything negative for concern of hurting someone's feelings, but even then if you dislike the subject of your review you could always abandon the project. But otherwise, you get to attend a play or movie, read a book or dine in a restaurant, think about it, and then write the review. So, the following assignment that you can repeat as many times as you wish, goes beyond writing or even research but requires you to experience your subject firsthand.

EXERCISE 1, 2, 3 . . .

Pick the type of review you want to write. Read the book or attend the play or watch the movie or dine at the restaurant. Once that is accomplished, just apply what you have learned and write the review, keeping it to less than 500 words. In fact, this may be the most difficult part, so you'll have to do quite a bit of editing. Don't forget to provide information as well as your opinion.

With review 1 complete, you can choose to do a second or third review. You can move from one type of review to another and see what you feel most comfortable with. It just might be that you'll discover the critic inside you and now you'll have the skills to give voice to that critic.

CHAPTER 15

Writing Opinion Pieces

If you feel passionately enough about an issue that you want to persuade others to think the same way, expressing yourself in writing provides an excellent vehicle to reach a larger audience. If this is your goal, you should consider writing opinion pieces but you'll need to know the precise requirements of this genre: the markets; what publishers look for in the subject matter; the contents and style expected in your piece; the specific length requirements; and the unique submission process.

The Art of Persuasion

To varying degrees and depending upon the genre, writers have articulated their opinions in the hope of convincing readers to think as they do about a certain subject or concern. However, it is only in the opinion piece that the writer's belief is the thrust of the article and influencing the attitudes of others its chief purpose.

ESSENTIAL

"A writer sometimes has dual loyalties. . . . He is a more or less respectable citizen of the kingdom of events, conscientious and law abiding. . . . And yet his mind is on the words that could be used to talk about the events, rather than on the events themselves."—Amos Oz, author, *Under This Blazing Light*

The Genre

Opinion pieces are also called "commentaries" and "op-eds," the latter because of their location on the page opposite the editorial page in newspapers. In a sense, the tactics in winning any debate or argument apply to writing opinion pieces. Consequently, while you should be passionate about your position, you have to write in a professional style and be aware of the factors that will strengthen your argument.

The Venues

The most popular market for submitting opinion pieces and one that remains open to the freelance writer is the newspaper. Consider every sort of tabloid from the local weekly to a daily with national circulation.

ALERT

Although issues that appeal to a broad audience are more common to newspapers and magazines with a large circulation, you can also submit such pieces to local newspapers. However, the reverse is not true. Commentaries about local matters will not be considered by publications with regional or national circulation.

Another venue for your opinion piece is magazines, although this is more limited than tabloids. While accepting commentaries, some periodicals restrict their consideration to the subject matter of the publication. For example, a magazine geared to hunting might consider an opinion piece about pending legislation concerning gun control but quickly dismiss a commentary about pending legislation on health care as not topical.

Factors to Consider Before Writing

Since the purpose of an opinion piece is to influence readers, getting your commentary published is of paramount importance. Therefore, you need to consider several crucial points before you even begin the writing process.

Importance of the Subject

Although you may be passionate about your position, it doesn't mean there are others who care one way or the other about the issue. For example, you may feel very strongly that four-way stop signs at intersections are more of a hazard than a benefit but no one else in the community seems to be troubled about it and certainly not the editors of the local and regional papers. That being the case, it's not likely you'll find an outlet for your commentary.

However, always keep in mind that circumstances can change, so given the same concern about the stop sign matter, if an accident occurs at an intersection with four stop signs, public interest may be aroused. This is why timeliness is so critical when it comes to opinion pieces.

FACT

The subject of your commentary must be an original position and not in response to an article, editorial, or other commentary that appeared in the publication. If you want to take issue with another published piece, you should express yourself by writing a letter to the editor and not a commentary.

Your Commentary Must be Timely

Since most opinion pieces are published in newspapers or weekly magazines, the subject of your commentary must be relevant to current concerns. For example, if you are writing about a political election, the time to submit your piece would be at the height of the campaign, or if you want to publish a commentary against shooting deer the appropriate time would be during hunting season. Consequently, as you will see when you learn about the unique procedure in submitting commentaries, there is a small window of time in which to write the piece and market it for publication.

However, if you miss the opportunity to write and circulate your opinion piece because it is no longer timely, in some cases, all you need to do is wait until the time returns when it becomes appropriate once again to market the article. Returning to the deer-shooting article, when the next hunting season is about to begin, you can circulate your opinion piece again.

Special Length Requirements

Publishers and editors have specific guidelines for word counts for manuscripts and articles that they will consider. Nowhere are these requirements more stringent than in the length of opinion pieces, especially since they often appear opposite the editorial page of newspapers where space is very much in demand. You must respect the maximum word count and stay within the limit, which means you need to rewrite and edit as much as it takes to achieve the appropriate length.

Generally, op-eds for newspapers are between 300 and 750 words. Commentaries for magazines and journals may be as long as 2,000 words.

Writing the Opinion Piece

Now that you are ready to sit down and compose your commentary, there are some techniques you should keep in mind in addition to what you have learned thus far about writing nonfiction. Some of these have been discussed before but require special attention here:

- Write in a clear and confident voice but do not appear arrogant or intolerant.

- Acknowledge the legitimacy of those on the opposing side while discussing and refuting their positions.
- You can write about a specific incident, event, or circumstance, but then you ought to draw a wider message.
- Keep your audience in mind—especially those who are indecisive over the issue or in the opposition—and use information and facts as well as logic that you think will appeal to them.
- Feel free to suggest specific action that your readers can take.
- If you have some personal connection to the topic or personal experience you should rely on that to establish your authority.

Be Persuasive

While you need to apply the techniques of writing nonfiction when you compose a commentary, one factor commands special attention. Because your goal is to persuade, more than in any nonfiction genre, you must establish a voice of authority. In order to achieve this, there are two essential methods you need to employ in your composition.

Facts and Reason

Once again, you have to adhere to the nonfiction writer's mantra that facts are the keystone to your work. Simply stating your opinion and asking the reader to accept it at face value will only succeed if the reader is predisposed to agree with you even before reading your article. Since the purpose of commentaries is to persuade and not merely reinforce the opinion of those in agreement, your objective is to convince those uncertain or in opposition to your viewpoint to come around to your way of thinking. The only way you can accomplish this is to support your argument with facts and information.

QUESTION

Can I present a radical position and still sway readers?
You can state your view even if what you suggest is on the zealous side. The important thing is you must use information, logical reasoning, and a restrained argument to lead the readers to your conclusion.

The second key element in writing an effective commentary is to write in a voice of reason and moderation. Chances are that if you sound like a fanatic, readers will dismiss you as one. Extremists may be successful preaching to the choir but if you want to change the hearts and minds of others, you must be logical and judicious in your presentation while still remaining passionate.

The Submission Process

In Chapter 22, you will get an overview advising how to go about getting your work published, and in the interview with Larry Atkins at the end of this chapter; you'll receive some advice concerning the submission process regarding opinion pieces. However, it deserves emphasis that because of the critical importance of timeliness, submitting opinion pieces to newspapers deviates from the standard protocol generally followed in the other genres of nonfiction writing.

Because op-eds in newspapers must address a current issue, you normally have precious little time to compose your commentary. Of even greater concern if you want to see your piece published is that you cannot follow the customary procedure of submitting your work to one editor, waiting for an answer, and if rejected, submitting it to another publication, because by the time you receive your third or fourth rejection, the issue may no longer be timely. Consequently, subject to the clarifications Larry Atkins offers in his interview, you may submit to more than one tabloid at a time.

FACT

Unlike all other genres where you should not make electronic submissions unless it is indicated as a suitable method, almost all newspapers accept e-mails. However, your commentary should not be attached to the e-mail but embedded since most editors are reluctant to open attachments without personally knowing the sender.

You should be aware that op-ed editors of the major newspapers may receive more than a hundred submissions a day. Don't expect a reply unless it is accepted. In this case, "no news is not good news." If you receive an acceptance, you need to make certain it is not published by another tabloid in the same region as the paper that has accepted your article, and you might want to contact those editors within that area and withdraw your piece.

Excerpts

The standard advice that you should read and study material in the genre you want to write is applicable to commentaries. Fortunately, it is easy and inexpensive to read opinion pieces. You can access many online or just browse through magazines and tabloids in the library or bookstore and read the opinion pieces you come upon. And because they are short, you don't have to invest a great deal of time. To give you an example of how much you can learn by reading opinion pieces written by others, consider the excerpts that follow.

Acknowledge the Opposition

The following is the beginning of a commentary in *Newsweek*:

"Unless you've been living in the Himalayas, you know huge numbers of Americans—46 million last year, or almost one in seven of us—who lack health insurance. By impressive majorities, Americans regard this as a moral stain. At the Democratic National Convention, Sen. Ted Kennedy echoed the view of many that health care is a 'right' that demands universal insurance. This is a completely understandable view and one that is, I think, utterly wrong. Take note Barack Obama and John McCain.

"Whoever wins should put health care at the top of his agenda. But the central problem is not improving coverage. It's controlling costs. In 1960, health care accounted for $1 of every $20 spent in the U.S. economy; now that's $1 of every $6, and the Congressional Budget Office projects that it could be $1 of every $4 by 2025." (*Getting Real About Health Care, Newsweek*, September 15, 2008)

In this commentary, Robert J. Samuelson so convincingly states the other side's position that he almost lulls the reader into the false impression he is in favor of revamping health insurance and providing universal coverage when in fact he goes on to make a very credible case that the true culprit regarding our health care system is soaring costs. Note the complete lack of ill will to the opposing argument or any tone of fanaticism and the reference to facts that cannot be disputed. Finally, for a man who is a highly respected economist, consider how he writes in a down-to-earth tone yet at the same time establishes a voice of authority.

Recent Incident Spawns Op-Ed

It is very common that a recent occurrence, sometimes itself seemingly unimportant, serves as a springboard for writing an opinion piece on a much broader and weighty topic. An example can be found in the beginning of the following commentary:

"Until recently, I had no idea who Duane "Dog" Chapman was, nor do I care much about him even now. However, when I learned his television show was pulled because he used the "N" word in a private conversation, I became alarmed over what I perceive to be just one more instance of an insidious assault on the free exchange of ideas upon which any democratic society depends." (*Banning Offensive Language Diminishes Free Speech, Philadelphia Inquirer*, November 12, 2007, by Richard D. Bank)

David and Goliath

Don't hesitate to take issue with your government, the president, or public officials. As they say, the pen can be mightier than the sword. But if you do so, do not sound like an extremist. Make sure your position is supported by reason and don't hesitate to refer to the larger issues as in the following commentary, in which Lance Morrow raises concerns that the Bush administration skirts the Constitution in its fight against terror and the war in Iraq:

"Sometimes wars are necessary in order to rescue peace and enforce international law and order. I think that is what is going on now. . . .

"Meantime, the least we can do is reread the Constitution and refresh our gratitude and submission to it. Keeping the Constitution will be as vital to the American future as fending off terrorists. More so. If Americans win a war (not just against Saddam Hussein but the longer-term struggle) and lose the Constitution, they will have lost everything." (*TIME*, March 17, 2003)

Write an Op-Ed

This exercise consists of writing an opinion piece, and although you may not actually start writing for days or weeks, the work begins immediately. Be open to the world around you and see what stirs your passion. It can be something you read or observe on TV or on the Internet; it can be something you overhear spoken by a total stranger or what someone you know says to you; it can be newsworthy to the world community or just a happenstance of no importance to anyone but yourself (if the latter, remember to use it as a catalyst to an issue others can relate to).

Once you decide upon your subject, apply everything you have learned and write an opinion piece of no more than 500 words and do it within three days from when you settled upon the subject. When you're done, if you can, ask someone who either disagrees with your position or is neutral to read it and see what she thinks. Feel free to have more than one person read it. It's not so much a question of the writing as it is the power to persuade that matters.

Now you're done. If you found the experience exhilarating then perhaps you should seriously consider writing commentaries.

Interview with Journalist and Lawyer Larry Atkins

Larry Atkins is a journalist, a lawyer, and an adjunct professor at Temple University and Arcadia University. In 2005, he wrote "Larry the Liberal Lawyer Lashes Out" (ASJA Press), a "best of" compilation of his op-eds. Atkins is a member of the American Society of Journalists and Authors and he wrote a chapter on op-eds and essays for the *ASJA Guide to Freelance Writing*. Atkins has written over 300 articles, op-eds, and essays for many publications including the *Atlanta Journal-Constitution, Baltimore Sun, Chicago Tribune, Christian Science Monitor, Philadelphia Inquirer*, and *Los Angeles Daily News*.

RDB: How did you come to write opinion essays and op-eds?

LA: In 1992, I took a freelance writing course. One of the covered topics was writing op-eds and essays and I discovered that newspapers and magazines would actually pay freelancers to write opinion articles. It really sparked my interest. I started sending op-ed submissions to the *Philadelphia Inquirer* and they accepted the fourth one that I submitted. Eventually, I became a frequent contributor to the *Inquirer* and I ended up submitting and publishing op-eds in newspapers throughout the country.

RDB: Where do you get your ideas?

LA: I get ideas from many different places. First of all, it's really important to be a news junkie and to follow current events closely. Every day I read several newspapers, check news websites, and keep MSNBC or CNN on while I work at my computer. I've also gotten ideas from my own personal experiences. For instance, when my father's paratransit van didn't show up one day and left him stranded, it inspired me to do some research in which I discovered that this was happening frequently in Philadelphia. I ended up writing an op-ed on that topic.

RDB: What makes you want to respond to some issues rather than others?

LA: I have many diverse interests but I tend to care about some issues more than others. I am passionate about politics, sports, legal issues, education, media and journalism, psychology, entertainment, and local issues. There are some situations where something in the news makes me angry and I feel an urgent need to respond.

RDB: How important is timeliness?

LA: Timeliness is essential for most issues. When a news event occurs, many editorial pages run op-ed's on that event in the next day's paper or within the next few days. If you decide to write an op-ed on a breaking news event, you should try to write and submit it to a newspaper within one day. There are some issues that have more flexibility because they involve ongoing controversies, such as the Iraq war, homeland security, stem cell research, gun violence, and health care. You can also try to anticipate certain events and write op-eds on them in advance such as the Super Bowl, the beginning of the school year, and Thanksgiving.

RDB: What is the protocol regarding submitting op-eds?

LA: Always use e-mail or fax since timeliness is usually an issue. Don't use attached files; cut and paste the text of your op-ed into the body of your e-mail. National newspapers such as the *New York Times* and *Washington Post* require exclusive submissions for a certain period of time, meaning that for a period of about one week, they don't want you to submit your op-ed to other publications. If you don't hear from them within the specified period of time, you are free to assume they have rejected your op-ed and you are free to submit it elsewhere.

Similarly, local newspapers want exclusivity in their specific circulation area. This means that you shouldn't submit your op-ed simultaneously to the *Chicago Tribune* and the *Chicago Sun-Times*. You can simultaneously submit your op-eds to non-national regional newspapers as long as their circulation areas don't overlap. Therefore, you could simultaneously submit the same op-ed to the *Philadelphia Inquirer, Dallas Morning News,* and *Atlanta Journal-Constitution.*

RDB: Any advice to writers who want to write opinion pieces?

LA: Be persistent and don't take rejection personally. There is an incredible amount of competition for publishing op-eds in newspapers. One way to increase your chances is to write what you know. Try to focus on issues in which you have expertise or a personal connection. For instance, if you are a teacher, you have expertise in education issues such as school violence, No Child Left Behind, and school district strikes.

Add a short personal anecdote that connects you to the issue involved. You can also create a website or blog focusing on a certain topic and earn credibility and expertise by doing so. Also, don't just limit your submissions to newspapers. Consider marketing your op-eds and essays to magazines and online publications. Proofread your articles carefully and have a friend or family member read it over to get feedback. Finally, it can help your chances if you are making a unique point or argument or taking a contrarian position to what most people believe.

CHAPTER 16

The Literary Essay

The literary essay is one of three types of essays—the other two being the opinion essay and the personal essay. While some writing techniques are common to all three, you must know the characteristics of each. The purpose of the literary essay is to inform and sometimes suggest a message in a well-written piece. Because the subject can be anything, writing a literary essay affords an excellent opportunity to learn more about a topic that fascinates you and convey that information with attention to the craft of writing.

What Is a Literary Essay?

Like opinion pieces, literary essays are written to inform the reader while sometimes delivering a message; unlike opinion pieces, literary essays are not designed to persuade, although affecting the way people think is often a by-product whenever information and ideas are imparted. Literary essays are also distinguishable from opinion pieces by their length, which may be as long as 8,000 words.

Although literary essays may involve an individual experience and dwell upon personal reflections similar to personal essays, the focal point of literary essays is the subject of the essay and not the writer. What also makes the literary essay stand apart from all other forms of nonfiction including personal and opinion essays is that the writing must demonstrate a convincing command of writing techniques and evince a sense of language. In other words, they must be well written.

The Subject

The wonderful thing about literary essays is that you can pick any topic you desire to serve as the centerpiece of your essay. The subject may be very explicit, such as a particular species of butterfly, or the topic may be more general, such as describing a city. The important thing is that regardless of how expansive or narrow the topic, your literary essay must appeal to a wide audience and preferably deliver a message that addresses many readers.

FACT

You need not limit yourself to one subject in a literary essay; it is possible to write about two subjects. Often when doing this, one of the subjects is a personal experience or consists of personal reflections. When you do write about two subjects, you need to make certain they come together by the end of the essay.

Deciding upon the topic of your literary essay is half the fun. You can write about anything at all, choosing something that has always interested you that you want to study further or a subject that you have only recently been intrigued by and now want to explore. What is more, the venue for your search is everywhere and anywhere. You can surf the Internet, peruse the shelves of a library or bookstore, read articles in magazines and newspapers, or just consider the world around you.

What is critical in composing a respectable literary essay is that once you select your subject, you know the standards and writing techniques that is expected in the genre. If you simply convey information, then you have written an article; if you instruct in a didactic manner, you have written a scholarly piece. And while there is nothing wrong with either genres, it does not make for a literary essay.

Organizing the Essay

Thus far you have seen that regardless of the nonfiction genre, you rarely sit down before a blank screen and start striking letters to form something out of nothing. There is always some preparatory work that needs to take place before you reach the stage where you're ready to write. In this respect, the literary essay is no different than other nonfiction genres. A good place to begin is to understand the structure of an essay.

ALERT

You need not feel compelled to follow or even consider the format that generally defines essays. Many people believe it is just as effective to read in the genre you want to write and you'll come away intuitively knowing what you need to do to write successfully in that genre without following any "rules."

The Paragraphs

The first paragraph of your essay introduces the main idea in a way that grabs the reader's attention and makes him want to read further. The introductory paragraph should contain your thesis statement or main idea in one sentence with the remainder of the paragraph providing background information and laying the foundation for what will follow.

The paragraphs that ensue comprise the body of your essay and develop the central concept. In composing your essay, you should take the following considerations into account:

- Before writing, you might want to make a list of your major points.
- Each paragraph should focus on one of your main points.
- Support your positions with facts, details, and examples.
- The paragraphs should transition smoothly and flow in a logical sequence.
- The first and last sentences of your paragraphs can be used to connect to the paragraphs that proceed and follow.

FACT

In longer essays, there may be two or more paragraphs in the beginning that serve as an introduction to the body of the essay and at the same time, there may be two or more paragraphs providing the conclusion. It is not uncommon that in longer essays one major concept is discussed in several paragraphs.

The concluding paragraph of your essay should summarize the key points you made. You may want to make some suggestions to the reader and offer insights of your own.

Writing the Literary Essay

Like most nonfiction, providing information is one of the chief objectives of the literary essay, so writing in a voice of authority is critical. However, unlike many other nonfiction genres, you do not need to be an acknowledged expert in the subject to write a literary essay, although having expertise will certainly be a benefit.

Voice

While you must write with a voice of authority so the reader trusts that you possess the knowledge to instruct in the subject of your essay, this does not mean you need to write in a scholarly or formal voice. You're not lecturing but rather, you are having a conversation with the reader. In fact, your voice can be very personal and even friendly. If you have written in other genres and have found your voice, there is no reason you need to adopt a different tone when writing the literary essay.

The way to gain the reader's trust in you as an authority is by imparting information. As you have seen elsewhere, one of the best methods to reach this goal is to fill your essay with details and specific facts. Of course, you must do this without being boring and with graceful language, which is what makes for a literary essay.

Sense of Language

It goes without saying that everything you compose should be well written. This is particularly true when writing a literary essay. Attention to grammar, spelling, and punctuation is important as well as word choice. For example, although both the article and the literary essay are meant to instruct, you must exhibit a greater sense of prose when writing a literary essay.

ESSENTIAL

Literary essays must be well written in every sense of the word while educating the reader in the subject and offering some insights. This is not to mean that literary essays must be written with stilted verbiage or scholarly terminology. Literary essays are meant to inform—not to impress.

You should make use of language and your voice to establish the tone of the piece. A literary essay when read aloud is something beautiful to hear and it should not sound like a lecture given by a professor from a podium.

Literary Essays Enlighten

Although the literary essay should tell the reader something he does not know, this does not mean you are bound by the protocol required in a scholarly treatise or a specific methodology when conducting your research. What is most gratifying about writing literary essays is that you are like a guide blazing a trail through somewhat familiar but frequently unexplored territory and then returning to lead the reader over the path you have forged. Draw on what you learned in Chapter 5 to gather your facts and information.

FACT

The primary market for literary essays consists of literary journals and periodicals as well as some magazines. Generally, the audience will be well-read and receptive about learning new subjects as well as appreciative of finely honed prose. Write your essay with this in mind. You should read journals and periodicals where you might want to submit your essay.

Writing with the voice and style you have developed, enlighten the reader about your subject. Keep it lucid and be direct. You're not defending a thesis and you certainly do not want to bore the reader. Rather, write in the tradition of literary essayists by exhibiting fine writing, edifying your subject for the reader, and sharing what you have learned.

Excerpts Reflecting a Wide Range

It is frequently said that the best way to learn to write is to read the work of others—especially in the genre in which you have interest. While this does not mean you should imitate the writing style of other writers, it is an excellent way to study the genre so you can then proceed to develop your own unique voice and style. With this in mind, consider the following excerpts and if you are serious about the genre, you should read other literary essays in their entirety.

Combining Literary and Personal Essays

"Okinawa: The Bloodiest Battle of All" by William Manchester was first published in the *New York Times Magazine* and was subsequently selected for *The Best American Essays 1988* as well as *The Best American Essays of the Century*. In this article, the author uses his presence at a ceremony attended by Japanese and American war veterans to dedicate a monument of those killed in the bloodiest battle of the Pacific war to expound upon the battle of Okinawa. As you will see in the next chapter, by dwelling upon his own experience and then drawing more universal implications, Manchester has followed the path of the personal essay but since the essay at hand is fundamentally an exposition of the battle itself, it is more properly categorized as a literary essay. The point being, there is not always a clear demarcation between these two popular kinds of essays. Consider how the information and the writing style of Manchester's piece brings it into the domain of literary essays.

Manchester introduces his exposition of the battle the following way:

"No one doubted the need to bring Japan to its knees. But some Americans came to hate the things we had to do, even when convinced that doing them was absolutely necessary; they had never understood the bestial, monstrous and vile means required to reach the objective—an unconditional Japanese surrender. As for me, I could not reconcile the romanticized view of war that runs a red streak through our literature—and the glowing aura of selfless patriotism that had led us to put our lives at forfeit—with the wet, green hell from which I had barely escaped. Today, I understand. I was there, and twice wounded. This is the story of what I knew and when I knew it."

Note how Manchester establishes his voice of authority from personal experience and consider how he makes use of word choice and language in his composition. In the subsequent paragraph, Manchester goes on to describe the battle and provide basic information about the confrontation. Can you see the change in word choice and sentence structure? Even the tone has shifted from personal reflection to a clear and lucid reporting of facts.

"To our astonishment, the Marine landing on April 1 was uncontested. The enemy had set a trap. Japanese strategy called for kamikazes to destroy our fleet, cutting us off from supply ships; then Japanese troops would methodically annihilate the men stranded ashore using the trench-warfare tactics of World War I—cutting the Americans down as they charged heavily fortified positions."

The Incidental to the Notable

A device you might want to consider employing when writing a literary essay is to expand on a seemingly unimportant subject as a means to bring the reader to a larger topic. For example, in "The Creation Myths of Cooperstown" first published in *Natural History* (1989) and selected for *The Best American Essays of the Century*, the renowned anthropologist and essayist Stephen Jay Gould begins with the following account:

> "The Cardiff Giant, the best American entry for the title of paleontological hoax turned into cultural history, now lies on display in a shed behind a barn at the Farmer's Museum in Cooperstown, New York. This gypsum man, more than ten feet tall, was 'discovered' by workmen digging a well on a farm near Cardiff, New York, in October 1869. Eagerly embraced by a gullible public, and ardently displayed by its creators at fifty cents a pop, the Cardiff Giant caused quite a brouhaha around Syracuse, and then nationally, for the few months of its active life between exhumation and exposure."

Gould went on to consider what he calls "origin myths" and how it applies to the evolution of baseball. He is able to move from the Cardiff Giant to baseball because of what they share in common—the colossal was "discovered" in Cooperstown, New York, the location of the baseball hall of fame.

Finely Crafted Writing

In an essay titled "New York City: Crash Course," which first appeared in *Granta* and was included in *The Best American Essays 1991*, Elizabeth Hardwick informs the reader about some historical notes of interest concerning New York City—just as the title implies. She touches upon subjects as diverse as slavery, tenements, the opera house, jogging, early explorers, immigrants, and stock traders. Yet, despite the abundance of facts, the reader is never bored because the data selected is fascinating and is presented in a method of writing that pays great attention to language and style. Nowhere is this more apparent than in the opening paragraph.

> "The old New York airport was once called Idlewild, a pastoral welcome to the gate of a zoological garden of free-ranging species. Or so it seemed

to say before the names were changed to those of politicians, those who won. Kennedy Airport, international arrival to our hysterical, battered and battering, potholed, bankrupt metropolis. A spectacular warehouse this city is: folk from anywhere, especially from those sunny sovereignties to the south of us, coming to peer out of blackened windows, each one in his shelter of sorts."

Write about Setting

Writing a literary essay is an excellent medium to elucidate upon a specific location whether it be a nature preserve, a village, a museum, a bridge, a park, or as in the essay "City Out of Breath" (first published in *Manoa* and later included in *The Best American Essays 2006*) by Ken Chen, a literary explication of Hong Kong.

Consider how Chen relies on details and language to provide a sense of the uniqueness of the city of Hong Kong.

"Somehow you are supposed to teach yourself how to comprehend Hong Kong's energy and flashy contradictions: Asian and Western; the encroaching Chinese mainland and the remnants of England; the greasy night markets of sticky-rice tamales and knock-off leather boots that slouch right across from Tiffany, Chanel, and Prada. The only things common to these are the offices sending air-conditioned blasts into the street, a kind of longing for money, and, most important, the sense of storytelling that the city seems to require as a visitor's pass."

Writing Exercises

All the skills you learned writing nonfiction apply to composing literary essays with the added emphasis on sense of language and style. The following exercises are designed to help you perfect this technique.

EXERCISE 1

Select a subject with which you have a significant amount of knowledge so that without any research you can write two paragraphs on it. You can write about a person of interest, a sport, an armed conflict, an historical event—whatever you choose.

Write two paragraphs introducing the reader to the subject and provide some information. Do this in the form of an article consistent with what you learned in Chapter 13. Now, present the same information but as you would in a literary essay, paying special attention to word choice and tone. Compare the two pieces. While there should be a distinction in sense of language and style, in both instances the information should have been conveyed effectively to the reader. To see if this is the case, ask one or two people to read it for purposes of clarity. If they say the literary essay was more impressive but not as comprehensible, then you need to work on that issue.

EXERCISE 2

This exercise is designed to introduce you to the great adventure and challenge that awaits you should you choose to write literary essays.

Select a topic about which you have some knowledge and a desire to learn more. The subject you pick should not be too broad. For example, if you are a bit of a civil war buff and want to learn more about the conflict, do not choose as a subject Lincoln's generals but rather focus on one general and only for a precise time period.

Now, start your quest for fact gathering, relying on what you learned in Chapter 5, but you only need to do enough research to write ten pages or so (although literary essays can be longer, this is a good start).

When your research is complete, it's time to impart the information to the reader in a way that will pique her curiosity and maintain her interest while you write in the style of a literary essayist.

Congratulations, you have just written a literary essay.

CHAPTER 17

Personal Essays

The personal essay is the one nonfiction genre in which you are the most qualified person to write your essay. Yet, you need to know how to make your personal experience of interest to others if you want it to be more than a diary entry. Writing the personal essay is a stimulating experience because you can apply the skills of nonfiction writing and also employ some techniques of writing fiction. Composing a personal essay is like telling a story—but the story is yours.

What Is a Personal Essay?

In personal essays, the subject is you. Or more specifically, it is about one or more personal experiences or memories that you want to share with others through the medium of writing.

ESSENTIAL

> The "personal essay" is sometimes referred to as a "memoir" because the focus is about a personal experience or reminiscence. However, the term *memoir* typically applies to a book-length project, so it is best to classify your work as a "personal essay" when submitting it for publication.

Like the opinion essay and the literary essay, there is a considerable degree of flexibility in composing the personal essay. However, there are several basic attributes that define the personal essay that you should follow:

- The personal essay takes one or more personal experiences or recollections, ruminates upon them, and often suggests a message to which the readers can relate.
- If intended for an audience beyond friends and family, the personal essay must be of interest to the reader.
- Personal essays are written in the first person.
- Personal essays may employ techniques common to writing fiction.
- Length is flexible but the range is between 1,000 and 4,000 words.

It's All about You!

You have seen that when writing nonfiction, you need to establish yourself as an authority. You can attain expertise by formal education and letters after your name evincing degrees; by research and fact gathering as you have seen in Chapters 5, 7, and elsewhere; or by personal experiences, often augmented by the other means in which you establish your authority. But in writing the personal essay, you come to the topic with expertise in hand, because the subject matter is drawn from your own life.

Selecting the Subject

Determining the focal point of your personal essay is solely up to you. Generally, your topic will fall into one of two categories: either an event or reminiscence. If you choose an event, try to keep it to that one occurrence or at least maintain that as the focus of your piece. For example, perhaps you want to write about your experience attending the last game in a World Series. If so, you concentrate on that one game and you do not write about other baseball games you attended, unless they specifically relate to the subject of your essay.

ALERT

Just because the personal essay is about an experience or reminiscence in your life, do not think research, fact gathering, and interviews are no longer important. To give body and background to your piece as well as to confirm events that might have occurred decades earlier, you may need to do some investigation to support your essay.

Writing about memories can be more fluid. For example, you may want to write about a grandparent. In doing so, you might rely on a number of recollections you have of that person, in which case you need not limit yourself to one event. Just bear in mind that you are not writing the story of your life. Save that for an autobiography or book-length memoir, which we'll explore in Chapter 18.

Who Cares?

The first question you must ask yourself once you settle on a subject is: "Who cares?" If your answer is "I do! My family does and so do my friends," then you should feel free to write your essay and share it with those you mentioned. However, if you want to write for publication, you need to be a little more demanding of yourself and the subject and you must ask the following types of questions:

• Why would anyone care?
• Is there a specific target audience for my essay?

- Are there other people who can relate to what happened to me?
- Is there a universal message to my essay?
- Will my account stir feelings in the reader similar to mine?

If your answers indicate there should be an audience who might have interest in your experience, then you're ready to proceed. But before beginning to write, there is one more thing you need to decide.

Two Kinds of Personal Essays

There is no distinction between one personal essay and another so far as the basic characteristics are concerned. However, when it comes to writing for publication, where you intend to send your work does impact how you go about composing the prose. In this regard, there are two types of personal essays, which might be called the "popular" and the "literary."

The Literary Personal Essay

Personal essays that are destined for literary journals and periodicals generally range between 2,000 and 4,000 words but can be as long as 8,000 words. In terms of sense of language, style, and technique, this type of essay is very similar to the literary essay. What distinguishes the literary personal essay from literary essays is the subject matter.

Make no mistake: the literary personal essay is about your personal experience and memory. However, the manner in which you reach out to the reader and convey your insights or message is more subtle than might be the case in the popular personal essay. You should be able to discern this difference from the excerpts that appear later in this chapter.

The Popular Personal Essay

Because popular personal essays typically appear in newspapers, tabloids, and glossy magazines, their length rarely exceed 2,000 words. On average, the popular personal essay is 1,000 words.

Given the market for the popular personal essay, the writing style bears closer resemblance to articles and opinion essays than it does to literary essays. The writing should be straightforward and the language clear and concise but unlike articles, the tone should be personal. Once again, because it is a personal essay, the focus should be on your experience or reminiscence.

FACT

Some magazines feature a regular column open to freelancers where they can submit their personal essays. Many periodicals, especially those with a specific subject, also have recurrent features open to personal essays such as magazines about pets where freelancers can submit essays about their own pet.

Writing the Personal Essay

Writing the personal essay should be an exhilarating experience because you have a great deal of flexibility determining what writing techniques you choose to employ. However, you might want to keep your audience in mind and the publications where you wish to submit as you compose your essay, although you can always write the essay and decide after it is complete where to send it. You'll learn more about submitting your work in Chapter 22.

Be Creative

If you have ever taken a creative writing course and enjoyed it or have written fiction and took pleasure utilizing the techniques of the genre, you're in for a treat writing the personal essay. What applies to writing book-length memoirs (Chapter 18) and creative nonfiction (Chapter 19) can also be applicable in composing the personal essay.

QUESTION

Can I write a personal essay like any fiction?
While you are free to employ the techniques of creative writing to the personal essay, there is one important caveat: creativity may be applied to your writing style but not to the substance of your essay. As with all nonfiction, your material must be true.

Feel free to be descriptive of settings and characters. The people in your essays can be more than names and they should not be one-dimensional. Make use of dialogue and employ language to suggest metaphors and symbolism. In other words, be creative. You'll learn more about this in Chapter 19, where the genre of creative nonfiction is addressed.

Like Telling a Story

Writing a personal essay can be just like writing a short story. You might even have a plot running through the piece. So if you like storytelling, you'll enjoy writing personal essays. Of course, there is the stipulation that your "story" is true and not fantasy. This may sound easier than it is. Memory is not always accurate—not yours or even people you might interview. When and where to draw the line between what is and what may not be true will be discussed when considering the ethics of writing in Chapter 20.

Excerpts That Are Personal

Despite the common elements shared by all personal essays, each one is distinct in its own way. The following excerpts demonstrate both the general features of personal essays as well as the uniqueness of each.

A Popular Personal Essay

In Chapter 16, you saw an excerpt from a literary essay that also had features common to personal essays, but on the whole, since the thrust of the piece was to deliver information, it was categorized as a literary essay. The same condition holds for personal essays where elements of literary essays and opinion essays might be found.

It is not unusual for opinions and calls for action to be included in personal essays. In fact, offering insight is common to most essays. The best way to determine the classification of a particular essay is to evaluate and consider the essence and main features of the essay.

For instance, consider the following passage from "Batting for the Cure," which appeared in the My Turn column in *Newsweek*. The author, Michael Goldsmith, begins this way:

"I received my death sentence in September 2006 when doctors told me I had amyotrophic lateral sclerosis (ALS), a progressively paralyzing neuromuscular disorder. There is no cure. Commonly known as Lou Gehrig's disease after the Yankee Hall of Famer who died of it, ALS is so uncommon that medical researchers consider it an 'orphan' illness."

Notice the direct language and how Goldsmith gets to the point. See how the first sentence works to draw the reader into his essay. Goldsmith goes on to be informative by explaining the disease and lack of research money, which lends itself to a literary essay. Later, he opines that perhaps July 4, 2009 (the seventieth anniversary of Gehrig's farewell speech), should be ALS-Lou Gehrig Day, which suggests the style of a commentary.

But the essence of the essay is the author's individual experience, which makes "Batting for the Cure" a personal essay. You can see this in the following passage about attending the Baltimore Orioles baseball fantasy camp after his diagnosis:

"We hung out with former Orioles, most of who were blue-collar guys thrilled to have made it to the majors. . . . Everyone played, talked, and laughed baseball. Orioles manager Dave Trembley told us how he tried to get thrown out of a game without using cuss words: it wasn't easy, and he succeeded only after calling the umpire a 'den mother.'"

A Literary Personal Essay

It's not likely that you will find an essay more eloquently written and evincing a greater sense of language than E. B. White's "Once More to the Lake" that first appeared in *Harper's Magazine* in 1941 and was subsequently included in *The Best Essays of the Century*. But without a doubt, this is as personal as an essay is ever likely to be about a grown man returning to camp on the lake with his son and recalling how he had spent similar times at the same location when he was a boy with his own father.

"I could tell that it was going to be pretty much the same as it had been before—I knew it, lying in bed the first morning, smelling the bedroom and hearing the boy sneak quietly out and go off along the shore in a boat. I began to sustain the illusion that he was I, and therefore, by simple transposition, that I was my father. . . . I seemed to be living a dual existence. I would be in the middle of some simple act, I would be picking up a bait box or laying down a table fork, or I would be saying something, and suddenly it would be not I but my father who was saying the words or making the gesture. It gave me a creepy sensation."

White's essay is also literary given its length, use of literary techniques, and the subtle way he delivers his message and rumination over mortality. Examine how the essay concludes:

"When the others went swimming, my son said he was going in, too. He pulled his dripping trunks from the line where they had hung all through the shower and wrung them out. Languidly, and with no thought of going in, I watched him, his hard little body, skinny and bare, saw him wince slightly as he pulled up around his vitals the small, soggy, icy garment. As he buckled the swollen belt, suddenly my groin felt the chill of death."

Childhood Memories

Many personal essays are reminiscences over one's youth. However, there are various ways to go about this that exhibit different writing styles. In "They All Just Went Away," which was first published in the *New Yorker* in 1995, and subsequently included in *The Best Essays of the Century*, Joyce Carol Oates, in a more direct writing style than E. B. White, sets the scene for her essay using abandoned houses as a metaphor for broken families and damaged women and one empty house in particular she observed when growing up. This is how she begins her essay:

"I must have been a lonely child. Until the age of twelve or thirteen, my most intense, happiest hours were spent tramping desolate fields, woods, and creeks banks near my family's farmhouse in Millersport, New York. No one knew where I went. My father, working most of the day at Harrison's, a division of General Motors in Lockport, and at other times preoccupied, would not have asked; if my mother asked, I might have answered in a way that would deflect curiosity. I was an articulate, verbal child. Yet I could not have explained what drew me to the abandoned houses, barns, silos, corncribs. A hike of miles through fields of spiky grass, across outcroppings of shale as steeply angled as stairs, was a lark if the reward was an empty house."

Anything Goes

One of the stimulating aspects of writing personal essays is that you can employ so many varied and challenging writing techniques in a composition about yourself, your memories, and your thoughts. An example of this is the essay "Wounded Chevy at Wounded Knee," first published in *Missouri Review* and included in *The Best American Essays 1991*, in which Diana Hume George begins as follows:

"*Pine Ridge Sioux Reservation, July, 1989.* 'If you break down on that reservation, your car belongs to the Indians. They don't like white people out there.' This was our amiable motel proprietor in Custer, South Dakota, who asked where we were headed and then propped a conspiratorial white elbow on the counter and said we better make sure our vehicle was in good shape."

George employs dialogue and a character to set the scene and lay the foundation for the essay, which is about race relations and the subjugation of Native Americans. Later, she establishes her own authority on the subject:

"I grew up in the 1950s and 1960s in a small white community on the edge of the Cattaraugus Seneca Indian Reservation in western New York State. Relations between Indians and whites in my world were bitter."

Near the end of the essay, in which she describes her personal visit to the Wounded Knee Reservation, she offers an assessment on the sad state of affairs of Native Americans and she lays the blame on both parties:

"Over a century ago, American whites began this destruction [of the Native American society] by displacing and killing the *pte*, [buffalo]. . . .

The history of our genocide is available in many historical and imaginative sources. What is still elusive . . . is how and why the Indians seem to have participated in their own destruction by their failure to adapt to changed circumstances."

Writing Exercises

Because personal essays are more than diaries and journal entries, you need to remember that although the experience or memory is important to you, it must be of interest to people who do not know you. Therefore, selecting your topic and composing it in a writing style that will appeal to readers is the challenge of writing personal essays. These exercises are designed with this in mind.

EXERCISE 1

In several pages, write about a personal experience that is memorable to you. Do it in one draft and don't worry about the style—just get it down. It's the substance that matters. Read it over and ask yourself why this would be of interest to a perfect stranger. If you can't come up with a good answer, then you know you don't have the basis for a personal essay. On the other hand, if you think it does have appeal to a wide audience, ask a few people who are barely acquaintances to read it and see if it means anything to them. If they answer in the affirmative, press them to find out why to make sure they're not just being polite.

EXERCISE 2

Unlike Exercise 1, give the matter a good deal of thought and select a personal experience or reminiscence that you believe will be of interest to others. In ten pages or so, write the essay and feel free to suggest any insights or opinions you have while not transforming the essay into a commentary. Make liberal use of all the techniques discussed in this chapter. When you're done and before rewriting and editing, decide if the piece is best described as a popular or literary personal essay so you know where to submit it once it's polished and complete.

CHAPTER 18

Memoirs—Book Length

Many writers find it rewarding to recount their lives and share their memories through prose, and readers find the long-standing genre of memoirs equally compelling. If writing for publication, you must make your story interesting and you need to know how to prepare your material before writing. Like the personal essay, memoir writing can be an elating experience because in many respects it's like writing a novel, except the story is true. But in order to succeed, you must master the skills of memoir writing.

A Venerable and Popular Genre

People have been sharing their life stories since the beginning of time. At first, it was in the oral tradition when the patriarchs of the clan passed on their experiences, memories, and whatever wisdom they had to offer. But later, at least as far back as the fourth century, people began to commit their experiences to writing.

FACT

The word *memoir* is derived from the French word *memoire*, which means "memory." The earliest memoirs relied upon the religious and psychological experiences of the authors but subsequent memoirs evolved to include all aspects of the writer's life that could be considered important, whether pleasant or painful to recall.

What distinguishes the memoir from the personal essay is that the former is a book-length project. Sometimes, however, as you have seen in Chapter 17, the terms are used interchangeably. Because the memoir is hundreds of pages, it encompasses a larger segment of the writer's life. At times, a memoir focuses on a particular time period, such as the author's childhood. In other instances, a memoir encompasses a series of events that are connected, such as an on-again, off-again relationship with a particular individual.

Like the personal essay, the memoir is more than a recitation of facts. It also includes ruminations and insights. Consequently, memoirs need to go beyond what a journalist would report. You must deliberate over the events, sharing your reflections and thoughts.

Memoir or Autobiography

An autobiography is a book-length work about the life of a particular person written by the subject. Typically, an autobiography is about the entire life of the author and a memoir concentrates upon one aspect of the subject's life. However, in recent years memoirs have become such a popular genre that for marketing purposes, autobiographies as well as traditional memoirs are generally advertised as memoirs.

A Popular Genre

Memoirs is a bestselling genre because on the one hand, the public has displayed a voracious appetite to learn about the personal side of public figures and celebrities and on the other hand, there is a long line of would-be authors who want to share all or part of their life stories with the public. The proof lies in the numbers: there are more than 27,000 memoirs in print.

ALERT

A number of memoirs are not written by the author but by another individual called a "ghostwriter." Sometimes, the author may have an active role in the actual writing and at other times the subject does no more than provide material, information, and verbal accounts.

Another reason for the proliferation of the memoir is that authors are not limited to write merely about their own lives. Frequently, the focal point for the book is based on the relationships of the family members. Indeed, there are normally 2,000 family memoirs in print.

So if you have a desire to share your story in book-length form—something more than a personal essay—there is definitely a large market awaiting your memoir. But first, there are some things you need to do before writing if it's publication you seek.

Is There a Memoir in You?

Many of the questions you had to consider in Chapter 17 when deciding whether or not to write a personal essay are even more applicable when contemplating whether to write a memoir. It's one thing to ask someone to read several pages in a journal, tabloid, or magazine in which your personal essay has been published but quite another to ask a person to spend twenty or thirty dollars to buy your book and take the time to read it. Therefore, you must give sober and objective consideration to the question, "Who will be interested enough to read my memoir?"

Naturally, if you have attained a degree of prominence and have significant name recognition, you will likely have an audience eager to purchase your memoir and you'll learn in Chapter 23 how important this can be. But do not despair if you are not a celebrity, because there still may be a memoir in you.

For one thing, you may have a compelling story to share that can inspire others. Or perhaps you can offer an inside look into an event that you were involved in that captured the national spotlight. Another possibility might be that you have a relationship with someone who is well known and you can write about that.

ESSENTIAL

"Unless you write yourself, you can't know how wonderful it is; I always used to bemoan the fact that I couldn't draw, but now I'm overjoyed that at least I can write. And if I don't have the talent to write books or newspaper articles, I can always write for myself."—Anne Frank, *The Diary of a Young Girl*

Benefits to You

Aside from the actual writing process, which can be rewarding and stimulating, there are other factors that make memoir writing a unique experience. It affords you an opportunity of recollecting your past—sometimes the recent past and sometimes a past spanning decades. You'll have the opportunity to recall people and events and the way you felt about them no matter how pleasurable or painful that might be. Memoir writing can offer a healing experience and you might re-establish relationships that had drifted apart. And of even greater significance, looking back can afford an opportunity to gain insight and wisdom, enabling you to proceed in the future in a new direction.

Preparing to Write Your Memoir

Because of the nature and style of memoir writing, which can be similar to fiction, you might be tempted to deviate from adhering to the facts or think that you can rely solely on your memory. However, remember that you are still writing nonfiction, so you still have an obligation to abide by the truth.

This will be explored more thoroughly in Chapter 20 where the ethics of writing nonfiction will be reviewed.

Since you need to be scrupulous in the accuracy of your material, you need to do more than ponder your past or dwell on reminiscences. Fortunately, there are a number of methods and resources you can utilize in your preparations for writing your memoir:

- Contact and interview persons familiar with the events, places, people, and time periods of your memoir.
- Employ the resources and methods you learned in Chapter 5 regarding fact gathering and research.
- Conduct a scavenger hunt through keepsakes, correspondence, records, photographs, diaries, and so forth.
- Use the Internet or library to confirm pertinent data such as events that occurred in a particular time period.
- Visit the physical locations and settings where the events took place.

Edit Your Life

Unless you're planning on writing the story of your life from birth to present, you're going to have to edit more than the words you put down—you're going to have to edit your life. Daunting as this may sound, it's quite simple.

As you recall time periods and events, ask yourself if this is anything the reader will care about and if so, is it an essential element to the theme. Even though it may be obvious that a particular situation doesn't belong in your memoir, it is sometimes very difficult to omit it. For example, your significant other may be the most important person in your life, but if your memoir is about your childhood and your significant other doesn't appear until a decade later, then that person has no business being in your memoir. To alleviate the difficulty that comes with making such necessary deletions, just keep in mind you can always write another memoir covering a time of your life in which this person or event does play a prominent role.

Afraid of Offending?

One of the most difficult aspects in memoir writing is how to portray the people who have played a real life role in the events. First and foremost, you must be truthful, but that may have the consequence of making you concerned about hurting feelings.

Portraying the people in a memoir accurately and truthfully to the best of your ability satisfies the ethical obligations of a memoir writer. However, you'll need more than good intentions and best efforts to defend a libel suit, where truth is an absolute defense only if it can be proven.

If you're still concerned about hurting the feelings of some of the people depicted in your memoir even though they are portrayed correctly, you can disguise them by changing their names, their physical appearances, where they live, and the jobs they have. Chances are they still may be recognizable to themselves and perhaps to others who know them, but it will assuage any sense of embarrassment they might feel vis-à-vis the general public. Still, there is no guarantee that sensibilities will not be offended and this is something you must be prepared to accept if you choose to write a memoir.

Diary or Memoir

In every other nonfiction genre, you're writing to an audience—or at least so you hope. But when you sit down to write about your life, you have to decide whether it is primarily for you that you're writing or whether you want to reach out to others. If it's the former, you are making entries into a diary or as some might say, "journaling." If it's the latter, you're writing a memoir. This is the final issue you must resolve before you begin writing.

Whether a work is a memoir or diary is not determined by the format but rather by conforming to the guidelines of writing nonfiction, in which case it's more likely a memoir. Another difference is that memoirs are written keeping the reader in mind by eliminating facts and events that would be of no interest to a stranger.

An example of this distinction is two prominent accounts of living under Hitler's specter and the shadow of the Holocaust. Perhaps because of its straightforward, impassive chronicle about life as an assimilated Jew married to a gentile woman, *I Will Bear Witness, A Diary of the Nazi Years* by historian Victor Klemperer is extremely effective in portraying the day-by-day deterioration of life under the Nazis. But so far as the writing goes, it is a diary:

> "New Year's Eve '39, Sunday evening. This Christmas and New Year's Eve we are decidedly worse off than last year, we are threatened with the confiscation of the house—despite that I feel better than I did then. . . . I am now convinced that National Socialism will collapse in the coming year. Perhaps we shall perish with it—but it will certainly end, and with it, one way or another, the terror."

Probably the most famous "diary" to emerge from that era is *The Diary of a Young Girl* by Anne Frank. Originally, Anne set out to compose a diary written strictly for herself, but at some point she decided that after the war she would publish a book based on her diary. Consequently, she rewrote and edited what she had previously written, keeping the reader in mind by deleting what was not of interest to others and making the text more readable. She continued in this style, writing her entries to her imagined reader, *Kitty.* Consider how personal and universal the following passage is and how easygoing the tone.

> *Tuesday, March 7, 1944*
> *Dearest Kitty,*
> "Oh, I haven't forgotten how to laugh or toss off a remark . . . and I can still flirt and be amusing, if I want to be. . . .
>
> "But there's the catch. I'd like to live that seemingly carefree and happy life for an evening, a few days, a week. At the end of that week I'd be exhausted, and would be grateful to the first person to talk to me about something meaningful. I want friends, not admirers. . . . The circle around me would be much smaller, but what does that matter, as long as they're sincere?"

Writing the Memoir

The fun in writing a memoir comes with the actual writing. In no other nonfiction genre do you come closer to storytelling than you do when you write a memoir. You have the opportunity to utilize all the techniques of creative writing. In essence, you will be composing your craft under the umbrella of what has become known as "creative nonfiction," which will be explored in Chapter 19.

ESSENTIAL

One of the indispensable features of creative writing that applies to memoirs is to follow the mantra "show, don't tell." A direct exposition of facts and details belongs to other nonfiction genres. Description, setting, bringing the characters to life, and even dialogue are the ingredients to a successful memoir.

The Elements of a Memoir

Because you are writing a memoir and not simply making entries into your diary, you need to recount your story with clarity and skill so that it can be read and appreciated by others. In order to do this, it is helpful to be aware of three key elements: summary, exposition, and drama.

Introducing the reader to your memoir requires providing some background information. Unlike a diary, it is not simply a matter of indicating the date and place; rather, you need to do this in narrative form in the first section. Following the summary, you'll go into the exposition, which is the story development that allows the reader to learn everything necessary to understand what is transpiring. From there, proceed to the main "meat" of the story, which equates to the plot in fiction. Finally, like every good story, make sure the narrative dramatically builds toward, and reaches, a climax.

Excerpts from Diverse Memoirs

Memoirs are as varied as the lives of the people on the planet. Although sharing some basic elements that have been discussed in this chapter, memoirs are written in different styles. Sometimes memoirs are written by famous people with little to offer the reader other than providing a window into their lives. But the better memoirs that may or may not be written by someone well known normally have something important to convey, as the following excerpts suggest. As you consider these passages try to discern the distinctive writing techniques.

Novel or Memoir?

In every respect, Elie Wiesel's *Night* reads like a novel written in the first person. Yet, because it is a true account, it is a memoir.

"We looked at the flames in the darkness. There was an abominable odor floating in the air. Suddenly, our doors opened. Some odd-looking characters, dressed in striped shirts and black trousers leapt into the wagon. . . .

"'Everybody get out! Everyone out of the wagon! Quickly!'

"We jumped out. I threw a last glance toward Madam Schächter. Her little boy was holding her hand.

"In front of us flames. In the air that smell of burning flesh. It must have been about midnight. We had arrived—at Birkenau, reception center for Auschwitz."

A Healing Message

Memoirs sometimes serve the function of providing an example with which the reader can identify and thus no longer feel isolated. Indeed, it can even offer a source of hope and inspiration or suggest a healing process. Examples abound with memoirs recounting stories of physical, mental or sexual abuse; addictions to alcohol or drugs; battling diseases and infirmities, or as in the following excerpt, mental illness. These memoirs may be written by someone well known or someone unknown whose account is particularly poignant. In the following passage from *Darkness Visible*, the novelist William Styron writes of his struggle with depression.

"For years I kept a notebook . . . whose contents I would not have particularly liked to be scrutinized by eyes other than my own. I had hidden it well out of sight. . . . The small volume was one that I fully intended to make use of professionally and then destroy before the distant day when the specter of the nursing home came too near. So as my illness worsened I rather queasily realized that if I once decided to get rid of the notebook that moment would necessarily coincide with my decision to put an end to myself. And one evening during early December this moment came."

Need Not Be Famous

While being a celebrity or otherwise renowned will certainly help having your memoir published, it is not the only avenue to getting your book into the bookstores. You may have life experiences that will provide your memoir the material it needs to attract an audience. For example, have you ever heard the name "Victor Rabinowitz?" Chances are that you do not know this attorney, but you probably have heard of some of his clients: Alger Hiss, Jimmy Hoffa, Benjamin Spock, and Fidel Castro. Consequently, his career spanning fifty years working on behalf of civil rights activists, trade unions, and war resisters makes for captivating reading. Yet, his book, *Unrepentant Leftist: A Lawyer's Memoir*, is not written in legalese but reads like a memoir, as the following excerpt illustrates.

"I remember Grandpa, too. He seemed very old. He was in fact seventy-four years old, and I was only five or six. Every grownup, especially a man with a beard, seemed truly ancient. Like many Jewish male immigrants, especially the Orthodox ones, Grandpa had a full white beard. . . . Grandpa, my mother's father, was very kind. He took me on his lap and he smelled of sweet tobacco. We didn't communicate much—in fact, we didn't communicate at all, since I spoke no Yiddish and, so far as I knew, he spoke no English. However, he did give me JuJubes, a popular sweet of the day."

Writing Exercises

Writing a memoir is like writing a personal essay except that it is much longer. Consequently, you need to master the same skills and writing techniques that you learned in Chapter 17. But if it is a book-length memoir you are considering, you might want to try the following exercises to get you started.

EXERCISE 1

With what you have learned in this chapter, focus on a segment of your life that you find compelling; that you want to write about; and that will also interest others. Draft an outline of the people, places, events, and what occurred. You can also make notes on any thoughts or insights you want to share with the reader. Finally, check all the facts to make sure what you present is accurate.

EXERCISE 2

After a few days or more, critically examine your outline and decide if it fits the criteria of a memoir. If so, proceed to write in a range between twenty-five and fifty pages. Following that, rewrite and edit and so on. . . . You know the drill by now.

CHAPTER 19

Creative Nonfiction

People have been writing nonfiction creatively for thousands of years, but only since the 1960s has creative nonfiction been considered a genre unto itself. While you can apply some of the skills of creative writing to your works of nonfiction, if you want to write exclusively in this genre, you must know its distinct features; what distinguishes it from other genres; the requirements and ethics of writing in the genre; and of most importance, how to apply the techniques of fiction writing to nonfiction.

What Is Creative Nonfiction?

It has been previously suggested that as soon as you put words on a blank computer screen, you have created something. Yet, to truly satisfy the desire to be creative, you will need to do more than that, which is why some non-fiction writers have availed themselves of various techniques used by fiction writers. This creative impulse in writers of nonfiction ultimately led to the rise of a new genre—creative nonfiction.

ESSENTIAL

"The arts are not a way to make a living. They are a very human way of making life more bearable. Practicing an art, no matter how well or badly, is a way to make your soul grow. . . . Do it as well as you possibly can. You will get an enormous reward. You will have created something."—Kurt Vonnegut, *A Man Without a Country*

Creative Nonfiction Defined

You know by now that the keystone of nonfiction is that the content of your work must be true and accurate, with only a touch of literary license (this will be discussed in more detail in Chapter 20, along with other ethical issues). The second defining factor for creative nonfiction has to do with the "creative" aspect, which focuses on the style and the writing itself rather than the substance.

Thus, a good working definition for creative nonfiction is this: creative nonfiction is writing nonfiction (true and accurate content) employing the creative techniques of fiction writing including the use of literary devices. Later in this chapter when you reach the point of how to write creative nonfiction, you'll see what techniques you should consider and how to apply them.

Not a New Genre

Although the term *creative nonfiction* is fairly new, the genre has been around a long time. Indeed, depending on your perspective, the genre is as old as the Bible. If you examine the Bible as literature apart from any divine attributes and accept that the content is basically accurate, then you have an example of creative nonfiction—factual material in story form exhibiting techniques of fiction writing such as suspenseful and intriguing plots, action, complex human characters, descriptive settings, and powerful dialogue.

Although many fine examples of creative nonfiction have appeared over the years, it was not until the publication of *In Cold Blood* (1965) by Truman Capote and *The Armies of the Night* (1968) by Norman Mailer that the genre of creative nonfiction came into its own.

FACT

In conducting his interviews for *In Cold Blood*, arguably the first modern work of creative nonfiction, Truman Capote never took notes nor recorded the conversations. Nonetheless, he claimed the contents of his book to be completely accurate because of his ability to recall verbatim whatever was said to him.

In Cold Blood and *The Armies of the Night* could not be more different in their subject matter. The former reconstructs the murder of four members of a family and the investigation leading to the capture of their killers, whom Capote interviewed and came to know well. The latter focuses on a single event when thousands, including the author, marched on the Pentagon to protest the war in Vietnam. What the books do share, and what makes them models for creative nonfiction, is that they read like riveting novels with all the ingredients that keeps the reader turning the pages. Given the critical acclaim both books received as well as their impressive sales, a popular new genre was spawned that has come to be known as creative nonfiction.

A Genre or Style

You have seen throughout this book as you examined each of the nonfiction genres that it is not unusual to make use of some of the techniques used in writing fiction. This is more applicable to some nonfiction genres than others and is especially true of personal essays and memoirs. Consequently, one might argue that writing nonfiction creatively is more of a style of writing than a genre unto itself, and to some extent this is correct. However in recent years, agents, editors, and publishers have begun to seek manuscripts that are called creative nonfiction. Moreover, a growing segment of the public looks for this category when seeking books that are factual in content but read like a novel. Consequently, acceptance has grown that a genre called creative nonfiction exists.

ALERT

Creative nonfiction is also known as "narrative nonfiction" and "literary journalism." Indeed, because of some ethical lapses leading to the discovery that several bestselling books of creative nonfiction were not factual, avoiding the word "creative" has become a useful way to reaffirm the accuracy of the contents, and thus the genre has been increasingly referred to as "narrative nonfiction."

The Genre

Merely applying creative techniques customarily used in fiction to the nonfiction genre in which you are working is a matter of style and does not place your project in the separate category of creative nonfiction. But when you embark on a nonfiction book project and you set out to convey a true account in narrative form using all the literary and fictional devices at your disposal, then it's likely you're working in the genre of creative nonfiction.

However, do not work yourself into a frenzy over whether you're writing in the genre or not. Although it is important to identify your project's genre and target market as you have seen and will learn more about in Chapter 22, the creative nonfiction genre is an exception, because it is relatively new and still fluid. What does matter is that if you set out to write creative nonfiction, you know how to do it well.

How to Write Creative Nonfiction

Writing creative nonfiction is where the fun begins, because you get to apply the techniques of fiction writing to your narrative. Keep in mind that while your "story" is true, you're still writing a story and you'll want to draw in the readers and keep them turning the pages by dramatizing the subject. You'll be writing like any other novelist except you won't be mining your imagination for material—instead, you'll be relying on facts and memory for content.

While your subject matter is factual, you will have a plot running through your work and though your characters are real, you need to present them in a way that will make the readers care about them.

FACT

Feel free to make ample use of dialogue and description when writing creative nonfiction. Like fiction writers who employ these devices to portray their imagined characters and their invented world, you can utilize these techniques to enliven your factual account by presenting stimulating conversations and vivid settings.

Plot and Characters

Like fiction, most works of creative nonfiction contain a plot but with an important difference; in creative nonfiction, the account must be true. In order for a plot to exist in your narrative, you need to make certain that something happens and tension is created. During the course of your story, you must also ensure there exists a recognizable beginning, middle, and end accompanied by a resolution. Your narrative also must contain rising action, a climax, and falling action.

Since the people populating your pages are real, it is easier to avoid writing one-dimensional characters. However, because they are real, you may find yourself wanting to disguise them for purposes of privacy or other considerations. Nonetheless, you still need to be certain that your characters are fleshed out, three-dimensional, and complex—in other words, that they are human. To help you accomplish this, you can describe their physical attributes, mannerisms, behavior, personality, and employ dialogue manifesting how they speak. Like all characters, it's not necessary for the reader to like them but the reader must care about them.

Literary Techniques

There are many devices used in writing fiction that you can consider:

- *Personify:* Treat inanimate objects as though they were alive.
- *Dramatize:* Surround your subject with action, and create tension.

- *Literary devices:* Make use of foreshadowing, symbolism, similes, and metaphors.
- *Senses:* Involve all the senses—sight, sound, smell, taste, and touch.
- *Dialogue:* Place the reader in the scene by allowing the characters to speak.
- *Pacing:* Use short, punchy sentences and paragraphs when you want the action to be fast-paced; use longer sentences and paragraphs for exposition.

Almost all of the techniques relied upon by writers of fiction that you might employ will further the goal of showing and not telling. Because this is the mantra for writing fiction, you need to know how to accomplish this objective in writing creative nonfiction.

ALERT

Do not provide too much information at one time or you risk boring the reader. While this is true of fiction, it is equally important for writing creative nonfiction. Follow the dictum to "spoon-feed" the information and spread it over the pages. This applies to describing both characters and settings.

Show, Don't Tell

Show, don't tell is the keystone of fiction and it means exactly what it says—show the readers through your words; don't just tell them about it. You'll rely upon description, dialogue, and action to help achieve this aim. Showing rather than telling is not only more effective in getting the reader to remember and believe what she is reading; it also makes for a more enjoyable reading experience. And for the same reasons, showing and not telling applies to creative nonfiction.

How to show in lieu of telling is the stuff of writing workshops, classes, and writers' groups—things you'll be informed about in Chapter 24. You'll also be given an exercise at the end of this chapter to practice this very important skill. But for now, just remember while you are writing to keep that third eye on the lookout to see if what you are composing can be shown instead of being told. And when you rewrite and edit, keep this in mind as well.

ESSENTIAL

In nonfiction, *show, don't tell* is used less frequently than in fiction not only because of the difference in writing style but for a practical reason as well. It takes more words to show rather than tell and in nonfiction more attention has to be paid to word count, so showing must be used more sparingly.

Don't Disregard Telling

Some of the best fiction is filled with *telling* and this mode has been a hallmark of some of the greatest novelists. When this occurs it is because the writer's voice is so compelling that the reader is receptive to being addressed. In nonfiction, there is even greater occasion to make effective use of your voice, thus reinforcing the importance of the telling portion of your prose. Showing in place of telling is a technique you should employ when and where it is most effective to do so. If the *telling* portion of your narrative doesn't seem to be working, don't try to fix it by showing but rather work on your voice and apply other means to polish your prose.

There are also times when showing is inappropriate, such as when you are providing information to the reader. This is especially true of nonfiction, in which informing the reader is one of the primary purposes of the project.

The Best of Both Worlds

In fiction, the writer wants to entertain, and informing the reader is a by-product. In nonfiction, the chief goals are to inform and persuade with entertainment as a by-product. But in creative nonfiction, you need not favor one over the other; you can pursue informing and entertaining at the same time. This is what makes writing creative nonfiction so rewarding and exciting while also challenging. Consider how successfully this is accomplished in the excerpts that follow.

The Setting

The opening of Truman Capote's *In Cold Blood* places the reader in a setting as effectively as any novel could ever achieve. Through the use of details, description, and appealing to the senses, the first paragraph of the book exemplifies how successful showing can be while not disregarding the need to convey information by telling.

"The village of Holcomb stands on the high wheat plains of western Kansas, a lonesome area that other Kansans call 'out there.' Some seventy miles east of the Colorado border, the countryside, with its hard blue skies and desert-clear air, has an atmosphere that is rather more Far West than Middle West. The local accent is barbed with a prairie twang, a ranch-hand nasalness, and the men, many of them, wear narrow frontier trousers, Stetsons, and high-heeled boots with pointed toes. The land is flat, and the views are awesomely extensive; horses, herds of cattle, a white cluster of grain elevators rising as gracefully as Greek temples are visible long before a traveler reaches them."

Author as Protagonist

The Armies of the Night is subtitled *History as a Novel, the Novel as History.* Mailer recognized that he was onto a relatively new way to write a factual account and this is clear in the following passage. But what makes Mailer's book even more extraordinary is that while he was a participant at the war protest, which is the book's subject, he writes from the distance of an eyewitness. Writing in the third person, Mailer portrays himself as the story's protagonist and as a character the reader can care about—a necessary ingredient in fiction and creative nonfiction.

"On a day somewhat early in September, the year of the first March on the Pentagon, 1967, the phone rang one morning and Norman Mailer, operating on his own principle of war games and random play, picked it up. That was not characteristic of Mailer. Like most people whose nerves are sufficiently sensitive to keep them well-covered with flesh, he detested the phone. . . .

"Still, Mailer had a complex mind of sorts. Like a later generation which was to burn holes in their brain on Speed, he had given his own head the texture of a fine Swiss cheese . . . by consuming modestly pro-miscuous amounts of whiskey, marijuana, seconal, and benzedrine. It had given him the illusion he was a genius."

Not Only Humans

Fiction is either plot driven or character driven. To some degree, the same holds true for creative nonfiction except that the plot and characters are real. For example, *In Cold Blood* is filled with suspense as the execution of a multiple homicide is carried out in excruciating detail. Nor are you likely to find fictional characters more intriguing than Norman Mailer in *The Armies of the Night*. So you would think a book about a horse must be plot driven, because how many people would ever care enough about a horse that they would read a book about the animal. And yet, while there is an exciting storyline, the compelling feature of *Seabiscuit* by Laura Hillenbrand is indeed its central character—a racehorse.

FACT

In creative nonfiction you need not be concerned whether your book is plot or character driven as is the case for fiction, where this can determine the genre in which the book belongs. However, in creative nonfiction, there must be some tension and anticipation as well as fully formed characters the reader will care about.

Consider how the opening paragraph hooks the reader as effectively as any work of fiction could aspire. Also note how succinctly the setting and time period is presented and how the reader is primed to turn the pages.

"In 1938, near the end of a decade of monumental turmoil, the year's number-one newsmaker was not Franklin Delano Roosevelt, Hitler, or Mussolini. It wasn't Pope Pius XI, nor was it Lou Gehrig, Howard Hughes, or Clark Gable. The subject of the most newspaper column inches in 1938 wasn't even a person. It was an undersized, crooked-legged race-horse named Seabiscuit. . . .

"For the Seabiscuit crew and for America, it was the beginning of five uproarious years of anguish and exultation. . . .

"Along the way, the little horse and the men who rehabilitated him captured the American imagination. It wasn't just greatness that drew the people to them. It was their story.

"It began with a young man on a train, pushing west."

Writing Exercises

To write creative nonfiction, not only do you need to master the techniques of fiction writing, but you must know how to apply them effectively and sparingly as well. And even though you are writing like a novelist, your work must remain true and accurate. The following exercises are meant to help you become proficient in these skills.

EXERCISE 1

One way to become competent in a task is to practice the opposite of what you are trying achieve. With this in mind, go back to Capote's excerpt and rewrite it as straight nonfiction or how it might appear in a newspaper article.

EXERCISE 2

Removing your journalist's hat and putting on your creative hat, scour a newspaper for an article that piques your interest. It can be on the sports page or in the metro section, reciting the facts of a crime or a piece of international news. Rewrite the first several paragraphs or more as creative nonfiction being careful to retain the accuracy of the piece while applying some techniques of writing fiction.

EXERCISE 3

Time to practice *show, don't tell*. Write about an event or a person that was important in your life. Do this as you might for an article or standard nonfiction book. Make certain to provide detailed information. It should be at least one page but feel free to write more.

Once this is complete, rewrite the piece, showing and not telling about specific aspects of the person or event without losing sight of the need to be accurate. After rewriting, the person or event should become more real and visible in your mind's eye.

CHAPTER 20

The Ethics of
Writing Nonfiction

Most authors and writers of nonfiction acknowledge they are subject to ethical considerations when composing their work, but it is not always clear what these principles entail. Formal codes of ethics are few and exist mostly among journalists, so it is largely left to each individual writer to recognize when an ethical issue arises and how best to deal with it. Consequently, you need to be aware of the standards and expectations you may be held to with particular attention paid to plagiarism and the authenticity of memoir writing.

Codes of Ethics

Professional organizations frequently have a code of conduct to which their members are expected to comply. Different occupations seem to fall into one of three groups in this regard: associations with extensive and exacting standards such as those regulating lawyers, doctors, and accountants; those where the canons are vague and infrequently applied; and vocations where it's merely a matter of not breaking any laws or violating government regulations. Writers and authors, for the most part, are in the latter two groups.

QUESTION

When must I take ethics into account in my writing?
You may write anything you wish so long as you are the only one who reads it. Once other people read your work or it is published in a tangible form, including the Internet, you should be prepared to hold yourself accountable to others and any ethical issues that arise.

Official Canons

Journalists take their work very seriously and have established codes of conduct. If you find yourself engaging in journalism, you might want to consider joining one of the professional organizations and becoming aware of the standards to which you will be held. However, many journalists do not belong to a professional association, nor do all these groups have prescribed codes of conduct.

Although the code of ethics embraced by thousands of journalists and officially adopted by the Society of Professional Journalists applies to journalism, some of it is relevant to a writer of nonfiction:

- Be honest and fair in gathering and reporting information.
- The accuracy of the information should be tested and the motive of sources examined.
- Distinguish between advocacy, advertising, and news reporting.
- Never plagiarize.

- Treat sources and subjects as human beings deserving respect.
- Avoid conflicts of interest.
- Acknowledge mistakes and correct them without delay.
- Avoid stereotyping.
- Support the open exchange of viewpoints.
- Be sensitive to those who may be adversely affected by your reporting.

The vast majority of writers and authors do not belong to any professional association. With 8,000 members, the Author's Guild is the largest organization of authors and also includes literary agents. The American Society of Journalists and Authors has 1,100 members comprised of journalists, authors, and freelance magazine writers.

Your Own Code of Ethics

If you do join a professional association of writers, authors, or journalists and that group expects its members to abide by its rules and regulations then you have your ethical requirements in place. However, if you're like most writers and authors, it is going to be a matter of paying attention to your own conscience, maintaining a sense of right and wrong, and considering the advice and examples from fellow writers.

However, there will be occasions when you will find yourself provided with a set of principles that you will be expected to follow. For instance, when you sign a book contract, you will normally be required to make certain guarantees including: the content is factual (if nonfiction); nothing has been plagiarized; there are no copyright infringements; and your work is not libelous. In other instances not involving a book contract, similar assurances must be confirmed by you in writing, while at other times it is assumed to be the case.

Except for behavior that rises to the level of illegal conduct, most of the issues you face will not be a matter of black and white. Instead, you'll find yourself forced to navigate a difficult gray area.

Plagiarism

You saw in Chapter 5 that plagiarism is different from copyright infringement; the latter is reproducing the copyrighted work of another without permission. On the other hand, plagiarism is using or copying someone else's work and representing it as one's own. "Work" should be broadly interpreted to include both language and ideas.

ALERT

Substituting some words for others will not make the work one's own, because plagiarism goes beyond language and encompasses the thoughts, ideas, and even the writing style and sentence structure of the material. Although ideas that have not been put in tangible form are not subject to copyright protection, they can be plagiarized.

What Constitutes Plagiarism

There are a number of areas where plagiarism can occur. To avoid even inadvertently committing plagiarism, be aware that any one of the following circumstances may amount to plagiarism:

- Representing someone else's work as your own.
- Copying the work of another without providing credit to the author.
- The failure of inserting quotation marks when reproducing the work of another.
- The failure to cite sources when relying on one or more works that forms the majority of your own work.
- Incorrectly citing the source of the material.

There are a number of contexts where plagiarism is most likely to take place. Probably foremost is the academic world, which you would enter when writing scholarly books and articles for journals. You must take exceptional care in this area because scrutiny is rigorous and the standards are high.

Ethics for Writing Nonfiction

Writing nonfiction in and of itself demands a strong ethical commitment that what you are presenting to the reader is factual. Simply put, if you want to write nonfiction, you must hold yourself to the highest standard that will ensure the content of your work is true and accurate. Should this present a problem, abandon the project or transform it into a work of fiction.

Due Diligence

Due diligence is a term frequently employed by lawyers drafting contracts on behalf of clients interested in acquiring assets, property, or a business that signifies care will be taken to properly inspect and evaluate what is being purchased. To the party engaged in making the acquisition and to laypeople as well, due diligence implies that all reasonable steps are made to authenticate and substantiate that what is being represented is true.

The standard of due diligence applies to the writer of nonfiction. As the writer, you are assuring your material is true and accurate. As you have seen, you will base this representation on research, interviews, fact gathering, personal experience, your own knowledge, and memories. However, it is not enough that you can cite sources or interviewees or your memory to fulfill what is ethically required of you as a nonfiction writer. Rather, you must exercise due diligence to verify what you have relied upon in your work.

Some of the procedures you should consider when undertaking due diligence as a nonfiction writer are:

- Investigate the credentials of your sources to make certain they are qualified and are who they say they are.
- Obtain confirmation from unrelated sources to support what your primary sources provided.
- When depending on your memory or personal experiences, secure independent corroboration.
- If something does not seem correct, even though the source is trustworthy, satisfy whatever doubts you have about the veracity of the material.
- Whenever possible, go the extra distance to confirm from secondary sources what you learned from your primary sources.
- Try to avoid relying upon one eyewitness account or what one person remembers and secure confirmation from others.

How Factual Must You Be?

The degree of accuracy to which you will be held accountable depends upon the nonfiction genre in which you are writing. Clearly, if it's scholarly nonfiction, a biography, history, or medical and health advice, you had better try to be 100 percent correct. In most other kinds of nonfiction, your goal should also be to achieve complete accuracy, but there is room for error. The more difficult issue arises when you are writing an autobiography, memoirs, and creative nonfiction.

ALERT

When you knowingly stray from a complete factual account or suspect you might have done so, make a disclaimer or declaration indicating that what is presented is not entirely true or that the depiction of certain people has been changed. An appropriate place to present this statement might be in the acknowledgment page of a book.

There are two reasons there is a greater tolerance for some deviation from the truth in creative nonfiction. First, both the memory of the author and that of others are relied upon for much of the material—particularly with memoirs. Second, for the sake of the narrative and writing style, some embellishment may be appropriate. The question in such cases is how much less than total accuracy is acceptable?

Literary License

Just how much literary license or divergence from the truth can you take in the nonfiction genres where you need not be completely factual? While there is no hard and fast rule and it is largely a matter left to the author's good faith judgment, you probably would be wise to ask yourself whether the embellishments, alterations, or omissions will have a significant impact on the accuracy of the material and if so, how necessary are these changes.

For example, altering the names and descriptions of people to protect their privacy or to make them unrecognizable for libel purposes, which will be reviewed later in this chapter and in Chapter 21, is not an ethical lapse especially if it is disclosed. But suppose you were to convert a quiet unassuming and mild-mannered college professor who bungled a goodnight kiss on your first and only date into a sly and vicious predator who slipped you a date rape drug and brutally violated you? While this will likely make the narrative more riveting it is clearly a major departure from the facts and has no place in nonfiction.

How to Avoid Committing Libel

For the nonfiction writer, avoiding libel suits can be like stepping around a field filled with buried landmines; in order to prevent being blown up, you must know what you are facing and where to step. If you want to minimize your exposure to libel you need to understand what constitutes libel; the privileges that exempt you from committing libel; the added latitude you have toward public officials; and the defenses to a libel suit.

What Is Libel?

A good working definition for libel is this: a false statement that damages the reputation of a living person or entity that has been published or read by someone other than the subject of the defamation. A defamatory statement that is not written but spoken is considered slander. Because the declaration must be false, truth is an absolute defense to libel.

FACT

Although a deceased's reputation can be assailed, because the person defamed is dead there can be no harm or damages and therefore no libel action can be brought against the author of the defamatory statement. This restriction also applies to the estate of the deceased.

Two Types of Libel

There are two types of libel. *Libel per se* is a written statement that on its face contains all the elements necessary to constitute libel. For example, the following published statement is libel per se: "Franklin Thompson, the owner and operator of the auto repair shop at Third Avenue and Main Street is a crook who will charge you double to fix your car and leave it a worthless wreck." On its face, this defamatory statement is libelous subject to whether or not it can be proven true.

The other type of libel is *Libel per quod*, or libel by implication. It exists when the statement is libelous because of the false facts it implies. An example might be publishing a wedding announcement in the local paper that Franklin Thompson married Eleanor Smith when in fact not only did Franklin Thompson not marry Eleanor Smith but he was already married to someone else. On its face, there is nothing defamatory about the announcement but by implication, it made Franklin Thompson a bigamist.

Four Elements of Libel

In order for you to have committed libel, the plaintiff in the case against you will have to prove that four conditions have been met:

1. The statement is false.
2. The statement has a defamatory meaning.
3. The allegedly injured party is clearly identified in the statement.
4. The statement has been published.

If all four conditions are not met, an action for libel will not prevail. Therefore, you must be familiar with these four elements and what a plaintiff must do in order to prove they have been satisfied.

Proving Libel

Because the statement must be false, truth is an absolute defense to libel. However, unless the plaintiff is a celebrity or public official, the burden of proof generally lies with the author to establish the material is true. Since the statement must possess a defamatory meaning, the plaintiff must prove that what is written has caused or is likely to cause harm to his reputation.

The third element of libel requires that the plaintiff is identifiable. It is not necessary that the plaintiff be named for this condition to be met so long as the party would be identifiable by someone who knows or knows of the plaintiff. For instance, returning to the preceding examples, a statement in the local paper read by community residents that refers to the owner of the auto repair shop at Third Avenue and Main Street would identify Franklin Thompson for libel purposes without actually naming him.

The fourth and final element to establish libel is satisfied if the statement has been published and read by a third party. Publication occurs when the work is printed in the traditional manner such as books, magazines, and newspapers or if it appears over the Internet. It can also be satisfied by a letter to a third party, the distribution or posting of flyers, or e-mails.

It is not necessary to prove that a third party read the statement so long as it is reasonable to assume this is the case. For example, if the statement appears in a newspaper, the condition will have been fulfilled without the need to parade witnesses to testify they read the article in the paper.

Privileges That Protect from Libel

As a matter of public policy, libel law has carved out special categories of statements that are considered to be "privileges" and though defamatory, they are exempt from libel actions. These privileges are designed to protect people who make the statements pursuant to a legal or moral obligation.

There are two categories of privileges. The first group has little to do with writers and authors and exists to shield persons engaged in governmental proceedings, including the judicial, executive, and legislative branches. These exemptions fall under what is known as "absolute privileges."

The second class of privileges is called "conditional privileges" and frequently applies to writers, authors, and publishers. Unlike absolute privileges, conditional privileges require that the party making the statement acted in good faith. There are three types of privileges in this category: statements made to protect the public interest; accurate reports of public proceedings; and the right to reply, which is often raised by authors and publishers in response to statements made against them.

Defenses to Libel Actions

It's relatively easy to avoid committing libel; all you have to do is abide by the mantra of the nonfiction writer: make certain your material is accurate and true. Since the first and foremost element for a libel suit is that the statement is false, truth is an absolute defense.

ESSENTIAL

Since you may have to defend yourself in court against an accusation of libel, it is not enough that you know your statements are true; you need to be able to prove the accuracy of the statements in question. Therefore, be certain to have undertaken due diligence in all your research and fact finding and maintain records of your sources.

Some jurisdictions will absolve a defendant in a libel action if it can be shown that the statement was made in good faith but to be safe, it is best to do everything you can to ensure the accuracy of your content. You should not rely on the argument that all your facts are correct. If it can be shown that taken as a whole, the content of the statement gives a false impression, libel may be found to exist even if everything is technically factual.

Obtain Consent

A second defense against a libel accusation occurs when consent had been obtained from the plaintiff. The consent must be specific and apply to the precise words that comprise the defamatory statement.

Keep in mind that when raising the defense that consent was secured, the question of whether or not the statement is defamatory is no longer the issue. A person is free to consent to having a defamatory statement published.

ALERT

To obtain consent, you should secure a release from the party providing the permission. Because the release might become the central issue in a lawsuit, although it can be verbal, it is best that it be a written document prepared by an attorney competent in publishing law or provided by your publisher.

Opinions Are Protected

Expressing an opinion cannot be subject to an accusation of libel because it is not a statement of fact—whether true or false. Consequently, you can articulate the most insulting opinion imaginable about someone and not be sued for libel.

However, do not assume that merely by prefacing your statement with something like, "In my opinion," you can safeguard yourself from a libel suit. If your statement implies facts that are libelous, you could be held responsible for *libel per quod*, or libel by implication.

FACT

Name-calling by itself is insufficient to form the basis for an allegation of libel. Known by the legal term *rhetorical hyperbole*, these statements are similar to opinions and thus do not represent a statement of fact. However, any additional information going beyond the derogatory name can be grounds for a libel suit.

Clearly, writers of op-eds, commentaries, and opinion pieces generally can avail themselves of this defense if they are accused of libel. Writers of reviews are likewise shielded from libel suits to the extent their articles are the expression of an opinion. However, as you saw in Chapter 14, reviews are also written to inform the reader. Consequently, if the facts presented in the review are alleged to be defamatory statements, you would need to rely on one of the other defenses to libel such as truth or consent in order to avoid liability.

Freedom to Criticize Public Officials

The First Amendment provides for freedom of speech and of the press and helps form the foundation of our democratic society, which is predicated upon the free exchange of ideas whether spoken or written. Perhaps in no instance can this be more important than the ability to level criticism against the government and its elected and appointed officials. While concern for being sued for libel can inhibit the expression of statements critical of public officials, it was not until 1964 that the matter was finally resolved by the United States Supreme Court.

In *New York Times Co. v. Sullivan*, the United States Supreme Court held that under the First and Fourteenth Amendments, a state cannot award damages to a public official regarding a defamatory statement concerning his official conduct even if it is false and libelous unless it can be proven that the statement was made with "actual malice." The Court went on to require that unlike libel claims asserted by private individuals, public officials have the burden of proving the statement to be false and maliciously made.

QUESTION

What is "actual malice?"
As defined by the majority opinion written by Justice Brennan in *New York Times Co. v. Sullivan*, the term *actual malice* means that the statement was made with the knowledge it was false or with reckless disregard to whether it was true or not.

Public or Private Persons

Public officials are not difficult to identify since they are persons who are substantially involved in government. Some of the more obvious categories are:

- Candidates for an elective office
- People who hold a position in government
- Law enforcement officials
- Public school teachers and coaches
- Public employees who have policy-making authority

The more complicated matter concerns the identity of "public figures" upon whom the Supreme Court in subsequent cases extended the *New York Times Co. v. Sullivan* requirement that "actual malice" must be proven to sustain a libel action. The Supreme Court reasoned that when someone voluntarily places themselves in the public arena, they must be prepared to accept public criticism.

There are two types of public figures. The "all purpose public figure" is a person who is well known to the public, such as professional athletes and celebrities. The "limited purpose public figure" is someone who is not easily recognized but because he has thrust himself into the forefront of a specific public debate, he would be considered a public figure for purposes of that issue only.

A person does not automatically become a "limited purpose public figure" just because she finds herself in the middle of a public controversy and placed in the public eye. It is necessary that the person voluntarily put herself in that position and sought the attention.

Libel Insurance

In one sense, whether you should obtain insurance that will minimize what you may have to pay for a libel claim involves the same consideration you would give to any insurance coverage; it's a question of determining if the cost for the premium is worth the potential risk and liability you might face. However, unlike the standard insurance policies you may have to cover your health, life, home, and auto, it's not very likely you'll find yourself as a defendant in a libel suit—especially if you follow the guidance provided in this chapter and in Chapter 5 concerning your fact gathering.

To minimize your exposure and risk to a libel claim, you can ask your publisher to name you as an "additional insured" under its publisher's liability policy. This is standard practice in book contracts but it's not common if you freelance for newspapers, magazines, journals, and other media.

Once again, the best guidance to avoid libel is to be as certain as you can that your representations are accurate, because truth is not only an absolute defense to libel but the best defense as well.

CHAPTER 21

The Right of Privacy and Publicity

As a writer of nonfiction, you will frequently find yourself writing about real people who have expectations of privacy and a right of publicity. Should you improperly intrude upon either of these rights, you can be liable for monetary damages and be compelled to take remedial actions. Therefore, you need to be acquainted with these legal doctrines and know how to minimize your exposure to lawsuits claiming an infringement of these rights. Taking precautionary steps such as disguising your characters, obtaining releases, and securing insurance can be helpful.

The Right of Publicity

The right of publicity is an individual's entitlement to manage the use of her name, likeness, or identity for a commercial purpose. Like the right of privacy, the right of publicity is a property right and is governed by statutory law or common law.

Since there is no federal law regarding the right of publicity or privacy, there is no uniformity among the states and therefore, you should be familiar with the laws of the states in which your work is published or sold. However, as a practical matter since you probably will not know the laws of all fifty states, it is best to conduct yourself in accordance with the laws that are most protective of the rights of publicity and privacy. For example, even though some states permit only celebrities to assert the right to publicity, it would be prudent to assume the subject of your work has a right to publicity whether she is a celebrity or not.

ALERT

In most states, only a living person can bring suit for a violation of the right to publicity. However, in a minority of states, the right to publicity survives the decedent, so to be cautious it would be wise to always contact the estate of the deceased or the heirs to obtain consent when appropriate.

Commercial Use

A person can claim their right to publicity is violated only when it has been usurped for a commercial use. Commercial uses include advertisements, promotions, and the sale of products or services. Clearly books, magazines, journals, and newspapers that are available for purchase are commercial uses and as the writer, your work also meets this criterion and therefore you could be liable for violating someone's right to publicity.

The right to publicity cannot be raised for purposes other than a commercial use because it would violate the First Amendment's freedom of speech and freedom of the press provisions. Consequently, permission need not be obtained for what is considered an "editorial" use. Examples of editorial uses are: matters of public concern, news reporting, education, political issues, and cultural events.

The Right of Privacy

The right of privacy safeguards a person's personal and confidential information from being published without their permission. It is irrelevant whether the information is derogatory or embarrassing or whether it is true or false. Like the right to publicity, laws pertaining to the right of privacy are not uniform among the states, so unless you are certain of the laws of the states having jurisdiction over your work, it is best to comply with the laws that are the most protective of the right of privacy.

ESSENTIAL

There is no explicit right to privacy in the United States Constitution, although an implied right to privacy has been held to exist. However, this is designed to guard against intrusion by the government and is not relevant to an individual's right to privacy from publications, which relies on the laws of the states for protection.

Generally, the right to privacy applies to three distinctive areas: the publication of private and embarrassing facts; the publication of facts that produce a false and offensive impression or create a "false light"; and the intentional intrusion upon a person's privacy.

Private and Embarrassing Facts

A person's right to privacy can be violated by the publication of private information that could be an embarrassment because a reasonable person would deem it offensive. The fact that the information is true is not a defense, but there are two defenses that can be raised.

First, if the information is of public concern or otherwise newsworthy it may be published. Obviously, public records may be published as well as accounts of public hearings, legislative proceedings, trials, criminal activities including arrest records, and calamities such as fires and floods. Information that is not free to be published and is considered private includes:

- Medical records
- Private letters and e-mails
- Financial information
- Sexual orientation and behavior
- Diaries and journals

If the information has a connection to the official or public function of a public person, it can be published no matter how odious. Therefore, you should determine if your subject is a public official, public figure, or a private individual.

The second defense to a claim that the right to privacy was violated is if it can be shown the information is not offensive nor will it cause any embarrassment to the party identified. The standard determining what might or might not be an embarrassment is based upon what might be distasteful to a reasonable person.

False Light

A person can take legal action claiming an invasion of privacy if the publication creates a false impression that a reasonable person would find highly offensive; this is frequently referred to as a "false light invasion of privacy." In order to prove a false light claim, three conditions must be satisfied: the impression must be highly offensive to a reasonable person; the defendant was at fault in some way; the aggrieved party is alive and identifiable.

ESSENTIAL

In some ways, false light invasion of privacy is very similar to defamation. A number of states do not recognize a distinction and require that a libel suit be brought instead of a false light case. While libel is meant to provide redress for damages to one's reputation; false light suits are designed to compensate for embarrassment.

Keep in mind the aggrieved party need not prove the information is patently repugnant but only that it gives a distasteful perception. There are four sets of circumstances that can give rise to a false light allegation:

- True events are fictionalized.
- Facts are distorted or omitted creating a false negative impression.
- Facts are embellished or mixed with fiction.
- Photographs are published with unrelated contents.

Intrusion Upon Privacy

Unlike libel, false light, and the publication of embarrassing facts, intrusion upon one's privacy does not require publication to establish a claim that a person's privacy has been violated. The justification for this distinction is that the law recognizes a person has a right to solitude and to not have it intruded upon in an objectionable fashion.

Generally, claims that one's privacy has been encroached upon focus on the actions of writers and reporters in the process of obtaining information and photographs. Trespassing on someone's private property will normally constitute a violation of privacy while remaining on public property, even if conducting surveillance is usually permissible.

The most effective way to protect yourself from being accused of interfering with a person's privacy is to be respectful and act in good taste. For example, if you walk up to a person's door, ring the bell, and when the door opens ask politely for an interview, there is no offensive conduct that would justify a lawsuit for intrusion of privacy even though you have technically trespassed. On the other hand, if you are stalking someone on public property and surreptitiously taking unflattering photographs of the subject, an intrusion upon privacy might be established.

First Amendment Concerns

American jurisprudence is often a balancing act between competing rights. At one end of the scale you will find the rights to privacy and publicity and at the other end you have the First Amendment guaranteeing freedom of the press and freedom of speech upon which writers, authors, journalists, editors, and publishers frequently rely. Not infrequently, a conflict arises between the First Amendment and either statutory law or common law that protects the right to privacy and right of publicity.

Two Exceptions

Responding to these contending rights, in deference to the First Amendment the courts have created two exceptions to a person's right of publicity. The first exemption is the "newsworthiness" exception that provides a person cannot object to the use of his name or likeness so long as the following conditions are satisfied:

- The content involves a matter of general public interest.
- There is nothing false or misleading.
- There is a connection between the person and the subject matter.
- The material is not a pretense for advertising.
- If the book is a biography and not authorized by the subject, there must be a statement indicating that it is an "unauthorized" biography.

ESSENTIAL

Common law is the result of a series of decisions made by the courts on a specific issue. Statutory laws are enacted by the legislative bodies at the local, state, and federal levels. Constitutional law emanates from the federal Constitution and the constitutions of the states as interpreted by the courts and takes precedence over statutory and common law.

The second exception is the "incidental use" exemption, which applies when a person's name or depiction is merely incidental to a privileged use. For example, in a biography of a celebrity, mentioning the names of actors who played roles alongside the subject of the book is an incidental use.

Defenses to Invasion of Privacy

There are a number of defenses that can be raised when a claim is made that one's privacy has been violated. First and foremost, in most cases the plaintiff must be alive, because the purpose of protecting privacy is to prevent the disclosure of intimate and personal matters. Obviously, this cannot apply when the information revealed is about someone dead.

However, the time of the publication is critical when the defense raised is that the person is deceased. If the subject of the disclosure was alive when the information was revealed but died thereafter, the estate of the deceased can commence a lawsuit. Moreover, because the law of privacy varies from state to state, you need to be aware that the right to prevent photos used for commercial purposes as well as the right to publicity survives the death of the subject in some states.

When an allegation is made that one's privacy was violated by the publication of private and embarrassing facts or creating a false light, a defense can be raised that the information disclosed is not offensive to a reasonable person. Of course, this would have to be proven based upon the facts of the case. Another defense to a claim of privacy violation is that the information is of legitimate concern to the public or otherwise newsworthy. But bear in mind that a newsworthy defense requires that it be timely, so while the subject and information might have been newsworthy at one time, years later that may no longer be the case and publication of the information might not be protected by this defense.

A defense can also be made that the subject consented to the information being published. As in the case of libel law, it is wise to obtain the subject's consent and this should be secured by a written and signed release prepared by an attorney or furnished by your publisher.

Disguise Your Subjects

Since an intrusion upon one's right to privacy as well as a violation of one's right to publicity both require that the subject is identifiable, disguising the subject so that she is not recognizable is a defense to lawsuits based on either or both claims. However, whether or not the subject is no longer recognizable will be a question for trial and you will have to do more than merely change a person's name.

For example, in *Ruzicka v. Conde Nast Publications, Inc.*, a federal appellate court held that where an attorney provided information conditioned on anonymity, merely changing her name but still identifying her as a "Minneapolis attorney" who helped draft the state's law criminalizing therapist-patient sex was specific enough to make her recognizable and the defendant was liable. Another example is the "Finch" family from Augusten Burrough's memoir *Running with Scissors* who claimed they were easily identifiable as the Turcottes for a number of reasons including the fact that anyone who knew Burroughs knew he had spent part of his youth with Dr. Turcotte and his family. Nor did it help that Burroughs identified them in subsequent interviews.

ESSENTIAL

The standard used to determine whether or not a person is identifiable is generally based upon the "reasonable person" persona created by the courts. The question you must ask yourself is whether the subject can be "reasonably" identifiable from the facts you have disclosed in your contents.

While you need not go so far as to make the subject unrecognizable to himself or to individuals who are closely involved with the subject and the information you are providing, you need to be confident that your readers cannot ascertain the subject's identity. Besides the name, features you might consider altering are occupation, physical characteristics, geographic location, and marital status.

Obtain a Release

You were advised in Chapter 20 that whenever possible you should obtain the consent of the person about whom you are writing and that the best way to verify consent had been given would be by the execution of a written release. The same holds true for matters of privacy. It was also suggested that although verbal consent is enforceable, since you may have to prove you received permission it is best to have the consent in writing. However, if you obtain oral permission, you may want to record the subject, but if you do this, make certain the subject agrees to the recording. Having witnesses present to a verbal consent will also be helpful.

If you prepare a written release to be signed, it is best that you do not write it yourself. There are standard forms you can utilize and customize for your specific purpose. You can also consider having an attorney who is familiar with publishing law prepare a release for you or you might obtain a form from your publisher.

Releases for Photographs

As a writer you may be wondering why you would ever need to be concerned with releases for photographs. But the fact is that nonfiction writers frequently have photographs contained in the body of their work—especially journalists writing for newspapers; freelancers writing for magazines; and authors writing biographies and histories. So you do need to know how the law of privacy and right to publicity pertains to photographs.

Since photographs are subject to copyright law, you will need permission from the owner of the copyright and obtain a release. Insofar as publicity and privacy is concerned, you should obtain a release from any person recognizable in the photograph so long as the photo is being used for commercial purposes. If a person is a public figure or public official, you will only need a release if there is a commercial purpose to the photograph.

Photographs of public places and people whose presence is incidental to the photograph do not require releases. However, the photo of a unique building such as an historic landmark will necessitate a release. As for sex and nudity, it is always wise to obtain a release from the individuals in the photograph.

If a release is sought from a minor, you need to obtain consent from a parent or guardian. The voting age of eighteen has nothing to do with contract law and the ages of maturity vary among the states, so it is prudent to secure permission from a parent or guardian whenever the person is under twenty-one years of age.

Insurance as an Added Protection

There is insurance coverage available for libel claims under what is called a media perils policy. This type of policy, accessible to publishers, editors, and writers, provides coverage for invasion of privacy claims as well.

The factors discussed in Chapter 20 apply equally here with one exception. Because intruding upon someone's privacy does not require publication should a claim be made against you for this violation, you may find that even if you were added as an additional insured to your publishers policy, you may not have protection for this specific liability. Consequently, you may want to consider your own insurance policy, although like most writers, you may find the cost does not warrant the potential benefit.

CHAPTER 22

Getting Your Work Published

Should you desire a readership beyond friends and family, you'll discover that the odds of getting your work published can be daunting. However, you can gain an advantage over competing writers if you understand the market, the submission process, and the publishing options available. You also need to know where to send your work; how to catch an editor's interest; and how to obtain an agent when appropriate. Finally, you must be mindful of protecting your work and what rights to retain.

The Marketplace

The bad news is that there are millions of writers and authors seeking to have their work published. The good news is that there is actually two parts of good news. First, the marketplace has never offered more opportunities to a writer to have his work published than now. The second piece of good news is that most of the writers submitting their work do not have the foggiest notion how to go about securing a publisher and because you will have read this chapter you'll have put the odds in your favor.

You saw in previous chapters that there are specific markets for the respective genres: newspapers and some magazines for opinion pieces; literary journals for literary and personal essays; consumer magazines for general articles; university presses for scholarly books; and so on. But finding out exactly where to submit isn't always easy, especially if you want to consider a national audience. Fortunately, there are a number of resources at your disposal to compile a list of potential publishers.

FACT

Once you determine the types of publishers that comprise your market, you need to investigate further to determine which specific ones will be receptive to your project. For instance, newspapers provide an excellent market for op-eds but not all newspapers publish op-eds or take submissions from freelance writers.

Identifying Your Market

Years ago, you could amble over to the library or a bookstore and peruse the shelves to survey the publishers of books in your subject or to make a list of periodicals where you could send submissions. But today, this is no longer the most practical solution and you have other options available.

There are a number of books listing book publishers, magazines, periodicals, and journals that you can purchase at the bookstore or examine in the library. Some of these books like *Writer's Market* contain publishers in almost all the genres while other books are more specialized, such as *The International Directory of Little Magazines and Small Presses.*

A number of these resource books have websites, such as *Writer's Market* (*www.writersmarket.com*). In some instances a subscription is required to access information. Other websites you might consider to ascertain the market for your work include:

- *www.travelwriters.com*
- *www.food-writing.com*
- *www.writingfordollars.com*
- *www.literarymarketplace.com*
- *www.absolutemarkets.com*
- *www.writersweekly.com*

ALERT

Because of the fluid nature of the publishing industry, publishers' requirements, submission procedures, personnel, and interests can change frequently, so the information provided in resource books and general websites is not always accurate. It is always wise to review the website of each publisher you have targeted for your submission.

Know Your Market

The standard and best advice is to be familiar with the publications and publishers where you want to send your work. For book publishers, it's fairly easy. You can visit their websites, examine their catalogs, or even peruse their books at the bookstores. For example, if it's a biography you have written, you can make a list of publishers that publish biographies by going to the biography section of the bookstore, library, or booksellers on the Internet.

For periodicals and journals, it's suggested you review a copy or two and perhaps buy a back issue. Unfortunately, you may find it a strain on your budget to purchase these issues, so you might want to consider other options. There are a number of ways other than reading back issues that will enable you to familiarize yourself with these publications:

- Consider the periodicals to which you subscribe or read as a potential market for your work.

- Never fail to leaf through an available magazine whether waiting at the doctor's office or browsing the shelves of a bookstore or library.
- Check the listings in resource books and websites to see which publications provide free back issues.
- Visit the website of publications where you might be able to read a portion of an issue online.
- Review the writers' guidelines provided by most publications either at their websites or available upon request.

How to Submit

Now that you have determined where to send your work, you are ready to begin the submission process. This is where you can distinguish yourself from the vast majority of submissions made to publishers and editors, and you can do this by simply following the proper protocol.

If you want to write an article or review, you should send what is known as a "query," which is discussed later in this chapter. Essays, memoirs, and op-eds are submitted in their entirety with a brief cover letter. Book proposals are sent with a cover letter or sometimes preceded by a query, depending upon the submission policy of the respective publisher, editor, or agent. It is always best to check the websites to review the current and specific submission procedure of each publisher or publication where you intend to submit.

ESSENTIAL

The submission process can be disheartening and you may receive many rejections before an acceptance. To avoid giving up, you might want to make a list of where you will be submitting; check off the name when you submit your work; cross it out upon its return; and then just move down the list for the next submission.

Tips and Terms

In order to appear professional in submitting your work, you need to know some of the terminology and what is expected from you at the receiving end of your submission. Although there are no absolute rules and you should comply with the submission guidelines where you are sending your work, the best course is to maintain the protocol of the industry. To do this you should guide yourself by the following points:

- Include a self-addressed, stamped envelope (SASE) with your submission for a response and any material you wish returned.
- Unless the intended recipient specifically requests or agrees to receive electronic submissions, send your material via regular mail.
- All material should be double spaced with the exception of query letters, which can be single-spaced.
- If appropriate, mention your publishing history or include a list of publications. Only send "clips" (copies of your articles) if requested or suggested in the submission guidelines.
- If you are granted an "assignment," that means you are authorized to proceed with the project subject to the terms of the assignment; an indication that your work will be read "on spec" means that your piece will be seriously considered but may be rejected for any reason whatsoever.

ALERT

Do not make first contact with someone you do not know with a telephone call. Likewise, to determine the status of your submission after an appropriate length of time has elapsed, your request should be in writing. Telephone calls are only appropriate after acceptance or if you have had a previous relationship with the individual.

Simultaneous Submissions

For many years, the standard procedure required the writer to make one submission at a time; a decision was rendered timely—usually in several weeks; and if rejected, the writer was free to submit elsewhere. With the dramatic rise in submissions and response time often taking many months, some writers began to submit to more than one publisher, editor, or agent at a time. This is called "simultaneous submissions."

From the recipient's standpoint, simultaneous submissions are undesirable because it means time is wasted considering a work when it has already been accepted somewhere else. From the writer's perspective, simultaneous submissions only aggravate a growing problem by generating even more submissions. Nonetheless, simultaneous submissions are becoming more acceptable, but you should consider the guidelines where you are sending your work, where you will find one of three policies concerning this issue: simultaneous submission is accepted; it is accepted only if the submission indicates it is being submitted elsewhere; it is not acceptable (no indication means it's not acceptable).

The Query and the Hook

A query letter may be the most important thing you'll write, so make certain it is your best writing. After all, it's your initial contact and amounts to the first impression you are making on an editor or agent. Whether you'll be asked to send your book proposal, manuscript, or essay or be given an assignment depends upon the effectiveness of your query.

Because editors, agents, and publishers receive hundreds of queries a week, they don't read every one from beginning to end. If their interest is not piqued by the end of the first paragraph, they are not likely to read on. Therefore, the most crucial portion of the query is the first few sentences, sometimes referred to as the "hook" because this is where you "hook" the reader in. Other elements of a good query are:

- Be concise and compelling. The query can be single spaced but only one page.
- Tell why your work should be published and why it will attract readers or interest the current readers of the publication.
- Summarize your project in a paragraph or two.
- Explain why you are the one to write it. Discuss your expertise and other qualifications.
- The tone of the query should reflect the tone of your work.
- Indicate how long your project is and when you predict you can have it complete.

A Writer's Rights

Writers are often so enthused at the opportunity to see their work published they sometimes forget to protect their own rights. As a result, almost every writer has at least one or two "horror" stories about not being paid or an inability to republish their own work or having their work usurped by others. While the bargaining positions may not be equal and you still may do almost anything to see your work in print, if you know your rights at least you can understand what you are giving up.

Copyrights

Some writers are practically paranoid their work will be lifted, but the truth is copyright infringement of a writer's work is rare. Another misconception people have is the belief that it is necessary to file with the Library of Congress in order to copyright one's work. While you can secure a copyright with the Library of Congress, the fact is that once you write your work it has been copyrighted so long as three conditions are satisfied: the work is original; it is fixed in some tangible form; and it falls within one of the statutory categories of "eligible work," which includes the work of most writers.

ALERT

Ideas by themselves cannot acquire copyright protection. It is necessary to transform an idea into a tangible form. Nor can you obtain a copyright for a title, which explains why movies and books may have the same titles. However in rare instances, you can copyright a title if it has a unique meaning, such as *Gone with the Wind* which has been recognizable to generations of Americans.

Copyright protection emanates from the federal Copyright Act and applies to all fifty states. As the holder of a copyright, you have certain rights that prohibit anyone from using your work without your authorization, which include reproducing the work, making new versions of the work, and distributing copies. However, copyright law is complex. You should seek the services of a copyright attorney if you feel someone has infringed upon your copyright or you are concerned about violating the copyright of someone else.

Retaining Your Rights

Absent an indication to the contrary, it is generally assumed that when offering a work to be published you are representing that it has never been previously published and you are selling "first serial rights," which allows you to retain the rights after the first publication. Should you have transferred "all rights" and subsequently want to include the work in an anthology or have it published elsewhere, you would need permission from the party holding the rights even though you are the writer of the work. If your work has been previously published and you are offering it for publication, you must indicate you are offering "one-time rights."

The rights that are retained by the author and the rights that are sold to a book publisher are often the heart of the negotiations. The book contract will reflect exactly how the rights are divided and unless you have expertise in this area, it is wise for you to be represented by an attorney experienced in publishing law or by a literary agent.

Getting Paid

How you are paid for a book is governed by the contract and is subject to negotiations. Once again, it is suggested you have representation. In most instances, an advance is paid at signing the contract that is credited against royalties earned. With traditional book publishers, authors are reimbursed by royalties, which is explained later in this chapter. Alternative publishing houses provide other means for payment.

FACT

Although more common with writers of fiction, writers of nonfiction do not always receive monetary payment for their work. Literary journals where you might send your essays sometimes pay in contributors' copies or provide a one-year free subscription. Some newspapers do not pay for opinion pieces or reviews.

Other than books, you are normally paid either when your work is accepted for publication or after your work has been published. Having no control over the publication date, you may have to wait months and sometimes years to receive payment if you are to be paid on publication. If you received an assignment, delivered the manuscript, and it was accepted but the publisher decided not to publish the work, you are often entitled to a "kill fee," which is a percentage of what you would have been paid had the work been published. The amount of the "kill fee" is usually stated in the letter or contract offering the assignment.

Literary Agents

Until the middle of the twentieth century, literary agents were barely a blip on the literary horizon and even then there were only a handful of agents spending their days having lunches and drinks with editors. Most authors found their own editors and publishing houses and were likely to remain with them throughout their career.

However, in the past several decades everything has changed. Most large publishers will only consider work submitted by an agent; editors and authors move from publisher to publisher with the same frequency one may buy new shoes; and contracts are convoluted with negotiations sometimes conducted like a game of hardball. As a result, if you are in search of a publisher for your book, your first step is to try to obtain a literary agent.

ESSENTIAL

Literary agents represent book projects exclusively, although some agents may handle nonbook projects for their existing clients. Many literary agents will limit their efforts to large publishing houses and will not contact midsize or small publishers, which an author can generally approach without an agent.

Finding an Agent

Almost all agents are listed along with editors and publishers in *Literary Marketplace*, a multivolume text available in libraries that contains basic information. If you want to know more about an agent, you should review books like *Writer's Market* and *Literary Agents* that are available in the publishing section of bookstores.

There are also several websites you can examine to find an agent. Many agents are members of the Association of Author's Representatives and you can learn about them at *www.aar-online.org*. Other websites to visit are *www.literaryagents.com* and *www.writersservices.com*.

Literary agents sometimes attend writers' conferences where you might have an opportunity to discuss your project. If you know someone who has a literary agent, ask if you can drop her name to make contact.

Choosing an Agent

Other than associations such as the Association of Author's Representatives, there is no formal code of professional conduct to which agents must comply. Anyone can be an agent, so you must be careful in selecting one. Of course, keep in mind that agents reject approximately 99 percent of the queries and unsolicited manuscripts they receive, so be grateful to have an agent take interest in your work.

ALERT

The most common mistake writers make submitting to agents is to send work in which the agent has no interest. This is a sure way to guarantee a rejection. Do not send your nonfiction proposal to an agent who handles children's books exclusively or send your memoir to an agent who only represents authors of general nonfiction.

However, once an agent does express interest, learn more about him. Visit the agent's website or read his listing at other websites or in reference books. Determine how many sales the agent made in the previous year or two. Find out what the commission will be; it is usually 15 percent but can be between 10 and 20 percent. Ask whether you have to pay copying costs and other charges. Finally, determine whether the agent charges a fee to read your work before offering representation. Most agents do not charge a reading fee.

Standard Publishing

Traditional publishing houses pay their authors in one of two ways: a royalty that is usually a percentage of the retail or wholesale price of the book; or a flat fee which is a "work for hire" where the author is considered an independent contractor and retains no rights to the work. There are three tiers of publishing houses with each having their respective advantages and disadvantages: large publishers, often owned by conglomerates, can offer wide distribution and publicity but frequently this is allocated to authors of potential blockbusters; midsize publishers that usually maintain a strong backlist, adding a longer life to your book, but lack the clout large publishers have in obtaining greater visibility in bookstores; and the small publisher where you can receive individual attention but are largely left to on your own to promote your book.

The Contract

The terms and conditions that define the author-publisher relationship are found in the contract. Unless you are well versed in publishing contracts, you should have an attorney experienced in publishing law or a literary agent represent you. Some of the important clauses you should examine are:

- The rights that are sold to the publisher and the rights that are retained by the author
- The advance and the royalties
- Time period for the author to deliver the manuscript
- Right of the publisher to reject the manuscript; what determines acceptability; the procedure and time period for the author to revise the manuscript to make it acceptable
- Insurance coverage available to the author
- Time period for the author to review the galleys

Large publishers generally use a contract modeled on the standard publishing contract, which consists of many "boilerplate" clauses. Midsize and small publishers are more likely to customize their contracts. The contract furnished to an author for signature tends to favor the publisher and should be critically examined and negotiated before signing.

Alternative Publishers

Anything other than the traditional author-publisher relationship that provides for payment by the publisher to the author with the publisher responsible for all costs of production and distribution is considered an alternative form of publishing by contemporary standards. However, publishing began with the publishing of religious books where no payment was made to authors. Thereafter, self-publishing became quite common and respectable. For example, Benjamin Franklin published most of his own writing. Thus, alternative publishing has a long history and you should not hesitate to consider it so long as you are aware of the advantages and disadvantages of the different types of alternative publishing.

Vanity Publishing

Vanity presses publish a book on behalf of the author and in turn are compensated for their costs and services. Some vanity presses help with distribution and even advertising but often this is left to the author. Because the author incurs all the costs, the author retains all proceeds from sales.

Subsidy Publishers

Subsidy publishing houses are a cross between standard and vanity publishers. The author pays the subsidy publisher a portion or all of the production costs but generally not for editorial, layout, or art. The publisher is responsible for promotion and distribution. In return for her investment, the author earns a higher percentage than the standard royalty traditional publishers pay.

Self-Publishing

If you cannot secure a standard publisher for your book and it's important to you for it to appear in print, you might want to consider self-publishing. Indeed, it is possible to generate more sales and earn more money from self-publishing than from a traditional publisher, although you have to be willing to take on greater responsibilities in the editing and production of your book as well as promotion and distribution. However, if you decide to self-publish because you believe that as a "published author" you will have a better chance securing a publisher for your next book, you would be making a mistake. Self-published books are not considered a publishing credit that will impress agents or editors unless thousands of copies are sold.

It was not long ago that self-publishing meant assuming every aspect of the publishing process including hiring a printer to print the initial run (usually a minimum of 1,000 copies) and spending thousands of dollars. Today, there are a number of respectable e-publishing companies where copies can be printed on demand as well as in larger numbers and you only pay a set-up fee of several hundred dollars, a per-book print fee, and optional costs such as the preparation of press kits for publicity. Moreover, in addition to your own distribution efforts, your book can usually be purchased at the publisher's website or even at the websites of Amazon.com and national booksellers.

ALERT

Do not be misled by the number of sales e-publishers report. Although the figures indicating annual sales of hundreds of thousands of books may be accurate, generally the average number of books sold per title is less than fifty. In a recent year, 1 million e-published books were sold, representing 25,000 titles or an average of forty sales per book.

For writers of nonfiction, self-publishing offers a viable option, especially if your book is intended to be part of a program to promote yourself to the public and to be sold at seminars or speaking engagements. Self-publishing also has the advantage of faster publication and the potential of earning more per book sold. But there are disadvantages as well and before you make a final decision you might want to research your options further and consult one or more books and articles on the subject.

To Succeed, Persevere

Of one thing you can be certain: your work will never be published if it remains tucked away in a drawer. You need to submit your work for it to see the light of day and be read by others. While this means you will receive rejections and sometimes even reach the point of putting a particular project aside, you need to persevere if you want to be published.

To do this, keep two thoughts in mind. First, rejection is very subjective and many times has nothing to do with the quality of your work. An editor may actually love what you submitted but it's just not right for her or at least not at that particular time.

Second, rejection has been endured by every writer—even the best:

- Robert Pirsig received 121 rejections before *Zen and the Art of Motorcycle Maintenance* was published, which went on to become a highly acclaimed classic and bestseller.
- The first *Chicken Soup* book was self-published because no publisher wanted the manuscript.
- William Saroyan claims to have had a stack of rejection slips three inches high before his first acceptance.
- Jack Kerouac's *On the Road* traveled among publishing houses for six years before it was accepted for publication.
- *Ulysses*, considered the best novel in the English language published in the twentieth century, was left in limbo by the publisher for nine years until James Joyce sued to force publication.

Exercise

Write a one-page query letter for a real project you have in mind or for one imagined. This must be your very best writing, so write as many drafts as you want but to stay realistic, get in done within a week. Once it's complete, identify your market and send it off; or if it's about something you just made up, give it a second thought. Perhaps it is something you want to write about after all!

CHAPTER 23

Selling Your Book— The Book Proposal

In securing an agent or publisher, it's the book proposal and not the book you are going to circulate; and it's the proposal that will determine whether you're offered a contract. To write a successful proposal, you need to know what it must contain; how it should be organized; and how to write it so an agent or editor becomes enthusiastic about the book. While there are nuances for the different genres, you can follow a general format to make your proposal professional and convincing.

It's the Proposal That Sells Your Book

There was a time when an author of a nonfiction book upon reaching the last page of the final draft, boxed the manuscript, walked it to the post office, and mailed it to an agent or editor for their consideration. But that day is long gone, because what editors and agents look for to decide which projects to take on involves much more than what is written in the manuscript. Perhaps it shouldn't be this way but it is; and the result is the decisions to accept or reject a project are based upon the book proposal.

ESSENTIAL

While some university presses and publishers of scholarly books require a complete manuscript before offering a contract, almost all publishers base their decision on the book proposal and do not want to see the entire manuscript. However, if you want to write the book, you should do so but with the knowledge that you still need to write a book proposal.

You learned in Chapter 22 that your first wave of submissions will be directed to literary agents if you are writing a book that might interest a large publisher and a general audience or has a very strong niche market that could generate thousands of sales. The other group to whom you will send your proposal are editors of midsize and small publishing houses. Thus you must bear in mind when writing your proposal who will be reading it—not the general public but rather professionals with a specific set of expectations. And the purpose of the proposal is to convince at least one of these people to offer you representation or to publish your book.

Most writers have little desire to become involved in the commercial aspects of the publishing industry. It would be nice to write your book, send it off, and have it published even while you're at work on your next book in your idyllic writer's garret. This may work for writers of articles, essays, and other nonfiction pieces, but this is not the case for authors of nonfiction books. The author is expected to help sell the book and the "selling" begins with the book proposal.

Writing the Proposal

There are two kinds of writers—writers who write for themselves and writers who write for the reader. There is nothing that makes one group superior to the other but there is one big difference. If you want to have your work published you had better keep the reader in mind. This is especially true in convincing an agent or editor that your book should be published, so the book proposal must be written just as if you were standing before an editor or agent and presenting your case.

This may sound as though you are a salesperson promoting a product. Or, perhaps like someone pitching a storyline for a movie or television series. In a sense, this is exactly what you are doing and to do this effectively you must have some knowledge about the people you are trying to convince.

Know Your Audience

You will be submitting your proposal to literary agents and editors. Sometimes, though rarely, a publisher is involved but normally publishing houses assign the task of reviewing proposals to editors. While literary agents and editors are distinct breeds, they have enough in common that you can direct one proposal to both groups, keeping several factors in mind.

Many publishing houses have acquisition editors whose sole responsibility is to obtain manuscripts for publication, and one of the ways this is accomplished is by reviewing unsolicited book proposals. In other publishing companies, especially smaller firms, editors may share the responsibility for acquisitions or it may be left to the editor in chief.

Since people in the publishing industry will be reading your proposal, do not be didactic or feel you have to explain anything other than the specifics of your project. Agents and editors are generally busy people with little time for much else than the work at hand, so be concise and get to the point. Because they lead hectic lives, editors and agents aren't looking for prima donnas or intractable writers; make it clear you're open to suggestions and guidance. All this and more makes for the tone of your proposal, which is critical if you are to succeed.

The Tone

First and foremost, your proposal should be written in the same tone and voice as your book. If you have a scholarly book, feel free to write your proposal in an academic style. If your book is a humorous memoir, your proposal should have a friendly and occasionally funny voice. However, there are portions of the proposal that are clear-cut, where the writing should be straightforward. And of course, always remain professional.

Since you are trying to sell your book, the tone of your proposal should reflect confidence and be upbeat. This holds true even if you have written a memoir of childhood abuse or a book about genocide in Rwanda. You also must make a convincing argument that you are the person to write the book and to do this effectively, you must convey a command not only of the book's contents but of all aspects of an author's role in the project as set forth in the book proposal.

The Contents of the Proposal

Although some genres have specific requirements and some editors and agents prefer a certain format, a standard table of contents will consist of the following sections:

- Overview
- Target market
- Promotional plan and platform
- Author's vita and bibliography
- Competitive books
- Chapter-by-chapter outline

In addition to the sections that comprise the table of contents, two sample chapters should be included in the submission. These chapters need not be consecutive nor need they be the first chapters of your book.

The Overview

In many ways, the overview is an extension of the query and consists of approximately ten pages. The overview must hook the reader in the first paragraph and provide a "selling handle" that pitches and succinctly states in a sentence or two what the book is about—something that could become the subtitle on the front cover.

QUESTION

How long should my book proposal be?
A typical book proposal ranges between thirty to forty pages. This is exclusive of the sample chapters. Some agents and editors have specific requirements as to format and length that you might want to review before submitting.

The overview expands upon the other issues touched upon in the query:

- A summary of the book
- Why the book is important and should be published
- Why the book will attract readers
- Why you are the one to write the book
- The length of the book and time needed to complete it

Author's Vita and Bibliography

This section of the proposal should be presented as you would any professional resume or vita. It can list all the relevant information or provide a narrative written in the first or third person. In the overview you have already addressed why you're the one to write the book and later in the promotional portion you'll explain what you intend to do to help sell the book. Consequently, all you have to do in this segment is provide basic information about yourself.

Be certain to include anything that qualifies you to write the book and your experience as a writer. If you have previously published, you should add a "bibliography" or a "list of publications." If you have only several cred-its, you should incorporate them into your vita.

ALERT

The chapter-by-chapter outline is not an "outline" in the strict sense of the word. It should be written as a narrative in the same style as the tone of your book. While summarizing the information, it should demonstrate how the book will actually read in addition to the sample chapters provided.

Outline

This section of the proposal should be about ten pages and summarize your book chapter by chapter. Obviously in order to write this, you will have thought out the book from beginning to end, which is exactly what an agent or editor is looking for. The form of the outline is chapter by chapter with one to three paragraphs describing each chapter's contents.

Sample Chapters

Although part of the book proposal, the sample chapters stand by themselves and should be page numbered separately. You were informed that the chapters need not be from the beginning of the book nor consecutive and in fact, it is wise to provide chapters that offer different perspectives of the book. Should you have an introduction to your book, you can include that as a sample chapter if it is the approximate length of your chapters. And speaking of length, two sample chapters will generally suffice unless they are short (less than ten pages), in which case you should submit three chapters.

Target Market

Even if you believe your book has the potential of being a blockbuster and interest everyone, this is not what an agent or editor wants to see. Although they would love a bestseller with an unlimited audience, the fact is almost all nonfiction books are directed at a specific segment of the population and marketed accordingly. This portion of your book proposal should identify the market for your book and explain why these people would buy it.

FACT

There is almost no such thing as too narrow a target market. You may have a potential audience only in the tens of thousands but if you can show a high percentage will want to purchase your book, generating several thousand sales, many midlist and small publishers will have interest in your proposal.

Clearly Identify the Audience

Once you're past the temptation of proclaiming your book is for everyone and you identify a target market, you must get even more specific. For instance, if your book is about the benefits of meditation for people with difficulty sleeping, you must say more than people with sleep disorders will be interested in the book. You need to do some research and cite an approximate number of people suffering with sleep deprivation who form your target market. Or, your meditation book might be focused on alleviating hyperactivity in children and adolescents, so you would ascertain the number of cases diagnosed with hyperactivity with their parents forming the core of your market. Another possibility is that your meditation book establishes how meditation makes for a more relaxed lifestyle, so while it would still address people with sleep disorders and parents with hyperactive kids, it is potentially of interest to tens of millions of people, because almost everyone could benefit from relaxation techniques.

Promotional Plan and Platform

It's been decades since you could rely on the maxim that if you build a better mousetrap the world will beat a path to your door. But the fact is this is precisely how books were once sold—by word of mouth beginning with a few favorable book reviews and advice from the independent bookseller while you browse the shelves. True, there were author signings and readings, but this was conducted in deference to the cultural importance of books as much as to stimulate sales. But today conditions and expectations are different and it's not enough to turn out another good book for your publisher; you are expected to help sell the book you just wrote.

The Platform

"Platform" in publishing jargon means your existing audience—people whom you can easily reach and who might purchase your book. If your only "platform" is friends and family, it's best not to mention a platform at all. In fact, many publishers are even dismissive of authors with a built-in audience made up of thousands of listeners to a radio program or readers of a newspaper column if it is not national in scope. However, chances are if you really think about it, you may discover you have a platform larger than you think.

For one thing, an Internet presence such as your own website or blog with thousands of hits is a good start to establishing your platform. Consider organizations of which you are a member that relate to your book. For instance, if you're writing a scholarly book and you teach at a university, the entire campus can be included in your platform.

ALERT

Do not confuse your "platform" with your promotional or marketing plan. Your platform is your existing audience who will listen when you speak and who have an interest in the subject of your book. The promotional plan is what you intend to do to promote the book and stimulate sales.

The Promotional Plan

This part of your book proposal is where you toss the author's hat on the shelf and shamelessly throw yourself into the commercial aspects of your project touting what you will do to sell your book. Not very long ago, it was enough to say that you were amenable to attending book signings and appearing on radio and television programs, leaving it to the publisher's publicity department to make the arrangements. Today, you are expected not only to attend these events and cooperate in promotional activities but you are expected to make them happen.

Some of the promotional functions you should consider including in your proposal are:

- Media events such as arranging for radio and television interviews
- Interviews in the press or for publications on the Internet
- Having articles written by you on the book's subject published around the time the book is released
- Groups and organizations you plan to visit for speaking engagements
- Book signings and talks at bookstores
- Well-known people who will write a blurb (endorsement) for your book or help in some way to promote your book
- Your own website to promote the book

Competitive Books

For many agents and editors, the most important section of the proposal concerns the competition. Not only must you be thorough in providing the information but how you present it is equally important; it is also an opportunity for you to distinguish yourself from other authors who do not appreciate the significance of competitive titles.

FACT

The fact that there are books similar to your book does not necessarily dissuade publishers from having an interest in your project. On the contrary, if there have never been books published addressing the same subject as your book, publishers will question if there is a market for the book at all.

Finding the Competition

The first step in identifying the competition is to see what books have been published that resemble your project. *Books In Print* is a multivolume set that lists all the books currently in print and is indexed in several ways including by subject matter. You can also visit Amazon.com or BarnesandNoble.com and search the category where your book would be assigned.

Do not be discouraged if you see titles similar to your book, because this is where your work is just beginning. Make a list and be sure to obtain the following information:

- Title
- Author
- Publisher
- Price

- Year published
- Number of pages
- ISBN

When you list the books in your competitive book section, be sure to include all this information—especially the ISBN, because editors and agents can track sales of a title with this identification and they appreciate that you are providing this number.

Distinguish Your Book

The fact that books have been published similar to your project actually helps make your case because it shows there is a potential market for your subject. What you must do is demonstrate why your book should still be published, and you can do this by distinguishing your book from the books on your list, which can be done in several ways.

First, it may be that the book is no longer in print; or, if it is in print, it is not on the shelves and therefore it would not hamper sales of your book. Second, the book may be different from your project. In order to make the distinction, you must familiarize yourself with each book and then explain why that book is distinguishable from your book.

ESSENTIAL

There are several ways to become familiar with competing titles without buying the book. You can examine the book at a library or bookstore; you can read book reviews that provide essential information; visit a bookseller's website where the book is sold and glean information from the title, subtitle, table of contents, and excerpts.

In differentiating your book from the competition, you should consider not only the contents but the target market. For instance, if your book and another book are both about swimming but your book is directed to swimming as an exercise for senior citizens while the other book is about developing swimming skills in young children, then the books are no longer competitive in the marketplace.

Finally, you must address the books left on your list that are readily available for purchase, have a similar subject matter, and target a comparable audience. This is where the meaning of "competition" comes into play and you must demonstrate why your book is superior to the other books. Of course, this can be a subjective matter, but try to be as objective and professional as possible in evaluating your competition.

Exercises

As you have seen throughout this book, writing nonfiction involves more than just "writing"; there is a significant amount of preparation involved and this is certainly true when composing a book proposal. The following two exercises are not writing exercises but require you to develop other skills.

EXERCISE 1: COMPETITIVE BOOKS

Determine the subject of your project and identify the competition. Gather the information and make your list. If you want to go further, pare down your list by eliminating what is no longer available or is distinguishable and then demonstrate why your book would be better than the remaining books on your list.

EXERCISE 2: PROMOTIONAL PLAN

Prepare a marketing plan for your proposed book. Consider anyone who could help you obtain publicity; specific bookstores for books signings; groups and organizations you can address; people to provide endorsements for your book; reviewers to send advance copies for review; local media where you can appear.

CHAPTER 24

Perfecting Your Skills as a Nonfiction Writer

The moment you wrote your first piece of nonfiction you became a nonfiction writer. The real question is whether you will be a good nonfiction writer, and if this is your goal, there are a number of ways to sharpen your skills. You can attend writers' conferences; writers' groups and workshops; formal educational programs from noncredit to advanced degrees; and join writing organizations. To advance your career, you might want to consider a publicist. But the real secret to success is simple—just keep writing.

Writers' Conferences

There are many reasons you might want to attend a writers' conference. For one thing, writing is a solitary endeavor and if nothing else, going to a conference affords you an opportunity to meet other writers; commiserate over rejections and realize you're not alone; receive opinions about your work; and network. Of course, the core of the conference will be the sessions and workshops designed to enhance your writing abilities. With so many conferences, you need to know where to look and how to choose one best suited for you.

Finding a Writers' Conference

There are hundreds of writers' conferences held every year but you won't necessarily see them advertised in the general media. Many of these conferences advertise in writers' magazines such as *Poets and Writers*, the *Writer*, and *Writer's Digest*. Most have a presence on the Internet, and *www.writing. shawguides.com* lists writers' conferences in the United States and all over the world.

Some of the conferences are well known and you might have heard of them. Other conferences are local endeavors or specialize in certain genres. Once you make your list of conferences in which you have an interest, you need to consider some factors so you select the right one and have a rewarding experience.

ALERT

Do not pick a writers' conference merely because famous writers will be present or a celebrity speaker is giving the keynote address. Many times the well-known writers are not accessible and do not teach the workshops but only make brief appearances because of their name recognition and ability to draw conferees.

Choosing a Conference

Many writers' conferences focus on a specific genre such as romance writers, writers of children's books, and speculative fiction, so there may be little benefit attending such a conference if you are not writing in that genre.

Indeed, a number of conferences concern only fiction and if it is nonfiction you are writing, these conferences may not be for you; although you can always benefit from learning fiction techniques especially if you are interested in creative nonfiction.

Aside from the genre, other factors you should consider in selecting a conference are:

- Geographic location
- Duration
- Cost
- Availability of scholarships
- Overnight accommodations
- Number and variety of workshops
- Quality of faculty
- Presence of editors and literary agents

Many writers' conferences are held in the summer because they are associated with a college or university. Conferences can be as short as one day or as long as the renowned Bread Loaf Writers Conference held for ten days. Some conferences such as the Philadelphia Writers' Conference, in existence since 1948, are held over weekends and try to be more intensive than one-day conferences by having several sessions for each workshop yet keeping costs more affordable than longer conferences. The important thing is not to select a conference because it is well known or expensive or has famous writers; do some homework and try to determine if it looks right for you.

FACT

Writers' conferences provide an excellent opportunity to make friends and network. Literary agents and editors who attend will be receptive to receiving your work and future queries. The faculty and other conferees may offer the names of editors and agents to contact. Writers' groups are often formed by some of the conferees and continue meeting after the conference.

Conference Tips

Just showing up and being present in the hope that by osmosis you'll learn how to be a better writer will not get you far. There are a number of things you can do to maximize your experience aside from common sense considerations like attending as many functions as you can and paying attention. Factors unique to writers' conference you should keep in mind are:

- If manuscript submissions are critiqued by faculty, make certain you submit your manuscript before the cutoff date and in the proper form.
- If there is a contest, be sure to enter before the deadline and comply with the submission rules.
- If agents and editors are available for individual appointments, sign up as early as you can.
- Do not bring your book-length manuscript to the conference.
- Have sufficient writing material to take notes; don't plan on bringing a laptop to workshops.
- Do not be intimidated or afraid to ask questions because you consider yourself a novice; most conferees are just like you in terms of experience.

Writers' Workshops

Another forum you might want to consider in honing your writing proficiency is to attend a writers' workshop. Writers' workshops may be as brief as one hour or as long as several weeks, but what they all have in common is affording an occasion to have your work read and critiqued by the workshop's leader and other participants.

ESSENTIAL

Writers' conferences provide a number of activities including meeting with other writers, editors, and agents; listening to presentations and speeches; attending classes and workshops; socializing; submitting work to be critiqued; and entering contests. Writers' workshops concentrate on the submissions, reading, and critiquing of the work of the participants; this process is sometimes called having a piece "work-shopped."

Most writers' conferences include workshops in their programs, especially if the conference is more than one day. But there are also programs that focus almost entirely on workshops such as the summer programs offered by the University of Iowa and Bennington College Writers' Workshop. Some programs concentrate on a specific genre while others are more general, so you should be certain there is a workshop relevant to your needs.

Writers' Groups

Writers' groups can be small or large, structured or informal, specialized or general, but they all provide a forum for you to receive feedback for your work. Some writers' groups invite speakers or discuss other aspects of writing but for the most part, the chief function is to enable the members to tender their work to other sets of eyes. The major difference between writers' groups and workshops is that workshops are generally sponsored by an organization or educational institution while writers' groups operate much like any club of like-minded individuals. Some writers' groups are open to every genre, while others may be specialized; some have only a handful of members, while others do not limit the number attending; some charge dues and meet in public forums, while others are free and meet in homes; some groups are completely open while others require a vote to admit new members; meetings may be held weekly or monthly or anywhere in between.

Family and friends rarely make for good readers to provide impartial criticism for your work. Workshops and writers' groups afford a forum to obtain objective opinions. Despite certain benefits from having others comment on your work, many writers prefer not to share their work and it is never read by anyone else until the submission process begins.

The most important factor to consider in deciding upon a particular group is the one thing you probably won't be able to answer until after you join; that is, whether you feel comfortable with the other members. Unless you will be forming a new group consisting of people you already know or you are already acquainted with several of the members of an existing group, it's going to be a matter of showing up, giving it a try, and seeing how it works out. If you are uncomfortable, you should move on to another group.

Keep in mind that you have two sets of responsibilities as a member of a writers' group. For one thing, most groups require that you submit material to be read and critiqued. The second role you must play is that of a reader providing constructive criticism and commentary. Flattering the writer with accolades is not fulfilling your responsibility; you need to offer suggestions and it should go without saying that you must do this in a civil way.

Finding a Writers' Group

Because writing is a solitary endeavor, many writers have little or no contact with other writers. The editors, publishers, and agents writers come into contact with do not form a pool of potential members for a writers' group. However, you can often locate a writers' group in one of the following ways:

- Writers' conferences
- Workshops and classes
- Search the Internet, especially links to writers' conferences
- The section of the newspaper that lists community activities, groups, and meetings
- Postings at libraries and bookstores
- Other writers you know

Noncredit Classes

Perhaps you prefer a more structured approach to develop your writing proficiency, in which case you should consider the traditional classroom setting in lieu of or in addition to workshops, conferences, and writers' groups. Yet at the same time, you are not about to spend tens of thousands of dollars and commit yourself to matriculating at a college or university. The good news is that noncredit classes may offer the right setting for you.

Noncredit writing classes almost always focus on a specific topic or genre such as writing short stories or magazine writing or getting published. Some courses concentrate on developing a specific set of skills such as researching on the Internet or employing literary techniques in your writing. Just make certain when you register for a course that it is one from which you can benefit and that it fits your schedule. Most classes are in the evening or on weekends and are held once a week for up to ten weeks.

ESSENTIAL

To obtain the best results from a noncredit class you should treat it just as you would any classroom situation: try to attend every session; complete every assignment; participate fully; and intermingle with your classmates. In fact, it is not unusual for the students in a class to form a writers' group to meet once the class ends.

Selecting Noncredit Classes

Many adult education programs that are operated by the local high school or municipality offer writing courses. A number of colleges and universities have noncredit programs. Occasionally, libraries and bookstores may hold classes and you may even find that writing classes are held on special theme cruises. Naturally, the Internet is a source for instruction as well.

If you want to maximize the benefit you'll obtain from a class, it's important to choose wisely and with care. Some of the factors to weigh are:

- The cost compared with competing programs
- The convenience of the location
- The quality and experience of the instructor
- The maximum number of students permitted
- The reputation of the program
- The classroom environment
- The course description
- The course matches your interest

Getting a Degree

There are many good reasons to obtain a degree related to writing: you'll learn skills to make you a better writer; a degree will open up employment opportunities; you can benefit from the community of faculty and fellow students; you'll develop knowledge, confidence, and professionalism. The one thing a diploma will not guarantee is that you will succeed in your goals to be published. While having a degree will certainly aid in your quest, do not expect editors, agents, and publishers to come knocking on your door pleading for material to publish.

One of the most important factors in deciding whether you want to pursue a degree and which program to choose should be how you intend to apply it to your vocation. In other words, it should either be related to your current "day job" or provide entry into a new field while at the same time complementing your skills and experience as a writer. This is particularly true of undergraduate programs.

Undergraduate Programs

There was a time when choosing a major best suited to foster a writing career was simple; if you want to write nonfiction, become a journalist (although many journalists like Hemingway wrote fiction), and if it's fiction you want to write, major in English. From a practical standpoint, you made your living working for newspapers and magazines or taught English, allowing you to pursue other writing activities. While these still remain viable options, it's no longer a simple matter, with many newspapers downsizing or closing and teaching English requiring a degree in education or an advanced degree. To complicate matters further, there are now numerous undergraduate majors pertaining to writing but these programs, though perfecting writing skills, do not always lead to many job opportunities.

Finally, in deciding upon an undergraduate major, think about how it will qualify you to obtain an advanced degree. On the graduate level, you will find many more programs designed almost exclusively to writing.

Graduate Degrees

Thirty years ago, you could easily count the institutions offering advanced degrees in writing, with the University of Iowa leading the list. Today, there are hundreds of graduate programs around the country designed to develop writing skills. However, it essentially comes down to two options; pursue an MFA (masters in fine arts) or an MA in English.

FACT

An MFA is generally inferior to an MA in English, so it may be more difficult to secure a teaching position if you have an MFA rather than an MA. On the other hand, an MFA is a "terminal" degree since it does not lead to a PhD and once a teaching position is secured, there is normally no expectation to continue for a PhD.

MFA programs usually consist of thirty credits while MA programs typically require the completion of sixty credits. MFA programs may focus on creative writing, poetry, plays, or writing in general. MA degrees are commonly obtainable in English with an emphasis on a number of subcategories. Several institutions offer an MA in English and publishing.

You really need to investigate the respective programs you are considering and in many ways this is similar to choosing an undergraduate degree. Once again, keep in mind that despite the value of an advanced degree, it does not provide a straight path to having your work published.

Publicists

Throughout this book you have learned that when it comes to promoting your nonfiction book, most of the burden is set on the author's shoulders. You will probably have to prepare a press kit; list newspapers and periodicals where reviews and publicity can be sought; arrange book signings; send requests for interviews and appearances to the media; and contact groups to schedule presentations. Although this has nothing to do with making you a better writer, without respectable sales on your current book, you may not have an opportunity to secure a publisher for your next project.

Is a Publicist for You?

Unless you are one of the lucky few with a real commitment from your publisher to promote your book, you must be ready, willing, and able to do what is necessary to promote your book. If not, then you should consider hiring a publicist. Before reaching a final decision however, you need to make one calculation. No matter how gratifying to your ego to have your own publicist and not be troubled with the mundane and sometimes awkward task of promoting your book, you should weigh the financial factors.

ALERT

Being assigned a publicist by your publisher does not mean you do not need to promote the book yourself or that you will not benefit from retaining your own publicist. Except for the author with a potential blockbuster and substantial sums allocated for publicity, most authors get scant attention from the publicist to whom they have been assigned.

Publicists do not come cheap nor do they work for a percentage of sales. You must pay them and while the rates vary, you will find yourself spending many hundreds and likely thousands of dollars. So the first thing to do is take the royalty you earn per book and determine how many books must be sold before you recoup what you pay the publicist. Then ask yourself if it's worth it.

If you do decide you want a publicist, you should take into account the fee, experience, location, and personality of each person you are considering. However, you also should determine if the publicist has represented authors before or is agreeable to working on a book promotion project. Check out firms that work with authors such as O'Connor Communications (*www.oconnorpr.com*) and Blackman-Brady Communications (*www.black manbradycommunications.com*).

The Secret to Being a Successful Writer

It's really not much of a secret to become the best writer you can be. In fact, all you need to know can be summed up in one word—*write*. It's as simple as that. Of course, what you have learned in this book and what you still can learn from courses, workshops, and other writers will help you hone your writing skills, but the bottom line is that the more you write, the better a writer you'll become.

You already know that you must persevere if you want to get published but you also must persevere while you work at your writing. It doesn't always come easy and as satisfying as it may be, there will be times you'll want to bolt from your desk and get as far away as you can from writing. At such times, feel free to do so and take a break. But as long as you find yourself returning to write some more, you're on your way to becoming a successful writer.

ESSENTIAL

In addition to writing, another key ingredient to becoming a better writer is to read. While you should read as much as you can in the genre you're writing, you should also read other genres. There is much crossover in terms of writing techniques and you will benefit not only from reading other nonfiction categories but fiction as well.

Lastly, just what is it that makes for a "successful" writer? If it's a question of getting published, making substantial sums of money, becoming famous and landing spots on television shows, then the standard for success is easy to discern and whether you reach it or not will be obvious. But on the other hand, if being a successful writer means finding your work fulfilling, setting personal goals and attaining them, having others appreciate your work even if it is only a handful of readers, taking pride in the finished product, and walking away from your writer's desk feeling good, then you'll know when you have become a successful writer.

APPENDIX A

Writing Samples

OPINION PIECE EXCERPT

"Some Muggles Aren't Impressed"

By Larry Atkins

Kids around the world are spellbound by J. K. Rowling's *Harry Potter and the Order of the Phoenix*. However, some people are out to muzzle the young wizard.

Throughout the country, parents, school districts, religious groups and others have attempted to censor the bestselling Harry Potter series because of the books' alleged occult/Satanic theme—its witchcraft, wizardry, encouragement of dishonesty, religious viewpoint, and violence. According to the American Library Association, the Harry Potter series has topped the list of books challenged for content or appropriateness.

Several elementary schools nationwide have banned the books, and there are efforts to ban Potter from public school classrooms in 26 states. During the last two years, religious groups in New Mexico and Western Pennsylvania burned the Harry Potter books, citing the witchcraft theme.

In 1999, a school superintendent and school board in Michigan banned classroom readings of Harry Potter, required parental permission for older students to check out the books from school libraries and forbade librarians from ordering future books in the series. A teacher and a reading tutor organized students, parents, teachers and others who opposed the ban to form "Muggles for Harry Potter." (In the Potter series, muggles are people without magical powers.)

Within nine months, 18,000 people nationwide joined the campaign. Through the protesters' efforts, the Michigan school district lifted all restrictions on the books, except for classroom readings for kindergarten through fifth-graders.

The Potter series joins a long list of challenged books such as Maya Angelou's *I Know Why the Caged Bird Sings*, J. D. Salinger's *The Catcher in the Rye*, and John Steinbeck's *Of Mice and Men*.

In *Board of Education v. Pico*, the United States Supreme Court held in a 1982 decision that local school boards may not remove books from school library shelves simply because they dislike the ideas contained in those books and seek by their removal to prescribe what shall be orthodox in politics, nationalism, religion, or other matters of opinion. The Pico plurality opinion indicated that removal of books is permissible where the book contained pervasive vulgarity or if the book was educationally unsuitable. The court stated that the First Amendment includes the right to receive ideas.

Readers could object to many great books on many counts. . . . But how far do you take it? Should parents prevent kids from reading the Bible because it contains bloody stories? Should you ban *The Diary of Anne Frank* because the Holocaust is a disturbing subject?

Authors of great books take creative risks and challenge the reader to use his or her imagination. Otherwise, kids' books would be as bland, non-controversial, sugarcoated and uninspiring as a Bob Saget sitcom or a Teletubbies script.

With all the evil and violence in society, it's natural for parents to want to protect their children from bad influences in the books they read, movies and television shows they watch, music they listen to, and video games they play.

But, a parent must view a book in its entirety. The Potter books do focus on magic and the occult. However, there are overwhelming themes of morality, love, bravery, loyalty and good triumphing over evil. Kids across the world have identified with and related to Harry as he works his way through life's struggles. Harry's even made it cool to read books and to wear glasses.

The greatest magic of the Potter series doesn't occur at the Hogwarts School of Witchcraft and Wizardry or at the World Quidditch Cup. It occurs when millions of kids around the world put down their X box video game and eagerly pick up a 870 page book.

Reprinted with permission of the author. Appeared in *Cleveland Plain Dealer*, June 27, 2003.

ARTICLE EXCERPT

"Raising Champions: Helping Your Children Reach Their Athletic Goals"

By Cory Bank, PhD

One of my primary responsibilities as a sports psychologist is to make sure each athlete is training intelligently in order to enjoy the process and ensure success. Parents often ask how they can assist in helping their child achieve their goals in a safe, enjoyable, and effective manner. The following are four common and crucial areas that can play a key role in helping parents increase their children's confidence, create more enjoyment and overall success with their respective sports.

Pay Attention To Your Child's Physical Training. Specifically, this involves avoiding the trap known as overtraining that many children who play organized sports fall into. Symptoms are feeling burned out . . . feeling sluggish, a decrease in athletic performance, and a higher resting heart rate. . . .

In my clinical practice, I recently worked with a female swimmer who was swimming for school and a club team and practiced two hours a day for six days a week. She did this routinely almost all year long for four years. Thanks to this grueling workout schedule, she tore her rotator cuff and had to have surgery. She rushed her recovery, tore it again, and the colleges that were scouting her withdrew their interest. By the time I began working with her she was very frustrated and depressed.

Be careful to avoid overtraining by working out the majority of days on the easier side. . . .

Implement A Bit Of Psychological Training. Teaching children to think positively can contribute significantly to the success and enjoyment of your child's sport. Use cognitive scripting, a branch of cognitive psychology that states the way we think about our situations will largely determine whether they will have a positive or negative outcome. . . .

Let's take an example where a runner estimates that her first mile time for a 5K race should be six minutes, but actually takes seven. She might ask herself, "How come I ran so slow and how am I ever going to make up all that time?" This might lead to a negative outcome in which she feels doubt, increased stress, increased body tension, and ultimately a slower time. However, if she asks herself, "How can I make up a bit of time in the next few minutes and enjoy the race as much as possible?" she will more likely realize a more favorable outcome because she is assuming she will enjoy the race and is focused on only the next few minutes. . . .

When we believe we have more control and power over a situation, we tend to feel more confident and respond more favorably. Practice with your child by asking effective questions to increase his or her sense of control, confidence, and power. . . .

Nutritional Training: re-hydrating and eating within a half an hour after training sessions, practices, and races. . . . If your child does not re-hydrate and eat within half an hour after training and racing, he or she is decreasing chances for maximum recovery. . . .

Pay Attention To Your Child's Preferences To Ecological Variables of Competition. . . .

If you are looking to maximize your child's performance, confidence and enjoyment in athletics, it is wise to find a good fit between your child's personality characteristics and the environment of the types of different sports.

For example, if your child prefers competing in a team environment then he would probably prefer basketball over golf. Does your child like short events such as a four hundred meter race or does she prefer entering and running the mile? . . . Knowing your child's answers to these questions should help you both select with greater accuracy fitness activities that will maximize confidence, performance and enjoyment!

_____

Reprinted with permission of the author. Appeared in *Parents Express*, December 2008.

BOOK EXCERPT

Mom, There's a Man in the Kitchen and He's Wearing Your Robe

By Ellie Slott Fisher

Preening in her new lavender underwear while contemplating a closetful of expertly tailored but boring business suits, newly single Gladys agonized over her first date in twenty-five years. She had no idea what to wear, where to go, or who would pay. When a friend suggested she feel romantic and treat herself to a teddy, Gladys was thinking stuffed animal.

She dug out her dog-eared copy of *The Sensual Woman*, dabbed on expensive perfume, applied new makeup, and carefully slid her first-ever issue of *Cosmo* under her bed like a teenaged boy hiding *Playboy*.

All suddenly single women can relate.

After years of feeling more at home in the bathroom than in the bedroom and being so clueless to think streaking meant she was out of Windex, Gladys had to update her knowledge of social rituals and take stock of herself.

Rewarding dating experiences are preceded by a boost in self-confidence, an improvement in attitude, and, if necessary, a refinement of appearance. Whether you exercise, enter therapy, order a subscription to the *New York Times* (at least read the front page), change your hair color, or undergo plastic surgery, if you feel good about yourself, mentally and physically, dating will not only be life altering and life affirming—it will be a blast.

Don't let a negative reaction from your children to your first date dissuade you from going on one. It's a first for them, too, and time, honesty and patience (especially yours) will ultimately result in their adapting to this change in your life.

————

Reprinted with permission of the author.

PERSONAL ESSAY EXCERPT

"Train to Nowhere"

By Richard D. Bank

Sometime on 9 November 1938, under the cover of night, my grandparents boarded a train bound for nowhere. Or, more precisely, the train pulling out of an otherwise empty station in the German town of Odenbach did have a destination. It's just that my grandparents did not.

While the house where they had lived and raised a family was being ransacked by SA troopers, assorted Nazi thugs, and anti-Semitic rabble, my grandparents slipped away unnoticed. With few worldly possessions, they stole down the street glancing back only once to see a neighbor rummage through the clothing piled on the curb. My grandparents never saw their home again. . . .

Using as an excuse the killing of a legation secretary in the German embassy in Paris by a Polish Jew named Herschel Grynzpan, the Third Reich unleashed the virulent throngs and added a new dimension to the persecution of Germany's Jews. When *Kristallnacht*, as the bleak hours of November 9th and 10th came to be known, reached a fiery end, Hitler had instigated the worst pogrom in German history: 500 synagogues were burned; seven thousand Jewish businesses were destroyed; tens of thousands of homes were invaded; 90 Jews were killed; hundreds of women were raped; and 30,000 Jews were arrested. . . .

In the ten months following *Kristallnacht*, another 100,000 to 150,000 Jews fled the country that had been their home for centuries. Those who stayed behind did so for one reason only—they had nowhere to go; which is what made my grandparents frantic hours endured on a lurching train both symbolic and prophetic.

A sympathetic conductor, who knew my grandfather from his frequent business trips, cautioned them not to disembark in Mainz where they had family. It was much too dangerous, he whispered. They had no money to go any farther, but he allowed them to remain until late the next day when they scurried off in the city of Furth, skulking through alleyways to a temporary haven with other family members.

Like all German Jews after *Kristallnacht*, my grandparents were without assets, dispossessed of their home, and in fear of their lives. The Nazis created the greatest "Catch-22" of all time. In order to avoid death, the Jews must leave . . . but in order to emigrate, they had to have the funds to pay the exorbitant exit fees and be able to demonstrate to the country of their destination that they had capital and would not be a burden. Much as the German government wanted the Jews gone, they made it practically impossible for them to comply.

Only two weeks earlier, my grandparents had managed to dispatch their two daughters to the United States, not knowing if they would see them again. After *Kristallnacht*, they had even less hope of reaching America. Instead, my grandparents felt the way they did during those interminable hours spent on a train rambling through the night.

But this time there was not even the promise of dawn, and the next train that would come for them would have a destination beyond their most horrific nightmare. Somehow, it was a train they managed to avoid.

————

Appeared in *Midstream*, November 1977

ARTICLE EXCERPT

"The Second Crash of '08: Our 'Derivative' World Series"

By Dan Rottenberg

As a former financial writer as well as a former sportswriter, I ask you: What do Wall Street and the World Series have in common? And the answer: Both require widespread suspension of disbelief in order to function effectively. And both collapsed this fall.

John Maynard Keynes once observed that the stock market is like a newspaper beauty contest in which readers must pick not the prettiest faces but the faces that other readers are likely to consider the prettiest. . . . The rise of derivatives—that is, financial instruments . . . mortgage-backed securities, for example, arose from the best of intentions. By repackaging a mortgage loan as a security and dicing it into small bits, the risk of lending money could be spread so widely that no lender would feel the pain of an individual default, and consequently home loans would be easier to obtain.

This ingenious system worked wonderfully until it collapsed this year. Only with the recent crash . . . has it occurred to us that pain and risk are good things: If no lender fears getting hurt in any transaction, no one will take the responsibility to make sure that borrowers are credit-worthy.

Baseball operates somewhat the same way. There is no intrinsic value in the ability of nine men to run around a field throwing, hitting and catching baseballs—unless huge numbers of people persuade themselves that such an activity is impor-

tant. That's why the integrity of the whole context . . . is so critical. If you tamper with it too much, the whole structure falls apart for lack of meaning.

Such a moment occurred . . . on Monday night, October 27, when the Phillies and the Tampa Bay Rays attempted to play the fifth game of the World Series in pouring rain and 39-degree weather. . . . As I watched drenched players wearing earmuffs slosh about in mud puddles and chase wind-blown pop flies halfway across the infield, the whole thing lost its logic.

"Game 5 is hopelessly tainted by what transpired between the time the game should have been called and the middle of the sixth inning, when it was finally suspended," wrote Phil Sheridan in the *Inquirer*. True enough—but Game 4 on Saturday night was tainted too. That contest was delayed 91 minutes by rain; it didn't start until after 10 P.M. and didn't end until 1:47 A.M. . . .

Sheridan raised the right question—why play an autumn game at night, when it is so much nicer and warmer in the afternoon?—but he didn't go far enough. The critical question is: Why is a summer game like baseball still being played at all at the very end of October?

The answer, of course, is the invention, a generation ago, of post-season playoffs . . . which not only extend the season but also render the regular season largely meaningless. And that raises another question that nobody . . . dares to ask: Did the two teams playing in this year's World Series really deserve to be there?

In the world of my youth, Major League Baseball consisted of two leagues of eight teams each. Each team played an equal number of games against every other team in its league. When the regular season ended, the winners of the two leagues played each other in the World Series. Simple, fair, and comprehensible. . . .

Today the end of the season is much more exciting but alas also much more pointless. Each league consists of 15 teams broken into three divisions. Each team plays barely more games against the teams in its own division than the teams in the other two divisions. Each team also plays a random assortment of games against teams in the other league. Despite this inequality, all games are counted equally. At season's end, the "winners" of the three divisions enter the playoffs, along with a fourth "wild-card" team that didn't win any division.

In other words, the team that compiled the best record all season long—this year the Chicago Cubs in the National League and the Los Angeles Angels in the American—won't necessarily play in the World Series. . . .

To put it another way: Major League Baseball today isn't really baseball; it's a *derivative* of baseball. No one really understands how it works. And as sages as diverse as Warren Buffet and the late Robert Montgomery Scott have observed, if you don't understand it, don't do it.

Reprinted with permission of the author. Appeared in *Broad Street Review*, October 28, 2008 (*www.broadstreetreview.com*).

Sample Permissions Agreement

Date:

_____ ("Licensor") of _____ (Address),

and

_____ ("Licensee") of _____ (Address)

hereby enter into this Permissions Agreement regarding the use of selected written materials from the Licensor ("Licensor's Work") in Licensee's Work tentatively titled

_____

on the terms described below.

1. Licensed Materials.
This Permissions Agreement applies to Licensor's Work as specifically described below:

_____

_____

_____

2. Grant of Rights.
Licensee has the nonexclusive right to reproduce, publish, distribute, and sell the Licensed Work as part of the Licensee's Work in all other languages throughout the world, including but not limited to book form, adaptation, anthology, collected works, book club, digest, abridgement, condensation, serialization, syndication, periodical, audio, visual, performance, dramatic, motion pictures, animation, radio and television, theater, filmstrip, microfilm, microcard, Braille and large type, foreign language editions, recorded readings, visual projections, information-storage and retrieval systems, all electronic versions (including without limitation software, electronic books or "e-books," interactive or multimedia versions, other screen-display technologies,

as well as verbatim text-only electronic editions), all other mechanical reproduction and transcription (including print-on-demand versions), all versions in any and all media and all technologies now existing or which may in the future come into existence, and all future editions and other derivative works; and

(2) to grant licenses to third parties to exploit any of the rights granted herein specifically related to the Licensee's Work.

3. Submission.
The Licensor agrees to provide the Licensee with the Licensor's Work by the following date: _____

4. Warrantees and Indemnities:
Licensor warrants to Licensee that Licensor owns and controls all rights to the Licensed Work as defined in this Agreement and agrees to indemnify, hold harmless, and defend Licensee from any claims, loss, or liability arising from a breach of the foregoing warranty.

5. Acknowledgement on Copyright Page.
The Licensee agrees to acknowledge the Licensor on the copyright page as follows:

_____

_____

_____

Agreed and confirmed:

_____   _____
Licensor   *Licensee*

_____   _____
Date   *Date*

APPENDIX C

Glossary

ASJA

American Society of Journalists and Authors.

Assignment

An authorization to proceed with a project as set forth in the terms of the assignment letter or contract.

Authorized biography

A project where the author was designated by the subject to write the biography.

Autobiography

A book about the author's entire life.

Bio

A short biographical sketch of the writer written in the third person.

Blurb

An endorsement that typically consists of one or two sentences praising the book found on the back cover, inside jacket, or in the front matter.

Book proposal

The submission made to editors, agents and publishers by an author marketing a nonfiction book project.

Bullets (bullet lists)

Lists that appear with dots or asterisks placed before each item.

Byline

The writer's name appearing in the publication.

Chronological double-helix

Writing an article beginning in the style of the double-helix but once the important facts have been presented, events are imparted in chronological order.

Chronological report

Writing an article by reporting the events in the order in which they occurred.

Clips

Copies of the writer's published pieces.

Copyright

Protection afforded to specific categories of original work fixed in tangible form so they cannot be copied or misappropriated without permission from the copyright holder.

Copyright infringement

The illegal misappropriation of work that is protected by copyright.

Creative nonfiction

Writing nonfiction utilizing the creative techniques of fiction writing including literary devices while the content remains factual and accurate.

Deadline

The date the completed work must be received by the editor or publisher.

Double-helix

Writing an article presenting the facts in order of importance but alternating between two separate sets of information.

Fair use

A defense to copyright infringement that permits researchers, scholars, educators, and others to utilize small portions of a copyrighted work for socially beneficial purposes without obtaining consent.

Fiction

Writing that arises from the writer's imagination.

First person

The writer speaks directly to the reader and frequently uses *I*.

First serial rights

The right to publish a piece for the first time, after which the rights revert to the holder of the copyright.

Foreword

Several pages introducing the book typically written by a well-known authority.

Hook

The opening sentences that are designed to pique the reader's interest and make the reader want to read more.

How-to books

Books that furnish information on a specific subject or task.

Inverted pyramid

Structuring an article presenting facts in order of importance.

ISBN

The international standard book number that is assigned to each commercial book as a means of identification.

Kill fee

A predetermined amount to be paid if an assigned work is not published for any reason other than it did not meet the requirements of the assignment.

Libel

A false statement that damages the reputation of a living person or entity that has been published or read by someone other than the subject of the defamation.

Literary essays

Essays that inform and sometimes deliver a message that are written in a style evincing a command of writing techniques and a sense of language.

Literary license

A term that refers to taking some divergence from truth or accuracy in writing nonfiction to enhance the narrative.

Memoir

A personal reminiscence about some part of the writer's life.

MS/MSS

Manuscript of a book or article.

Multiple submissions

Submitting more than one piece to a publisher at the same time.

Nonfiction

Writing that is based on facts and purported to be true and accurate.

Nonfiction books

Works of nonfiction generally between 50,000 and 90,000 words.

Novels

Works of fiction usually between 60,000 and 80,000 words.

On-spec

An offer to consider a submission "on speculation" retaining the right to reject the piece for any reason.

Op-ed

A term for an opinion piece that is located on the page opposite the editorial page of a newspaper.

Personal essay

An essay about one or more personal experiences or memories of the writer; sometimes referred to as a memoir.

Plagiarism

The failure to provide an acknowledgment to the author of the material and taking credit for oneself.

Platform

An author's existing audience consisting of people who might purchase the book.

Point of view (POV)

One of four ways in which the reader is addressed: first person; second person; third person omniscient; third person objective.

Profile interview

A piece in which the person being interviewed is the subject of the article.

Promotional plan

An author's strategy to market and sell the book.

Query

A letter that requests an assignment or permission to send work to be considered for publication.

Research-oriented interview

An interview in which the subject supplies information about the project.

SASE

Self-addressed, stamped envelope.

Scholarly books

Books directed to an academic audience.

Second person

The writer directly addresses the reader and commonly employs *you* and *your*.

Self-help books

Books that offer advice on improving oneself or some aspect of one's life.

Selling handle

One or two sentences succinctly stating what the book is about that could become the subtitle on the front cover.

Simultaneous submission

Submitting one piece to more than one publisher, editor, or agent at the same time.

SPJ

Society of Professional Journalists.

Storytelling model

An article that is written utilizing some of the techniques of fiction writing.

Target market

A specific segment of the population predisposed to have an interest in the book and to which the book is directed and promoted.

Third person objective

The writer describes things as they seem from the outside.

Third person omniscient

The writer knows everything there is to know and can enter the minds and thoughts of the subjects.

TOC

Table of contents

Voice of authority

Writing in a tone that manifests confidence.

Work-shopped

Having work read and critiqued by others as part of a writer's group or workshop class.

Index

THE EVERYTHING® SERIES!

BUSINESS & PERSONAL FINANCE

Everything® Accounting Book
Everything® Budgeting Book, 2nd Ed.
Everything® Business Planning Book
Everything® Coaching and Mentoring Book, 2nd Ed.
Everything® Fundraising Book
Everything® Get Out of Debt Book
Everything® Grant Writing Book, 2nd Ed.
Everything® Guide to Buying Foreclosures
Everything® Guide to Fundraising, $15.95
Everything® Guide to Mortgages
Everything® Guide to Personal Finance for Single Mothers
Everything® Home-Based Business Book, 2nd Ed.
Everything® Homebuying Book, 3rd Ed., $15.95
Everything® Homeselling Book, 2nd Ed.
Everything® Human Resource Management Book
Everything® Improve Your Credit Book
Everything® Investing Book, 2nd Ed.
Everything® Landlording Book
Everything® Leadership Book, 2nd Ed.
Everything® Managing People Book, 2nd Ed.
Everything® Negotiating Book
Everything® Online Auctions Book
Everything® Online Business Book
Everything® Personal Finance Book
Everything® Personal Finance in Your 20s & 30s Book, 2nd Ed.
Everything® Personal Finance in Your 40s & 50s Book, $15.95
Everything® Project Management Book, 2nd Ed.
Everything® Real Estate Investing Book
Everything® Retirement Planning Book
Everything® Robert's Rules Book, $7.95
Everything® Selling Book
Everything® Start Your Own Business Book, 2nd Ed.
Everything® Wills & Estate Planning Book

COOKING

Everything® Barbecue Cookbook
Everything® Bartender's Book, 2nd Ed., $9.95
Everything® Calorie Counting Cookbook
Everything® Cheese Book
Everything® Chinese Cookbook
Everything® Classic Recipes Book
Everything® Cocktail Parties & Drinks Book
Everything® College Cookbook
Everything® Cooking for Baby and Toddler Book
Everything® Diabetes Cookbook
Everything® Easy Gourmet Cookbook
Everything® Fondue Cookbook
Everything® Food Allergy Cookbook, $15.95
Everything® Fondue Party Book
Everything® Gluten-Free Cookbook
Everything® Glycemic Index Cookbook
Everything® Grilling Cookbook
Everything® Healthy Cooking for Parties Book, $15.95
Everything® Holiday Cookbook
Everything® Indian Cookbook
Everything® Lactose-Free Cookbook
Everything® Low-Cholesterol Cookbook

Everything® Low-Fat High-Flavor Cookbook, 2nd Ed., $15.95
Everything® Low-Salt Cookbook
Everything® Meals for a Month Cookbook
Everything® Meals on a Budget Cookbook
Everything® Mediterranean Cookbook
Everything® Mexican Cookbook
Everything® No Trans Fat Cookbook
Everything® One-Pot Cookbook, 2nd Ed., $15.95
Everything® Organic Cooking for Baby & Toddler Book, $15.95
Everything® Pizza Cookbook
Everything® Quick Meals Cookbook, 2nd Ed., $15.95
Everything® Slow Cooker Cookbook
Everything® Slow Cooking for a Crowd Cookbook
Everything® Soup Cookbook
Everything® Stir-Fry Cookbook
Everything® Sugar-Free Cookbook
Everything® Tapas and Small Plates Cookbook
Everything® Tex-Mex Cookbook
Everything® Thai Cookbook
Everything® Vegetarian Cookbook
Everything® Whole-Grain, High-Fiber Cookbook
Everything® Wild Game Cookbook
Everything® Wine Book, 2nd Ed.

GAMES

Everything® 15-Minute Sudoku Book, $9.95
Everything® 30-Minute Sudoku Book, $9.95
Everything® Bible Crosswords Book, $9.95
Everything® Blackjack Strategy Book
Everything® Brain Strain Book, $9.95
Everything® Bridge Book
Everything® Card Games Book
Everything® Card Tricks Book, $9.95
Everything® Casino Gambling Book, 2nd Ed.
Everything® Chess Basics Book
Everything® Christmas Crosswords Book, $9.95
Everything® Craps Strategy Book
Everything® Crossword and Puzzle Book
Everything® Crosswords and Puzzles for Quote Lovers Book, $9.95
Everything® Crossword Challenge Book
Everything® Crosswords for the Beach Book, $9.95
Everything® Cryptic Crosswords Book, $9.95
Everything® Cryptograms Book, $9.95
Everything® Easy Crosswords Book
Everything® Easy Kakuro Book, $9.95
Everything® Easy Large-Print Crosswords Book
Everything® Games Book, 2nd Ed.
Everything® Giant Book of Crosswords
Everything® Giant Sudoku Book, $9.95
Everything® Giant Word Search Book
Everything® Kakuro Challenge Book, $9.95
Everything® Large-Print Crossword Challenge Book
Everything® Large-Print Crosswords Book
Everything® Large-Print Travel Crosswords Book
Everything® Lateral Thinking Puzzles Book, $9.95
Everything® Literary Crosswords Book, $9.95
Everything® Mazes Book
Everything® Memory Booster Puzzles Book, $9.95

Everything® Movie Crosswords Book, $9.95
Everything® Music Crosswords Book, $9.95
Everything® Online Poker Book
Everything® Pencil Puzzles Book, $9.95
Everything® Poker Strategy Book
Everything® Pool & Billiards Book
Everything® Puzzles for Commuters Book, $9.95
Everything® Puzzles for Dog Lovers Book, $9.95
Everything® Sports Crosswords Book, $9.95
Everything® Test Your IQ Book, $9.95
Everything® Texas Hold 'Em Book, $9.95
Everything® Travel Crosswords Book, $9.95
Everything® Travel Mazes Book, $9.95
Everything® Travel Word Search Book, $9.95
Everything® TV Crosswords Book, $9.95
Everything® Word Games Challenge Book
Everything® Word Scramble Book
Everything® Word Search Book

HEALTH

Everything® Alzheimer's Book
Everything® Diabetes Book
Everything® First Aid Book, $9.95
Everything® Green Living Book
Everything® Health Guide to Addiction and Recovery
Everything® Health Guide to Adult Bipolar Disorder
Everything® Health Guide to Arthritis
Everything® Health Guide to Controlling Anxiety
Everything® Health Guide to Depression
Everything® Health Guide to Diabetes, 2nd Ed.
Everything® Health Guide to Fibromyalgia
Everything® Health Guide to Menopause, 2nd Ed.
Everything® Health Guide to Migraines
Everything® Health Guide to Multiple Sclerosis
Everything® Health Guide to OCD
Everything® Health Guide to PMS
Everything® Health Guide to Postpartum Care
Everything® Health Guide to Thyroid Disease
Everything® Hypnosis Book
Everything® Low Cholesterol Book
Everything® Menopause Book
Everything® Nutrition Book
Everything® Reflexology Book
Everything® Stress Management Book
Everything® Superfoods Book, $15.95

HISTORY

Everything® American Government Book
Everything® American History Book, 2nd Ed.
Everything® American Revolution Book, $15.95
Everything® Civil War Book
Everything® Freemasons Book
Everything® Irish History & Heritage Book
Everything® World War II Book, 2nd Ed.

HOBBIES

Everything® Candlemaking Book
Everything® Cartooning Book
Everything® Coin Collecting Book
Everything® Digital Photography Book, 2nd Ed.

Everything® Dog Obedience Book
Everything® Dog Owner's Organizer, $16.95
Everything® Dog Training and Tricks Book
Everything® German Shepherd Book
Everything® Golden Retriever Book
Everything® Horse Book, 2nd Ed., $15.95
Everything® Horse Care Book
Everything® Horseback Riding Book
Everything® Labrador Retriever Book
Everything® Poodle Book
Everything® Pug Book
Everything® Puppy Book
Everything® Small Dogs Book
Everything® Tropical Fish Book
Everything® Yorkshire Terrier Book

REFERENCE

Everything® American Presidents Book
Everything® Blogging Book
Everything® Build Your Vocabulary Book, $9.95
Everything® Car Care Book
Everything® Classical Mythology Book
Everything® Da Vinci Book
Everything® Einstein Book
Everything® Enneagram Book
Everything® Etiquette Book, 2nd Ed.
Everything® Family Christmas Book, $15.95
Everything® Guide to C. S. Lewis & Narnia
Everything® Guide to Divorce, 2nd Ed., $15.95
Everything® Guide to Edgar Allan Poe
Everything® Guide to Understanding Philosophy
Everything® Inventions and Patents Book
Everything® Jacqueline Kennedy Onassis Book
Everything® John F. Kennedy Book
Everything® Mafia Book
Everything® Martin Luther King Jr. Book
Everything® Pirates Book
Everything® Private Investigation Book
Everything® Psychology Book
Everything® Public Speaking Book, $9.95
Everything® Shakespeare Book, 2nd Ed.

RELIGION

Everything® Angels Book
Everything® Bible Book
Everything® Bible Study Book with CD, $19.95
Everything® Buddhism Book
Everything® Catholicism Book
Everything® Christianity Book
Everything® Gnostic Gospels Book
Everything® Hinduism Book, $15.95
Everything® History of the Bible Book
Everything® Jesus Book
Everything® Jewish History & Heritage Book
Everything® Judaism Book
Everything® Kabbalah Book
Everything® Koran Book
Everything® Mary Book
Everything® Mary Magdalene Book
Everything® Prayer Book

Everything® Saints Book, 2nd Ed.
Everything® Torah Book
Everything® Understanding Islam Book
Everything® Women of the Bible Book
Everything® World's Religions Book

SCHOOL & CAREERS

Everything® Career Tests Book
Everything® College Major Test Book
Everything® College Survival Book, 2nd Ed.
Everything® Cover Letter Book, 2nd Ed.
Everything® Filmmaking Book
Everything® Get-a-Job Book, 2nd Ed.
Everything® Guide to Being a Paralegal
Everything® Guide to Being a Personal Trainer
Everything® Guide to Being a Real Estate Agent
Everything® Guide to Being a Sales Rep
Everything® Guide to Being an Event Planner
Everything® Guide to Careers in Health Care
Everything® Guide to Careers in Law Enforcement
Everything® Guide to Government Jobs
Everything® Guide to Starting and Running a Catering
   Business
Everything® Guide to Starting and Running a Restaurant
**Everything® Guide to Starting and Running
   a Retail Store**
Everything® Job Interview Book, 2nd Ed.
Everything® New Nurse Book
Everything® New Teacher Book
Everything® Paying for College Book
Everything® Practice Interview Book
Everything® Resume Book, 3rd Ed.
Everything® Study Book

SELF-HELP

Everything® Body Language Book
Everything® Dating Book, 2nd Ed.
Everything® Great Sex Book
**Everything® Guide to Caring for Aging Parents,
   $15.95**
Everything® Self-Esteem Book
Everything® Self-Hypnosis Book, $9.95
Everything® Tantric Sex Book

SPORTS & FITNESS

Everything® Easy Fitness Book
Everything® Fishing Book
Everything® Guide to Weight Training, $15.95
Everything® Krav Maga for Fitness Book
Everything® Running Book, 2nd Ed.
Everything® Triathlon Training Book, $15.95

TRAVEL

Everything® Family Guide to Coastal Florida
Everything® Family Guide to Cruise Vacations
Everything® Family Guide to Hawaii
Everything® Family Guide to Las Vegas, 2nd Ed.
Everything® Family Guide to Mexico
Everything® Family Guide to New England, 2nd Ed.

Everything® Family Guide to New York City, 3rd Ed.
**Everything® Family Guide to Northern California
   and Lake Tahoe**
Everything® Family Guide to RV Travel & Campgrounds
Everything® Family Guide to the Caribbean
Everything® Family Guide to the Disneyland® Resort, California
   Adventure®, Universal Studios®, and the Anaheim
   Area, 2nd Ed.
Everything® Family Guide to the Walt Disney World Resort®,
   Universal Studios®, and Greater Orlando, 5th Ed.
Everything® Family Guide to Timeshares
Everything® Family Guide to Washington D.C., 2nd Ed.

WEDDINGS

Everything® Bachelorette Party Book, $9.95
Everything® Bridesmaid Book, $9.95
Everything® Destination Wedding Book
Everything® Father of the Bride Book, $9.95
Everything® Green Wedding Book, $15.95
Everything® Groom Book, $9.95
Everything® Jewish Wedding Book, 2nd Ed., $15.95
Everything® Mother of the Bride Book, $9.95
Everything® Outdoor Wedding Book
Everything® Wedding Book, 3rd Ed.
Everything® Wedding Checklist, $9.95
Everything® Wedding Etiquette Book, $9.95
Everything® Wedding Organizer, 2nd Ed., $16.95
Everything® Wedding Shower Book, $9.95
Everything® Wedding Vows Book, 3rd Ed., $9.95
Everything® Wedding Workout Book
Everything® Weddings on a Budget Book, 2nd Ed., $9.95

WRITING

Everything® Creative Writing Book
Everything® Get Published Book, 2nd Ed.
Everything® Grammar and Style Book, 2nd Ed.
Everything® Guide to Magazine Writing
Everything® Guide to Writing a Book Proposal
Everything® Guide to Writing a Novel
Everything® Guide to Writing Children's Books
Everything® Guide to Writing Copy
Everything® Guide to Writing Graphic Novels
Everything® Guide to Writing Research Papers
Everything® Guide to Writing a Romance Novel, $15.95
Everything® Improve Your Writing Book, 2nd Ed.
Everything® Writing Poetry Book

Everything® Drawing Book
Everything® Family Tree Book, 2nd Ed.
Everything® Guide to Online Genealogy, $15.95
Everything® Knitting Book
Everything® Knots Book
Everything® Photography Book
Everything® Quilting Book
Everything® Sewing Book
Everything® Soapmaking Book, 2nd Ed.
Everything® Woodworking Book

HOME IMPROVEMENT

Everything® Feng Shui Book
Everything® Feng Shui Decluttering Book, $9.95
Everything® Fix-It Book
Everything® Green Living Book
Everything® Home Decorating Book
Everything® Home Storage Solutions Book
Everything® Homebuilding Book
Everything® Organize Your Home Book, 2nd Ed.

KIDS' BOOKS

All titles are $7.95
Everything® Fairy Tales Book, $14.95
Everything® Kids' Animal Puzzle & Activity Book
Everything® Kids' Astronomy Book
Everything® Kids' Baseball Book, 5th Ed.
Everything® Kids' Bible Trivia Book
Everything® Kids' Bugs Book
Everything® Kids' Cars and Trucks Puzzle and Activity Book
Everything® Kids' Christmas Puzzle & Activity Book
Everything® Kids' Connect the Dots
        Puzzle and Activity Book
Everything® Kids' Cookbook, 2nd Ed.
Everything® Kids' Crazy Puzzles Book
Everything® Kids' Dinosaurs Book
Everything® Kids' Dragons Puzzle and Activity Book
Everything® Kids' Environment Book $7.95
Everything® Kids' Fairies Puzzle and Activity Book
Everything® Kids' First Spanish Puzzle and Activity Book
Everything® Kids' Football Book
Everything® Kids' Geography Book
Everything® Kids' Gross Cookbook
Everything® Kids' Gross Hidden Pictures Book
Everything® Kids' Gross Jokes Book
Everything® Kids' Gross Mazes Book
Everything® Kids' Gross Puzzle & Activity Book
Everything® Kids' Halloween Puzzle & Activity Book
Everything® Kids' Hanukkah Puzzle and Activity Book
Everything® Kids' Hidden Pictures Book
Everything® Kids' Horses Book
Everything® Kids' Joke Book
Everything® Kids' Knock Knock Book
Everything® Kids' Learning French Book
Everything® Kids' Learning Spanish Book
Everything® Kids' Magical Science Experiments Book
Everything® Kids' Math Puzzles Book
Everything® Kids' Mazes Book
Everything® Kids' Money Book, 2nd Ed.
**Everything® Kids' Mummies, Pharaoh's, and Pyramids
        Puzzle and Activity Book**
Everything® Kids' Nature Book
Everything® Kids' Pirates Puzzle and Activity Book
Everything® Kids' Presidents Book
Everything® Kids' Princess Puzzle and Activity Book
Everything® Kids' Puzzle Book

Everything® Kids' Racecars Puzzle and Activity Book
Everything® Kids' Riddles & Brain Teasers Book
Everything® Kids' Science Experiments Book
Everything® Kids' Sharks Book
Everything® Kids' Soccer Book
Everything® Kids' Spelling Book
Everything® Kids' Spies Puzzle and Activity Book
Everything® Kids' States Book
Everything® Kids' Travel Activity Book
Everything® Kids' Word Search Puzzle and Activity Book

LANGUAGE

Everything® Conversational Japanese Book with CD, $19.95
Everything® French Grammar Book
Everything® French Phrase Book, $9.95
Everything® French Verb Book, $9.95
Everything® German Phrase Book, $9.95
Everything® German Practice Book with CD, $19.95
Everything® Inglés Book
Everything® Intermediate Spanish Book with CD, $19.95
Everything® Italian Phrase Book, $9.95
Everything® Italian Practice Book with CD, $19.95
Everything® Learning Brazilian Portuguese Book with CD, $19.95
Everything® Learning French Book with CD, 2nd Ed., $19.95
Everything® Learning German Book
Everything® Learning Italian Book
Everything® Learning Latin Book
Everything® Learning Russian Book with CD, $19.95
Everything® Learning Spanish Book
Everything® Learning Spanish Book with CD, 2nd Ed., $19.95
Everything® Russian Practice Book with CD, $19.95
Everything® Sign Language Book, $15.95
Everything® Spanish Grammar Book
Everything® Spanish Phrase Book, $9.95
Everything® Spanish Practice Book with CD, $19.95
Everything® Spanish Verb Book, $9.95
Everything® Speaking Mandarin Chinese Book with CD, $19.95

MUSIC

Everything® Bass Guitar Book with CD, $19.95
Everything® Drums Book with CD, $19.95
Everything® Guitar Book with CD, 2nd Ed., $19.95
Everything® Guitar Chords Book with CD, $19.95
Everything® Guitar Scales Book with CD, $19.95
Everything® Harmonica Book with CD, $15.95
Everything® Home Recording Book
Everything® Music Theory Book with CD, $19.95
Everything® Reading Music Book with CD, $19.95
Everything® Rock & Blues Guitar Book with CD, $19.95
Everything® Rock & Blues Piano Book with CD, $19.95
Everything® Rock Drums Book with CD, $19.95
Everything® Singing Book with CD, $19.95
Everything® Songwriting Book

NEW AGE

Everything® Astrology Book, 2nd Ed.
Everything® Birthday Personology Book
Everything® Celtic Wisdom Book, $15.95
Everything® Dreams Book, 2nd Ed.
Everything® Law of Attraction Book, $15.95
Everything® Love Signs Book, $9.95
Everything® Love Spells Book, $9.95
Everything® Palmistry Book
Everything® Psychic Book
Everything® Reiki Book

Everything® Sex Signs Book, $9.95
Everything® Spells & Charms Book, 2nd Ed.
Everything® Tarot Book, 2nd Ed.
Everything® Toltec Wisdom Book
Everything® Wicca & Witchcraft Book, 2nd Ed.

PARENTING

Everything® Baby Names Book, 2nd Ed.
Everything® Baby Shower Book, 2nd Ed.
Everything® Baby Sign Language Book with DVD
Everything® Baby's First Year Book
Everything® Birthing Book
Everything® Breastfeeding Book
Everything® Father-to-Be Book
Everything® Father's First Year Book
Everything® Get Ready for Baby Book, 2nd Ed.
Everything® Get Your Baby to Sleep Book, $9.95
Everything® Getting Pregnant Book
Everything® Guide to Pregnancy Over 35
Everything® Guide to Raising a One-Year-Old
Everything® Guide to Raising a Two-Year-Old
Everything® Guide to Raising Adolescent Boys
Everything® Guide to Raising Adolescent Girls
Everything® Mother's First Year Book
Everything® Parent's Guide to Childhood Illnesses
Everything® Parent's Guide to Children and Divorce
Everything® Parent's Guide to Children with ADD/ADHD
Everything® Parent's Guide to Children with Asperger's
        Syndrome
Everything® Parent's Guide to Children with Anxiety
Everything® Parent's Guide to Children with Asthma
Everything® Parent's Guide to Children with Autism
Everything® Parent's Guide to Children with Bipolar Disorder
Everything® Parent's Guide to Children with Depression
Everything® Parent's Guide to Children with Dyslexia
Everything® Parent's Guide to Children with Juvenile Diabetes
Everything® Parent's Guide to Children with OCD
Everything® Parent's Guide to Positive Discipline
Everything® Parent's Guide to Raising Boys
Everything® Parent's Guide to Raising Girls
Everything® Parent's Guide to Raising Siblings
**Everything® Parent's Guide to Raising Your
        Adopted Child**
Everything® Parent's Guide to Sensory Integration Disorder
Everything® Parent's Guide to Tantrums
Everything® Parent's Guide to the Strong-Willed Child
Everything® Parenting a Teenager Book
Everything® Potty Training Book, $9.95
Everything® Pregnancy Book, 3rd Ed.
Everything® Pregnancy Fitness Book
Everything® Pregnancy Nutrition Book
Everything® Pregnancy Organizer, 2nd Ed., $16.95
Everything® Toddler Activities Book
Everything® Toddler Book
Everything® Tween Book
Everything® Twins, Triplets, and More Book

PETS

Everything® Aquarium Book
Everything® Boxer Book
Everything® Cat Book, 2nd Ed.
Everything® Chihuahua Book
Everything® Cooking for Dogs Book
Everything® Dachshund Book
Everything® Dog Book, 2nd Ed.
Everything® Dog Grooming Book